Amiga Tricks & Tips

Bleek Maelger Weltner

23529 1.

Abacus

A Data Becker Book

Table of Contents

1

Introduction

1
Introduction

1.   Introduction

Think back to the first time you sat down at your Amiga. You probably experienced the following reactions: excitement, astonishment, surprise and confusion—probably in that order. Yes, the Amiga really is a super personal computer. But there's so much you can do with an Amiga that you often don't know where to begin. How should you begin to apply the Amiga to your tastes? How do you make the most of the Amiga's many capabilities?

If you are new to the Amiga, you probably have dozens of questions by now. To start you off, Chapter Two of this book describes work with the Command Line Interface (CLI).

Part of this book explains methods and programming techniques for getting the most out of Microsoft's AmigaBASIC, with special emphasis on using existing system modules from the software supplied with your Amiga. You'll find handy AmigaBASIC program routines in this book that let you use the various fonts and type styles, use rubberbanding, create borderless windows, and even a disk monitor for exploring the machine language code of the disk drive.

Chapter Five describes the handling of AmigaDOS. It shows how to use the commands in the CLI, and how these commands can be useful to you.

Other subjects covered in Amiga Tricks and Tips include the handling and changing of the Workbench. This includes manipulation and editing of icons for your own purposes.

2
The CLI

2.   The CLI

CLI stands for Command Line Interface. This user interface is controlled from the keyboard. Neither the icons nor the mouse can be used
in the CLI. The CLI included in Workbench Version 1.2 recognizes
about 50 commands.

The CLI works closely with AmigaDOS, the disk operating system.
Many special CLI commands make working with diskettes faster and
more convenient than performing the same functions from the
Workbench screen. Some disk commands must be called from the CLI,
since they cannot be directly accessed by Intuition. Intuition is
the part of the Amiga's operating system that acts as an interface
between the user and the window-and-mouse technique of handling
diskettes, programs and files.

You usually access CLI from Intuition. However, you can also
call CLI commands from BASIC and C programs.

2.1 CLI questions and answers

Many new Amiga users ask questions about the CLI. Below are 20 of the most often asked CLI questions, and their answers.

Question 1:   **How do I get into the CLI?**

Answer: The CLI is contained on every Workbench diskette. Here's how you can access it:

a)   Accessing CLI with Intuition (the usual method):

- Boot your system with the Workbench diskette in the drive. You'll see the deep blue Workbench screen displayed.

- Click the Workbench disk icon. This opens a window named **Workbench**, which contains a number of icons.

- Click the System drawer. This opens a window called **System**, again filled with a number of other icons. We are interested in an icon named CLI, which either displays 1> (Version 1.1), or an icon of a little window with 1> displayed in it (Version 1.2).

  If you don't see a CLI icon, then the CLI gadget in the Preferences program is switched to Off. Click on the Preferences icon in the **Workbench** window. When the Preferences screen appears, click the On gadget next to the word CLI. Save the result by clicking Save. Now close and reopen the **System** window. A CLI icon should appear this time.

- Click on the CLI icon. This opens a window named **New CLI**. You can enlarge or reduce the size of this window, but you can't close it, since there is no close gadget. You now have your own CLI.

b)   Accessing CLI through AmigaDOS:

- AmigaDOS has a command called execute which executes CLI commands in a batch file.

- You can also access AmigaDOS through the system libraries, which is how AmigaBASIC and the C programming language communicate with the CLI.

c) Interrupting the booting process (the easiest method of calling the CLI):

- Boot your system as usual. When the Kickstart diskette (Amiga 1000) or Kickstart in ROM (Amiga 500 and 2000) has successfully loaded, the icon of a hand holding a Workbench diskette appears on the screen.

- Insert the Workbench diskette in the drive. The hand disappears and the system boots up.

- As soon as the AmigaDOS window (the blue screen) appears, hold down the <CTRL> key and press the <D> key. The following message appears:

```
** BREAK – CLI
1>
```

- You are now in the CLI. Enter:

```
1> loadwb
```

- You can now access all functions of the CLI.

Question 2: **How do I get out of the CLI?**

Answer: The CLI window doesn't have a close gadget. You exit the CLI by typing in the following:

```
1> endcli
```

If you have started programs from CLI, the CLI window remains open while the programs run.

Question 3: **I don't have a typewriter, but I have a printer connected to my Amiga. Can I use my Amiga to type?**

Answer: Yes. Type in the following CLI command:

```
1> copy * to prt:
```

The asterisk (*) represents the open CLI window. After this input the CLI prompt 1> disappears, but the cursor stays on the screen. Now everything you type goes to the printer when you press the <RETURN> key, like a typewriter with one-line correction capability.

Hold down the <CTRL> key and press the <\> (backslash) key to exit typewriter mode.

You can also copy text from the CLI window to another window. Type this and press the <RETURN> key to display your text in another window:

```
1> copy * to CON:10/10/300/100/copy_text
```

Re-activate the CLI window by clicking on it. Press and hold the <CTRL> key and press the <\> key to stop this command.

Question 4:

I only have one disk drive. Every time I call a CLI command, the Amiga wants the Workbench diskette. Can the Workbench be stored in memory?

Answer:

Each CLI command is a program stored in directory c: of the Work-bench diskette. When you call a CLI command, the Amiga loads this program from the Workbench diskette. This saves system memory because the CLI commands aren't taking up any of that memory. On the other hand, if you only have one disk drive, you spend a lot of your time swapping diskettes.

Buying a second disk drive is one solution to the problem. Or, if you have enough system memory, you can copy some or all of the CLI commands into a RAM disk. Here's the sequence for copying these commands:

```
1> makedir ram:c
1> copy sys:c to ram:c
1> assign c: ram:c
```

The Amiga creates a subdirectory on the RAM disk named c:. Next, the CLI command set is copied to this directory. The last command assigns the command directory c: to the RAM disk.

If your Amiga doesn't have enough memory available, copy only the CLI commands you need most. For example:

```
1> makedir ram:c
1> copy sys:c/copy to ram:c
1> copy sys:c/dir to ram:c
1> copy sys:c/list to ram:c
(..any other commands you want copied..)
1> assign c: ram:c
```

Type in the following to make the CLI accessible from the Workbench diskette:

```
1> df0:c/assign c: df0:c
```

Once you change to the Workbench-accessed CLI, you should delete the RAM-based CLI to release the memory it occupies:

```
1> delete ram:c#?
1> delete ram:c
```

Question 5:   **Are there wildcard characters on the Amiga like the * and ? found on the older Commodore computers?**

Answer: The Amiga uses the character combination #? as a wildcard. The asterisk * represents the current CLI window, so it isn't used as a wildcard on the Amiga. You can delete the entire RAM disk by typing in:

```
1) delete ram:#?
```

Try this command:

```
1) run amig#?
```

The Amiga can't execute this command because it doesn't know which program to execute. There may be several programs with names which start with the letters "amig".

Question 6:   **How can I print all the CLI commands on my printer?**

Answer: Type in this command sequence to print the complete CLI command list:

```
1> list quick sys:c to prt:
```

The quick option prints the command names only. The file creation date, the time, the protection status and the file size aren't printed. The CLI commands themselves are in the c: subdirectory, or in the system directory sys:. The list prints out even faster if you use the multitasking capabilities of the Amiga:

```
1> run list quick sys:c to prt:
```

This line opens another task for handling printer output. The Amiga prints the command words in the background, leaving you free to work on other things.

Question 7: **How can I determine the syntax of a certain CLI command while working in the CLI?**

Answer: Almost all CLI commands have some help messages. If you don't remember the exact syntax of a command, enter the command name followed by a space and a question mark. For example:

```
1> list ?
```

The Amiga displays:

```
DIR,P=PATH/K,KEYS/S,DATES/S,NODATES/S,TO/K,S/K,
SINCE/K,UPTO/K,QUICK/S:
```

DIR stands for a directory. The current directory is listed if DIR is omitted. All other options have a condition, or *argument*, added to the name of the option:

/A: This requires a specific argument
/K: This argument requires a parameter
/S: This argument has no parameters

This command prints the programs in df0: with the various starting memory blocks, but without dates:

```
1> list df0: keys nodates
```

Type in this command sequence to print the programs in df0: which were written between October 4th, 1986 and today.

```
1> list df0: since 04-Oct-86 upto today
```

Question 8: **How can I stop a CLI command as it executes?**

Answer: Pressing <CTRL><C> stops any command. <CTRL><D> sends an execute command to stop the program as soon as possible.

Question 9: **How can I copy a program using one disk drive?**

Answer: There are two methods of copying programs with one disk drive.

a) Using the RAM disk:

• Copy the program you want copied, as well as the copy program, from the source diskette into the RAM disk:

```
1> copy program to ram:
1> copy c/copy to ram:
```

- The `copy` program was copied by the second command sequence. This means that you won't have to insert the Workbench diskette during the copying procedure.

- Remove the source diskette and put the destination diskette in the drive.

- Type in the following to copy the program onto the destination diskette:

```
1> ram:copy ram:program to df0:
```

- Remove the destination diskette from the drive and insert the Workbench diskette.

- Enter this line to delete the RAM disk:

```
1> delete ram:#?
```

b) Using the `Intuition` icons:

- Insert the source diskette and click the source diskette's icon.

- As soon as the desired program's icon appears, remove the original diskette and insert the destination diskette.

- Open the destination diskette by clicking its icon. Now you can drag the program icon from the source diskette to the destination diskette's window.

- Requesters tell you when to exchange diskettes (remember not to remove a diskette from a drive until the disk light turns off).

Note: There are programs on your Workbench diskette which aren't listed in `Intuition` windows. This is because they have no icons assigned to them. Here's how you can assign icons to these programs.

- Insert the Workbench diskette. Type in the following lines:

```
1> copy df0:clock.info to ram:
1> rename ram:clock.info as ram:program.info
1> copy c/copy to ram:
```

- Insert the diskette which contains the original program. Enter:

```
1> ram:copy ram:program.info to df0:
```

- Now your program (here just called `program`) has an icon.

- Insert the Workbench diskette and delete the RAM disk:

```
1> delete ram:#?
```

Question 10:   **How can I copy a program using two disk drives?**

Answer: Enter this line in the CLI to copy the program:

```
1> copy df0:originalprogram to df1:
```

`originalprogram` is the name of your program. It must be in directory `df0:` of the diskette in drive 0 for this command to work correctly.

You can also copy a program by moving the program icon from one disk window to another (see b) in Question 9 above).

Note: Workbench diskettes with version numbers of 1.2 and above automatically copy info files when programs are copied. Info files contain the icon design of the program and other information. If your Workbench is earlier than Version 1.2, you must copy the info file and the program, if you want the program to have an icon:

```
1> copy df0:originalprogram.info to df1:
```

Question 11:   **How can I copy an entire diskette?**

Answer: Use the `diskcopy` command.

a)   If you have one disk drive:

•   Insert the Workbench diskette.

•   Enter the following CLI command:

```
1> diskcopy from df0: to df0: name "copy"
```

•   Requesters tell you to exchange the source and destination diskettes as needed.

b)   If you have two disk drives:

•   Insert the Workbench diskette.

•   Enter the following CLI command:

```
1> diskcopy from df0: to df1: name "copy"
```

•   Insert the source diskette in drive 0 and the target diskette in drive 1. No diskette swapping is required.

Note: Always write-protect the source diskette before you begin copying, so you won't accidentally overwrite the source diskette.

Question 12:   **What is a startup sequence, and what can I do with it?**

Answer: The startup sequence is a list of CLI commands executed when the
                 system is first booted up. You can also run the startup sequence while
                 in the CLI:

>   1> execute s/startup-sequence

Type this command to see what the startup sequence contains:

>   1> type s/startup-sequence

You can write your own startup sequences with the CLI editor Ed.
Type this to access Ed, and the startup sequence:

>   1> ed s/startup-sequence

The startup sequence for Workbench Version 1.2 looks like this:

```
echo "Workbench Diskette (Version 1.2/33.43)"
echo " "
echo " (Date and time can be set with 'Preferences')"
if EXISTS sys:system
   path sys:system add
endif
BindDrivers
Loadwb
endcli > nil:
```

Move the cursor to the line you want to change with the cursor keys.
Pressing the <ESC> key puts you into extended command mode. Pressing <ESC> <D> <RETURN> deletes the current line. Delete the line:

```
    endcli > nil:
```

Move the cursor to the line that says loadwb. Press <RETURN> to
move that line down. Move the cursor to that blank line. Enter this:

```
    echo"****  This is my startup sequence.  ****"
```

Press the <ESC> key, <X> key and <RETURN> key to save your
startup sequence.

Try out the new sequence:

>   1> execute s/startup-sequence

As the sequence executes, your message appears on the screen, and the
Amiga drops right into the CLI.

Note: The loadwb command must be present at the end of the startup
                 sequence to enable Intuition. If you exit the startup sequence
                 without loadwb, you'll get a blank blue screen without icons.

15

Question 13:   **Can the Amiga speak while in the CLI?**

Answer: Yes. The CLI command for speech is say. say works similar to a
                     print command in BASIC, except that the text is read through the
                     Amiga's sound system, and no quotation marks are needed for say.
                     Type this in to hear say in action:

                         1> say tobi is a real nice guy!

                     The default speech parameters can be changed by including a modifier in
                     the text you want spoken. These modifiers are: -f (female), -m (male),
                     -r (robot), -n (natural), -s # (speed; # is a number ranging from 40 to
                     400) and -p # (pitch; # is a number ranging from 65 to 320). say can
                     speak the contents of a file when you add the modifier -x filename
                     to the command. The following example recites the startup sequence in
                     a woman's voice with a pitch of 180 and a speed of 180:

                         1>say -f -p180 -s180 -x s/startup-sequence

                     You can also use say within the startup sequence (see Question 12 for
                     editing instructions). Imagine having your Amiga say hello to you
                     every time you turn it on!

Question 14:   **How can I send a C listing to a printer?**

Answer: Use the CLI type command. Say you have a C listing called test.c
                     in drive df1:. Enter the following:

                         1> run type df1:test.c to prt: opt n

                     run uses the multitasking capabilities of the Amiga here—while the
                     printer runs, you can work with another program. The opt n option
                     inserts line numbers in the C listing. These are helpful when tracking
                     down errors.

Question 15:   **How do I use the multitasking capabilities of the Amiga
                     in everyday work with the CLI?**

Answer: Normally the CLI processes one command after the other; there is no
                     option for multitasking. Remember that the CLI itself can't perform
                     more than one task at a time. However, the multitasking operating
                     system of the Amiga allows you to run several single task CLIs at
                     once.

                     For example, if you want to print the directory of the system diskette,
                     edit a document, and have the Amiga speak a sentence, all at once, the
                     usual command sequence would look like this:

```
1> list sys: to prt:
1> ed text
1> say hello user
```

This sequence executes faster if you use multiple CLI commands:

```
1> run list sys: to prt:
1> run ed text
1> say hello user
```

The run command passes the command sequence which follows it to a new CLI. The original CLI then has nothing to do, and goes on to the next task without waiting for the first one to finish.

There is a limitation: Two CLIs shouldn't access the same drive (or a drive and the printer) at the same time. In the case of the disk drives, the two CLIs share computing time, which takes the entire operation longer than if the two CLIs were executed one after the other.

Another way to initiate several tasks at once is by opening mulitple CLIs with the newcli command. This gives the user another complete input interface. This method works best when you execute several CLI functions over a long period of time, instead of executing CLI commands quickly. The following example makes this clear:

```
1> newcli
1> list df0: quick
2> type files opt h
```

Here a new CLI opens, and all of the filenames in the df0: directory appear in this window. Then the file contents of the second, new CLI print out. This way you can read filenames in the first CLI window and work in the second window without disturbing the list of names.

The newcli command also offers several options. The user can set the dimensions of the new CLI window. The syntax looks like this:

```
1> newcli con:0/10/639/100/newcli
```

The word con: refers to the console (keyboard and monitor). The first two numbers specify the x and y coordinates of the upper left corner of the window, and the last two numbers set the width and height of the window.

This lets you place new CLI windows so that they don't hide other windows. If you work with multiple CLIs, just leave each window's back and front gadgets visible. Clicking a front gadget allows you to bring any of the windows to the foreground.

Question 16:   **What options does the Amiga have for text output?**

Answer: The `copy` command is the simplest method:

      1> copy * to prt :

See Question 3 for more information about the `copy` command.

The built in `CLI` editor `Ed` can be used for writing letters:

      1> run ed letter

Immediately the **Ed** window appears, and you can write your letter.

`Ed` runs independently of your original `CLI`. You can enter as many documents as you wish. When the letter is done, enter the key combination <ESC><x><RETURN> to save it to diskette under the name "`letter`". You can print your saved file from the `CLI` by typing:

      1> type letter to prt :

One advantage here over the simple typewriter mode from Question 3 is that the text is on diskette. It can be printed at any time, or edited by typing:

      1> run ed letter

If you don't want the letter any more, enter:

      1> delete letter

The `Notepad` is a third option for editing text. You call it as follows:

      1> run utilities/notepad

This is an expanded notepad which allows access to the Amiga disk resident fonts. That is its only real advantage over `Ed`. We recommend using `Ed`, or a true word processor like Abacus' *TextPro* or *BeckerText*.

Question 17:   **How can I make the invisible files on my Workbench diskette visible?**

Answer: A file doesn't appear in an `Intuition` window unless it has a matching info file. This info file contains the icon data for the corresponding file.

There are many files on the Workbench diskette without info files. These files are invisible to windows. You can adapt these files to appear as icons.

Type in the following to load Ed:

```
1> ed S:show
```

Enter the following text in Ed:

```
.key file/a
.bra (
.ket )
if exists sys:cli.info
  echo "create info file"
  if exists (file)
    copy sys:system/cli.info to (file).info
  else
    echo "there is no such source file"
  endif
else
  echo "no .info original found"
endif
quit
```

Now press <ESC>,<X> and <RETURN> to save the text. This text is saved under the name "show" in the s: directory.

Now you can assign an info file to any file, and make the unseen file visible in a window. Just enter:

```
1> execute show NameOfTheFile
```

The execute command activates the command sequence show. The .key command uses NameOfTheFile instead of the word file. The /a option indicates that this argument must be entered.

The .bra and .ket commands define the characters which mark the start and end of the argument placeholders in the command sequence.

The command sequence checks for the existence of the info file "cli.info", since this info file is used as the source info file. If this file is not found in your directory, you must switch the CLI gadget in Preferences to On (see Question 1, part a)).

Sometimes new file icons are piled on top of each other, if they are identical. Separate the icons with the mouse (drag them apart), and use the Workbench option Snapshot to keep them in place.

Question 18:   **How can I combine various documents?**

Answer: A common operation is combining various separate documents into one. These can be parts of a C listing, or a letter heading, text and closing. Ed cannot merge documents like some word processing programs can. However, AmigaDOS has the `join` command available through the CLI.

Say you have three text files called `header`, `text` and `closing`. You want to create a single document out of these three parts. This is done with `join`:

```
1> join header text closing as letter
```

The three separate components combine in order and save to diskette under the filename "`letter`".

Question 19:   **How can I search for certain text passages in my files?**

Answer: The `search` command locates a specific word or sentence in files. C programmers can use this command to search for procedure and variable names in source listings. Here's the syntax of `search`:

```
1> search name search search_text all
```

`name`   = name of the file or disk directory being searched

`search_text` = text to search for

`all`   = all available directories are searched

This sequence searches all the files on the diskette in drive `df0:` for the word "`tobi.`"

```
1> search df0: search "tobi" all
```

This command sequence checks the file "`letter`" for the name "`Meier`".

```
1> search letter search "Meier"
```

This command searches all of the files starting with the letters "`docum`" in the current directory for the words "`Grand Rapids`".

```
1> search docum#? search "Grand Rapids"
```

Question 20:   **Can a text file's contents be sorted?**

Answer: Yes, the `sort` command allows text files of up to 200 lines to be sorted alphabetically. This is especially useful for address lists. For example, if the file "`addresses`" contains the unsorted addresses of your friends, just enter:

```
1> sort addresses to sorted
```

This line alphabetically sorts the file, and saves the sorted list as a new file named "`sorted`".

If you want to sort more than 200 lines of text, you must increase the size of the stack with the `stack` command.

2.2   New CLI commands

The newest version of the Workbench is here! There are a number of new CLI commands not documented in the Amiga manual. This section defines these new commands in alphabetical order.

AddBuffers

The AddBuffers command supplies a connected disk drive with more working memory. A disk drive can have a maximum of 24K, but only a fraction of this memory is used. The result is slow diskette operation. AddBuffers drive df0:buffers 10 assigns 10 buffer blocks of about 512 bytes each to the internal disk drive. You must decide for yourself which is more important—speed or memory.

BindDrivers

You use this command in the Workbench 1.2 startup sequence (see Question 12 in the preceding section). When you want to add a driver program other than the one controlling the disk drive, you place the program in the drawer marked Expansion. The BindDrivers command tells the CLI to look in the Expansion drawer for the necessary device driver.

ChangeTaskPri

When you test out the multitasking capabilities of the Amiga, you may have found one disadvantage: Multitasking sets up equal priorities. This is good for some tasks but not others: You don't want the disk drive starting up while you draw in a graphic program. On the other hand, you might like to sort a file or format 30 diskettes while something else is going on. However, the draw function of the graphic program is much slower because of the other task(s) happening at the same time. The microprocessor gives all tasks the same time allotment. It doesn't matter that the sorting or formatting takes longer. ChangeTaskPri −5 sets the background diskette functions to minimal priority. These diskette functions take longer to execute, but won't stop the other tasks at crucial times. ChangeTaskPri can theoretically use values from -128 to +127, but values below -5 or about +5 can result in a system crash.

DiskChange

This command is for those of you who own a 5-1/4" disk drive for the Amiga. The DiskChange command tells the Amiga that you have changed diskettes in the 5-1/4" drive. If you don't use this command, AmigaDOS will not handle the new disk correctly. The reason is that unlike the 3-1/2" drive, the 5-1/4" disk drive doesn't check for diskette exchanges. If you manually enter DiskChange dev df1:, the system solves the above problem.

DiskDoctor

Once you're through paying for your Amiga, you don't have much money left for diskettes. So like most users, you buy no-brand diskettes, which may not be very good media. One day, the requester appears that says, "Disk structure corrupted: Use DiskDoctor." This command has no description in the AmigaDOS manual. The Disk-Doctor program looks at a diskette track by track, and attempts to correct all the errors it finds. It displays a list of all files and tracks which are defective or in need of repair, and instructs the user to copy these programs to a new diskette. If you only have an internal disk drive, you should enter the command as follows:

DiskDoctor DRIVE df0:

Let the disk drive stop running after you insert the diskette containing the DiskDoctor, before you press the <RETURN> key.

Mount

The Workbench is a passive program. The first thing it does is check for the user-defined device drivers, and whether these peripheral devices are connected. Mount tells the Amiga what to do with these drivers. If this command is found, then the Amiga checks the MountList in the devs directory for the drivers. If the appropriate entry is present in the MountList, and you have a 5-1/4" drive, entering Mount df1: instructs AmigaDOS to access the drive.

Path

The Workbench diskette contains all the CLI commands. When only one command should be executed, the Amiga first checks the current directory (accessed by cd) for the command. If the command isn't in that directory, the directory named c is searched. In Version 1.2 of the Workbench, some of the commands are stored in the system directory. The list of directories may be expanded using the path command so that the user can add new commands. The syntax for adding to directories:

path directory_name add

The word add tells AmigaDOS to add directory_name to the search path. When you want to know which directories are searched, enter path alone, or enter show. If the previously given directory is no longer needed, then you can delete it with path reset.

SetDate

This command is particularly important for Amiga 1000 owners. When you turn on the Amiga and you want to edit a text or a program, the new version is saved with the date last set in Preferences. If you didn't set the date before editing the text/program, the date stamped on the file will not be accurate. This command lets you change the date and time stamped on any file. You can set your date and time by entering the following syntax:

SetDate FILE "text" DATE Da-Month-YR TIME 23:59

SetMap

The Amiga sells worldwide. Many countries have different keyboard settings and different alphabets. To get around some of these problems of language, Commodore Amiga created different keyboard drivers. The keyboard only comes in one configuration (American), but it can simulate the keyboards of other nations. The `SetMap` command sets the keyboard according to the codes in the table below:

Name	Country
ch	Switzerland
dk	Denmark
d	Germany
e	Spain
f	France
gb	Great Britain
i	Italy
is	Iceland
n	Norway
s	Sweden/Finland
usa()	United States

Version

This command returns the version number of the Workbench and KickStart systems currently in use.

2.3   New startup sequences

The following startup-sequence allows you to enter the current date on
every system start. The `startup-sequence` file must be in the `s:`
directory on the Workbench diskette to execute.

```
Echo " "
Echo "Startup-Sequence: ) 1987 by Stefan Maelger"
Echo " "
if exists sys:system
 Path sys:system add
Endif
BindDrivers
SetMap d
Date
Echo " "
Echo "Please enter the new date in"
Echo "the displayed format:"
Date ?
Echo " "
Echo "The new date is:"
Date
Echo " "
Info
loadwb
endcli >nil:
```

The sequence below sets the Amiga to tomorrow's date. If you remember to set the date in `Preferences` before you turn off the Amiga,
the date is correct, or close, the next time you turn on your Amiga.

```
Echo " "
Echo "Startup-Sequence by Stefan Maelger"

If Exists sys:system
 Path sys:system add
end if
Binddrivers
Setmap d

Date tomorrow
Echo " "
Echo "Today's date is:"
Date

Echo "Sytem:"
Info

loadwb
endcli >nil:
```

This is the ideal Workbench for CLI enthusiasts. It opens a second CLI window and changes the prompt slightly (you'll see how when you try it out).

```
ADDBUFFERS df0:C 20
Echo "This creates a new CLI window and prompt"
Echo " "
If Exists sys:system
 Path sys:system add
end if
Binddrivers
PROMPT CLI#%n>
NEWCLI
Info

loadwb
endcli >nil:
```

This is the startup sequence for the beginner. It closes the big CLI window, but opens a smaller CLI window. It also shows the RAM disk icon.

```
Echo " "
Echo "Workbench Version 1.2 33.45"
Echo " "
If Exists sys:system
 Path sys:system add
end if
Binddrivers
Echo "Welcome everyone"

loadwb
DIR RAM:
NEWCLI "CON:0/150/400/50/Alternative"
endcli >nil:
```

2.3.1   Printer spooler

Using a printer spooler with a multitasking computer allows you to work on something else while a file goes to the printer.

The CLI has a RUN command for executing a new task. You can treat the spooler program as a batch file using this command. The procedure is as follows:

Start the CLI and enter:

```
ED c:PRINT
```

Now enter the following program:

```
.key filename/a,typ/s        ;take the parameters

;--------------------------
;  Printer-Spooler
;--------------------------
;(c) 1987 by Stefan Maelger
;--------------------------

if not exists <filename>     ;check for file

echo "File not found"        ;no?
quit                         ;-then end here

else                         ;or:

copy <filename> to ram:<filename>
                             ;copy file to the RAM-Disk

if <typ> eq "DUMP"           ;Hex-Dump output?

 run >nil: type ram:<filename> to prt: opt h
                             ;-HexDump-Spooling

else                         ;or:

 run >nil: type ram:<filename> to prt: opt n
                             ;-normal Spooling
endif

delete ram:<filename>        ;free memory

endif
echo "printing"              ;Output message
quit
```

Save the file with <ESC><X>. You can call the routine by entering the following (the DUMP parameter is optional and can be omitted):

```
    EXECUTE PRINT filename (DUMP)
```

Since the EXECUTE command takes a while to type—and can easily be typed in incorrectly—enter the following:

```
    run>nil: copy sys:c/EXECUTE to sys:c/DO quiet
```

This creates a command named DO which does the same thing as EXECUTE. For example:

```
    DO PRINT filename
```

The ability to put a number of commands into a two-character word is a real time saver. Here's another example of DO:

```
    RENAME sys:c/EXECUTE TO sys:c/DO
```

2.3.2   CLI programming (batch files)

The CLI's flexibility in "programming" can make much of your work easier. This section shows you a couple of examples for bypassing the problem of accessing every AmigaDOS command from the Workbench diskette. Also, ideas are presented here for performing data exchange from the CLI.

The big hindrance to the CLI is that no loops can be constructed. The AmigaDOS interpreter reads every command from the execute file in order. Jumps cannot be executed. This goes for all CLI programming.

2.3.3   Resident CLI

The fact that the CLI must always access the Workbench diskette can be annoying. The program below makes the CLI resident in RAM:

```
; Program to copy all the CLI-commands to RAM
; ---------------------------------------------------
;
FAILAT 30
MAKEDIR ram:c                    ; RAM-Data create
;
IF FAIL
  SKIP ende
ENDIF
;
ECHO "CLI-commands being copied ..."
;
COPY df0:c TO ram:c QUIET        ; copy all commands to ram
ASSIGN c: ram:c                  ; commands now from ram:
ECHO "Ready!"
LAB ende
```

Program description

Before you go on, you should know that this is just a revision of the RAM-resident CLI command workings as listed in the AmigaDOS manual.

First the program creates a directory in RAM for storing all C commands. If no errors occur, the entire CLI directory moves from the currently inserted diskette into RAM. When all are ready, the ASSIGN command tells the operating system to look in RAM only for the CLI.

28

2.3.4   `Resi` (partial resident)

There is one small disadvantage to the RAM-resident CLI. A basic
512K Amiga can lose a lot of memory to the CLI. Selective copying
of CLI commands saves memory. Another advantage to Resi: Since
every command must be copied over one at a time, you can also change
the command names to abbreviations using the RENAME command. For
example, delete can become del, and execute can become ex.
This makes things much easier when you might otherwise have to enter
long strings of characters, and even frequently used commands like dir
or list.

```
;
; Program copies the most important CLI commands to RAM
; ----------------------------------------------------------
;
FAILAT 20
ECHO "The commands are being copied!"
MAKEDIR ram:c
COPY c/copy TO ram:c
ASSIGN c: ram:c
;
COPY c/cd  TO ram:c
COPY c/ed  TO ram:c
COPY c/dir TO ram:c
COPY c/echo TO ram:c
COPY c/type TO ram:c
COPY c/list TO ram:c
COPY c/info TO ram:c
COPY c/date TO ram:c
COPY c/execute TO ram:c
COPY c/makedir TO ram:c
COPY c/delete TO ram:c
COPY c/assign TO ram:c
ECHO "Ready!"
;
; End of copy
```

2.3.5   `ToDisk`

Once you finish using the CLI in RAM, you'll want to free up the
memory used by the resident commands. ENDCLI disables the resident
CLI, but leaves the commands in RAM. The ToDisk program below
assigns the CLI system in RAM to the diskette currently in the drive,
then clears the c directory from RAM. Other programs in RAM remain

```
EXECUTE Resident              ; CLI commands copied
;
ECHO "Please insert new formatted diskette ..."
WAIT 8 SECS
CD df0:
;new diskette initialization
COPY ram:copy/CLI TO CLI       ; CLI written
COPY ram:copy/CLI.info TO CLI.info
MAKEDIR DiskUtilities
COPY ram:copy/Resident TO DiskUtilities
;Help files written
COPY ram:copy/ToDisk TO DiskUtilities
COPY ram:copy/CLICopy TO DiskUtilities
COPY ram:copy/ReSi TO DiskUtilities
MAKEDIR c
COPY ram:c TO c QUIET
;CLI commands written
;
ECHO "Ready!"
```

Program description

The program copies the CLI icon in the main directory, the programs in the DiskUtilities directory and the CLI commands in the c directory from the current diskette (make sure that these programs and directories are on the current diskette). To avoid overwriting the copy routine for all CLI commands, the program uses the Resident routine as a subroutine. After 8 seconds the Amiga asks you to exchange diskettes. The inserted diskette is viewed as the target diskette, and the writing procedure begins. The CLI and its icon are copied and then the directories with the utility programs. Finally, the commands copy to the newly written c directory. Now you have a diskette that you can call the CLI from without having to change diskettes. Typing ASSIGN sys:c workdisk:c makes the diskette in drive 0 into the work diskette.

2.3.7   Data management

Why should you only want to delete, save and copy files. This section shows how you can use the CLI to create an address file. This has all the basic functions you need, such as data entry, search and deletion. Also, you can look for keywords and view any entry you wish.

Preparations

The address file cannot exist on the main directory of the diskette. The best bet is to create a subdirectory with the name AdrBook:

```
makedir "df0:AdrBook"
```

When you wish to work with the address file, you must change this directory to the current directory:

```
cd "df0:adrbook"
```

This subdirectory contains the program and the address directory. You have one of two options for creating the address directory. You can use the program DatDir.TXT below, or enter the CLI command MAKE-DIR "df0:AdrBook/AdressData". DatDir.TXT checks for an existing directory of the same name. If one exists, the user gets the option of cancelling the program, or deleting or recreating the directory.

```
;create directory in main directory
;------------------------------------------------
;
CD df0:AdrBook
;
IF EXISTS AdressData
 ECHO "The existing data files will be erased!"
 ECHO "You have three seconds to remove the disk"
 WAIT 3 SECS
 DELETE AdressData#?
 DELETE AdressData
ENDIF
;
MAKEDIR AdressData
;
ECHO "Directory created in AdrBook!"
```

Entry

Now you can continue. The Entry.TXT program lets you write individual address data into the AdressData subdirectory. You call this with EXECUTE Entry.TXT "name". "name" stands for the name section under which you want the address data arranged. This is always the main search criterion. Here you must decide whether the last name or the entire name is more important. You can naturally also use this program for keeping track of your record collection or library. The only important thing to remember is that text must be placed in quotation marks when it contains a blank space.

```
;Enter data in the address data file
;------------------------------------------------
;
;KEY Name/A
CD df0:AdrBook/AdressData
;
IF EXISTS "<Name>"
 ECHO "Existing data can only be edited!"
ENDIF
;
ED FROM "<Name>"
CD df0:AdrBook
ECHO "<Name> has been written!"
```

Program description

The EXECUTE command assigns a variable to the program through .KEY. It looks to see whether this name already exists. If so, the Amiga displays a warning that existing data can be edited only. You cannot manage multiple data under the same main search criteria.

The AmigaDOS screen editor executes so you can edit your data. When the input is done, AdrBook is declared as the current directory, which saves you the trouble of constantly stating the directory paths. You can exit input mode by pressing <ESC><X> (save data and exit) as well as <ESC><Q> (quit without saving).

Delete

When entering data, there are times that you either enter some data incorrectly, or no longer need that data. The following batch file lets you remove data entries without having to go directly into the directory.

```
;Delete name data from the address file
;------------------------------------------------------
;
;KEY Name/A
CD df0:AdrBook/AdressData
;
IF NOT EXISTS "<Name>"
 ECHO "Data not found!"
 SKIP Ende
ENDIF
;
DELETE "<Name>"
ECHO "<Name> has been deleted!"
LAB Ende
CD df0:AdrBook
```

Program description

After a short check for the existence of the file, the entry is removed from the data directory, and the program exits.

Search

If you have many friends and relations in your data file, there are times when you may want specific data on one particular person from a file. You can get an alphabetized list by typing DIR, but searching through a large directory can take time. The EXECUTE Search.TXT command searches through the directory for the name you want. If the name exists, this data appears on the screen.

```
;Search for one name in the Address file
;------------------------------------------
;
;KEY Name/A
;
CD df0:AdrBook/AdressData
.
IF EXISTS "<Name>"
 ECHO "Data found ..."
 TYPE "<Name>"
 SKIP Ende
ENDIF
```

Program description

The EXECUTE command assigns a variable to the program through .KEY. It looks to see whether this name already exists. If so, the Amiga displays a warning that existing data can be edited only. You cannot manage multiple data under the same main search criteria.

The AmigaDOS screen editor executes so you can edit your data. When the input is done, AdrBook is declared as the current directory, which saves you the trouble of constantly stating the directory paths. You can exit input mode by pressing <ESC><X> (save data and exit) as well as <ESC><Q> (quit without saving).

Delete

When entering data, there are times that you either enter some data incorrectly, or no longer need that data. The following batch file lets you remove data entries without having to go directly into the directory.

```
;Delete name data from the address file
;-------------------------------------------------------
;
;KEY Name/A
CD df0:AdrBook/AdressData
;
IF NOT EXISTS "<Name>"
 ECHO "Data not found!"
 SKIP Ende
ENDIF
;
DELETE "<Name>"
ECHO "<Name> has been deleted!"
LAB Ende
CD df0:AdrBook
```

Program description

After a short check for the existence of the file, the entry is removed from the data directory, and the program exits.

Search

If you have many friends and relations in your data file, there are times when you may want specific data on one particular person from a file. You can get an alphabetized list by typing DIR, but searching through a large directory can take time. The EXECUTE Search.TXT command searches through the directory for the name you want. If the name exists, this data appears on the screen.

```
;Search for one name in the Address file
;-------------------------------------------
;
;KEY Name/A
;
CD df0:AdrBook/AdressData
.
IF EXISTS "<Name>"
 ECHO "Data found ..."
 TYPE "<Name>"
 SKIP Ende
ENDIF
```

```
ECHO "Data record ?<Name>? not found!"
LAB Ende
CD df0:AdrBook
;
```

Keyword search

A variation on searching is the keyword search. This gives you an overview of which data records contain the keyword. The CLI has its own provision for this command—all it needs is the keyword. The program below is a short batch file to perform the keyword search. Enter the keyword text in quotes when you call the batch file.

```
;Key word search of the address data
; -------------------------------------------------------
;
;KEY Word/A
;
ECHO "The search begins..."
CD df0:AdrBook
SEARCH FROM AdressData SEARCH "<Word>"
;
ECHO "Search ended!"
CD df0:AdrBook
```

There you have a file manager for beginners. This can be a big help for those who don't own a professional file management program like *DataRetrieve Amiga*. You can send your data to screen or printer as you wish. And when you do buy a real database program, you can transfer the files over to and from this program using the ASCII import function.

3
AmigaBASIC

3.   AmigaBASIC

BASIC (Beginner's All-purpose Symbolic Instruction Code) was written when computer programs were assembled by hand. Compilers were not good systems for beginners because the programmer had to start over if the programs had errors. Two people at Dartmouth thought about this and developed a "beginner-friendly" language. This language had a command set made of English words, and an interpreter instead of a compiler. BASIC was born, and BASIC is probably the most used programming language in the world today.

Over the years BASIC has expanded and improved. An advanced BASIC like AmigaBASIC has the easily learned command words and the advantages of structured programming once found only in compiled languages.

AmigaBASIC is a product of Microsoft Corporation. Actually, Amiga-BASIC is more a version of Macintosh Microsoft BASIC adapted to the Amiga than an interpreter written specifically for the Amiga. AmigaBASIC supports the Amiga's windows and menu techniques, but many Amiga-specific features cannot be executed directly from AmigaBASIC. These features, like disk-resident fonts and disk commands, are accessible from the AmigaBASIC LIBRARY command. LIBRARY command demonstrations appear later on in this chapter.

Note: The AmigaBASIC programs in this book show where you should press the <RETURN> key at the end of a program line. The end of paragraph character <¶> means to press <RETURN>. These characters were added because some program lines extend over two lines of text in this book, and many of these lines must not be separated.

All of the BASIC programs in this book are also available on the optional diskette for this book, see the order information at the end of the book for more information on how to order the optional diskette.

3.1   Kernel commands

AmigaBASIC allows extremely flexible programming. In addition to the AmigaBASIC commands (such as PRINT, IF/THEN/ELSE, etc.), the interpreter can use unfamiliar commands if they are organized as machine language routines. This means that you can easily integrate your own commands into the BASIC command set.

Instead of writing new routines, it's easier to access existing machine language routines. The Amiga operating system contains a number of general machine language routines, called the *kernel*. Just as a kernel of corn is the basis for a plant, the Amiga kernel is the basis for the operating system.

The operating system can be divided into about thirty libraries, arranged according to subject. These additional routines require only five of these libraries:

1. exec.library

Responsible for tasks, I/O, general system concerns, memory management

2. graphics.library

Responsible for text and GELs (graphic elements)

3. intuition.library

Responsible for windows, screens, requesters and alerts

4. dos.library

Responsible for accessing the Disk Operating System

5. diskfont.library

Responsible for Amiga fonts stored on diskette

Each of these libraries is filled with machine language routines for accomplishing these tasks. To use these routines through Amiga-BASIC, you need three pieces of information:

1)   The interpreter must have a name for every single routine. You can assign each machine language routine its own name.

2)   The interpreter must convey in which library the corresponding routine can be found. Each library has an *offset table* for this

assignment: It begins with offset 6, and jumps in increments of 6. Every machine language routine has its own offset.

3)   AmigaBASIC must know which parameter register it needs for the routine. AmigaBASIC uses a total of eight data registers and five address registers:

```
1 = Data register d0
2 = Data register d1
3 = Data register d2
4 = Data register d3
5 = Data register d4
6 = Data register d5
7 = Data register d6
8 = Data register d7

 9 = Address register a0
10 = Address register a1
11 = Address register a2
12 = Address register a3
13 = Address register a4
```

Every library has a .bmap file. This file contains the necessary information for all commands organized in the library.

You can easily create the necessary .bmap files using the `ConvertFd` program on the Extras diskette from Commodore Amiga.

Before you continue, you should have the following files available:

```
graphics.bmap
intuition.bmap
exec.bmap
dos.bmap
diskfont.bmap
```

Copy these files to the `libs:` subdirectory of the Workbench diskette. An alternative is to ensure that these files are in the same subdirectory as the program using them. The copying procedure goes like this when using the `CLI`:

```
1> copy graphics.bmap to libs:
1> copy intuition.bmap to libs:
1> copy exec.bmap to libs:
1> copy dos.bmap to libs:
1> copy diskfont.bmap to libs:
```

3.2 AmigaBASIC graphics

The AmigaBASIC graphic commands are much too complex and exhaustive to describe in this brief section (see *Amiga BASIC Inside and Out* from Abacus for a complete description). The next few pages contain tricks and tips to help you in your graphic programming. We'll spend this section describing the commands in detail.

3.2.1 Changing drawing modes

The Amiga has four different drawing modes. When you create graphics on the screen, they can be interpreted by the computer in one of four basic ways:

JAM 1
When you draw a graphic (which also includes the execution of a simple PRINT command), only the drawing color is "jammed" (drawn) into the target area. The color changes at the location of each point drawn, and all other points remain untouched (only one color is "jammed" into the target area).

JAM 2
Two colors are "jammed" (drawn) into the target area. A set point appears in the foreground color (AmigaBASIC color register 1), and an unset point takes on the background color (AmigaBASIC color register 0). The graphic background changes from your actions.

INVERSEVID
AmigaBASIC color register 0 and color register 1 exchange roles. The result is the familiar screen color inversion.

COMPLEMENT
This mode works just like JAM 1 except that the set point inverts (complements) instead of filling with AmigaBASIC color register 1. A set point erases, and an unset point appears.

These four modes can be mixed with one another, so you can actually have nine combinations.

AmigaBASIC currently has no command to voluntarily change the drawing mode. A command must be borrowed from the internal graphic library. It has the format:

```
SetDrMd(RastPort,Mode)
```

The address for RastPort is the pointer to the current window structure stored in WINDOW(8). The AmigaBASIC format looks like this:

SetDrMd(WINDOW(8),Mode)

Here is a set of routines which demonstrate the SetDrMd() command:

```
'###########################¶
'#                         #¶
'# Program: Character mode #¶
'# Author:  TOB            #¶
'# Date:       8-3-87      #¶
'# Version: 1.0            #¶
'#                         #¶
'###########################¶
¶
LIBRARY "graphics.library"¶
¶
   Shadow "Hello everyone",11¶
   LOCATE 4,8¶
   Outline "OUTLINE: used to emphasize text." ,10¶
   ¶
   LIBRARY CLOSE¶
   ¶
   END¶
   ¶
SUB Shadow (text$,space%) STATIC¶
   cX% = POS(0)*8¶
   cY% = (CSRLIN - 1)*8¶
   IF cY% < 8 THEN cY% = 8¶
   ¶
   CALL SetDrMd(WINDOW(8),0)  ' JAM1¶
   ¶
   FOR loop% = 1 TO LEN(text$)¶
     in$ = MID$(text$, loop%,1)¶
     ¶
     CALL Move(WINDOW(8),cX%+1,cY%+1)¶
     COLOR 2,0¶
     PRINT in$¶
     ¶
     CALL Move(WINDOW(8),cX%, cY%)¶
     COLOR 1,0¶
     PRINT in$;¶
     ¶
     cX% = cX% +space%¶
   NEXT loop%¶
   ¶
   CALL SetDrMd(WINDOW(8),1)  ' JAM2¶
   PRINT¶
END SUB¶
¶
SUB Outline (text$, space%) STATIC¶
   cX% = POS(0)*8¶
   cY% = (CSRLIN -1) * 8¶
   IF cY% < 8 THEN cY% = 8¶
   ¶
   FOR loop% = 1 TO LEN(text$)¶
     in$ = MID$(text$, loop%, 1)¶
     CALL SetDrMd(WINDOW(8),0) 'JAM1¶
     FOR loop1% = -1 TO 1¶
       FOR loop2% = -1 TO 1¶
         CALL Move(WINDOW(8),cX% +loop2%,cY%+loop1%)¶
         PRINT in$;¶
       NEXT loop2%¶
     NEXT loop1%¶
     CALL SetDrMd(WINDOW(8),2)  'COMPLEMENT¶
     CALL Move(WINDOW(8), cX%, cY%)¶
     PRINT in$;¶
     ¶
     cX% = cX% + space%¶
   NEXT loop%¶
     ¶
```

```
        CALL SetDrMd(WINDOW(8),1)  'JAM2¶
        PRINT¶
END SUB¶
```

COMPLEMENT mode demonstrates another application: *rubberbanding.*
You work with rubberbanding every day. Every time you change the
size of a window, this orange rubberband appears, which helps you to
find a suitable window size.

Intuition normally manages this rubberband. This technique is
quite simple: To prevent the rubberband from changing the screen background, Intuition freezes all screen activities (this is the reason that
work stops when you enlarge or reduce a window in a drawing program,
for example). The COMPLEMENT drawing mode draws the rubberband
on the screen. This erases simply by overwriting, without changing the
screen background.

This can be easily programmed in BASIC. The following program
illustrates this and uses some interesting AmigaBASIC commands:

```
'###############################¶
'#                             #¶
'# Program:  Rubberbanding     #¶
'# Author:   TOB               #¶
'# Date:     8-3-87            #¶
'# Version:  2.0               #¶
'#                             #¶
'###############################¶
¶
LIBRARY "graphics.library"¶
¶
main:        '* Rubber banding demo¶
             CLS¶
             ¶
             '* rectangle¶
             PRINT "a) Draw a Rectangle"¶
             Rubberband¶
             LINE (m.x,m.y) - (m.s,m.t),,b¶
             ¶
             '* line¶
             LOCATE 1,1¶
             PRINT "b) ...and now a Line!"¶
             Rubberband¶
             LINE (m.x,m.y) - (m.s,m.t)¶
             ¶
             '* area¶
             LOCATE 1,1¶
             PRINT "c) Finally Outline an Area"¶
             Rubberband¶
             x = ABS(m.x-m.s)¶
             y = ABS(m.y-m.t)¶
             PRINT "width (x)   =";x¶
             PRINT "Height (y)  =";y¶
             PRINT "Area        =";x*y; "Points."¶
             ¶
             LIBRARY CLOSE¶
             END¶
¶
¶
SUB Rubberband STATIC¶
    SHARED m.x,m.y,m.s,m.t¶
    CALL SetDRMD(WINDOW(8),2) 'COMPLEMENT¶
    ¶
    WHILE MOUSE(0) = 0¶
```

```
        maus = MOUSE(0)¶
     WEND¶
      ¶
     m.x= MOUSE (1)¶
     m.y = MOUSE(2)¶
     m.s = m.x¶
     m.t = m.y¶
      ¶
     WHILE maus < 1¶
       m.a = m.s¶
       m.b = m.t¶
       m.s = MOUSE(1)¶
       m.t = MOUSE(2)¶
       IF m.a <> m.s OR m.b <> m.t THEN¶
          LINE (m.x,m.y) - (m.a,m.b),,b¶
          LINE (m.x,m.y) - (m.s,m.t),,b¶
       END IF¶
      maus = MOUSE(0)¶
     WEND¶
      ¶
      ¶
     ¶
      ¶
     LINE (m.x,m.y)-(m.s,m.t),,b¶
     PSET (m.x,m.y)¶
     CALL SetDRMD(WINDOW(8), 1)¶
 END SUB¶
```

3.2.2   Changing typestyles

The Amiga has the ability to modify typestyles within a program.
Typestyles such as **bold**, <u>underlined</u> and *italic* type can be changed
through simple calculations. This is useful to adding class to your text
output. Unfortunately, BASIC doesn't support these programmable
styles. The `SetSoftStyle` system function from the graphic library
performs this task:

```
SetSoftStyle (WINDOW(8),style,enable)

style:
```

0	= normal
1	= underline
2	= bold
3	= underline and bold
4	= italic
5	= underline and italic
6	= bold and italic
7	= underline, bold, and italic

The following program demonstrates these options:

```
'###################################¶
'#                                 #¶
'# Program:   Text style           #¶
'# Author:    TOB                   #¶
'# Date  :    8-12-87               #¶
'#                                 #¶
'###################################¶
¶
DECLARE FUNCTION AskSoftStyle% LIBRARY¶
DECLARE FUNCTION SetSoftStyle% LIBRARY¶
¶
LIBRARY "graphics.library"¶
¶
var:        'the mode assignments¶
¶
            normal%    = 0¶
            underline% = 1¶
            bold%      = 2¶
            italic%    = 4¶
            ¶
demo:       ' an example¶
            CLS¶
            Style underline% + italic%¶
            PRINT TAB(20); "This is italic underlined
text"¶
            ¶
            LOCATE 5,1¶
            Style normal%¶
            PRINT"This is the Amiga's normal text"¶
            PRINT"Here are some example styles:"¶
            PRINT"a) Normal text"¶
            Style underline%¶
            PRINT"b) Underlined text"¶
            Style bold%¶
            PRINT "c) Bold text"¶
            Style italic%¶
            PRINT "d) Italic text"¶
            PRINT¶
            Style normal%¶
            PRINT "Here are all forms available:"¶
            ¶
            FOR loop% = 0 TO 7¶
             Style loop%¶
             PRINT "Example style number";loop%¶
            NEXT loop%¶
            ¶
            ' and normal style¶
            Style normal%¶
            ¶
            LIBRARY CLOSE¶
            END¶
            ¶
SUB Style (nr%) STATIC¶
    bits% = AskSoftStyle%(WINDOW(8))¶
    news% = SetSoftStyle%(WINDOW(8), nr%, bits%)¶
    ¶
    IF (nr% AND 4) = 4 THEN¶
      CALL SetDrMd(WINDOW(8),0)¶
    ELSE                      ¶
      CALL SetDrMd(WINDOW(8),1)¶
    END IF¶
END SUB¶
```

Variables   bits%   style bits enabling these character styles
               news%   newly set style bits
               nr%   given style bits

Program   The program calls the Style SUB command immediately. The
description AskSoftStyle& function returns the style bits of the current font.
               These bits can later be changed algorithmically. The desired change is
               made with SetSoftStyle, which resets the previously obtained
               style bits. This function sets the new style when the corresponding
               mask bits in bits% are set. Otherwise, these bits remain unset.

               If the italic style is selected in any combination (nr% and 4=4), charac-
               ter mode JAM 1 is switched on (see Section 3.2.1 above). Italic style
               uses this mode because JAM 2 (normal mode) obstructs the characters
               to the right of the italicized text. If the italic style stays unused, then
               SetDrMd() goes to normal mode (JAM 2).

3.2.3   Move – cursor control

In some of the previous examples we used the graphics.library
command MOVE. AmigaBASIC can only move the cursor by characters
(LOCATE), or by pixels in the X-direction (PTAB), but it is easy to
move the cursor by pixels in both X- and Y-directions with the help of
the MOVE command.

Call the command in BASIC as follows:

        Move& (WINDOW(8),x%,y%)

To simplify things, we have written a command that can be extremely
useful:

        xyPTAB x%,y%

graphics.bmap must be on the diskette.

Note:

```
DECLARE FUNCTION Move& LIBRARY¶
¶
LIBRARY "graphics.library"¶
¶
var:¶
text$="Here we go..."¶
text$=" "+text$+" "¶
empty$=SPACE$(LEN(text$))¶
fontheight%=8¶
¶
main:¶
FOR y%=6 TO 100¶
 xyPTAB x%,y%¶
 PRINT text$¶
 xyPTAB x%,y%-fontheight%¶
```

```
    PRINT empty$¶
    x%=x%+1¶
  NEXT y%¶
  ¶
  LIBRARY CLOSE¶
  END¶
  ¶
  '------------------------------------¶
  ¶
  SUB xyPTAB(x%,y%) STATIC¶
    e&=Move&(WINDOW(8),x%,y%) ¶
  END SUB¶
  ¶
```

Variables

text$	demo text
empty$	empty string, provided for erasing when moving in the y-direction
fontheight%	font height
x%, y%	screen coordinates
e&	Move& command error message

Program description

The Move& command is declared as a function and the library opens. The demo text moves across the screen in the soft-scroll mode, the library closes, and the program ends.

The actual subprogram is extremely simple, since all that happens is that the necessary coordinates pass to the Move command.

Although this routine looks simple, it is also very powerful. It can move text in any direction, as in the example, either with the smear effect (SetDrMd mode%=JAM1) or with soft-scrolling (SetDrMd mode%=JAM2).

3.2.4   Faster IFF transfer

IFF/ILBM file format is quickly becoming a standard for file structure. IFF format simply means that data can be exchanged between different programs that use the IFF system. Data blocks of different forms can be exchanged (e.g., text, pictures, music). These data blocks are called *chunks*.

You have probably seen many loader programs for ILBM pictures in magazines, or even typed in the IFF format video title program from Abacus' *AmigaBASIC Inside and Out*. The long loading time of IFF files is the biggest disadvantage of that format. There are a number of reasons for this delay. First, it takes time to identify the different chunks and skip the chunks that are unimportant to the program. Second, there are a number of different ways to store a picture in ILBM format. For example, a graphic with five bitplanes must be saved as line 1 of each bitplane (1-5), line 2 of each bitplane (1-5), and so on.

Considering that a bitplane exists in memory as one piece, it takes time to split it up into these elements. Third, programs such as *DeluxePaint II®* present another problem: Each line of a bitplane is compressed when a graphic is saved, and must be uncompressed when reloading the graphic.

Many professional programs don't use IFF for the reasons stated above. Some programmers don't want graphics compatible with other programs (e.g., *Defender of the Crown®* graphics). Other programmers prefer to sacrifice that compatibility for speed.

You can add a professional touch to your AmigaBASIC programs with this routine. This program loads an IFF-ILBM graphic (you might not want to try this with *DPaint®*) and saves this graphic in the following format:

```
Bitplane 1 (in one piece)
Bitplane 2 …
…last bitplane
Hardware-color register contents
```

An AmigaBASIC program is generated which loads and displays this graphic after a mouse click. The AmigaBASIC program is an ASCII file, which can be independently MERGED or CHAINed with other programs, and can be started from the Workbench by double-clicking its icon.

The listing below is a fast loader for IFF-ILBM graphics. In-house tests of this loader could call up a graphic in 320 x 200 x 5 format with a loading speed of over 41000 bytes per second (IFF files take a hundred times longer to load).

```
' #####################################¶
' #   load pictures like a prof with  #¶
' #-----------------------------------#¶
' #    F A S T - G F X    A m i g a   #¶
' #-----------------------------------#¶
' #     (W) 1987 by Stefan Maelger    #¶
' #####################################¶
'¶
  DECLARE FUNCTION xOpen& LIBRARY¶
  DECLARE FUNCTION xRead& LIBRARY¶
  DECLARE FUNCTION xWrite& LIBRARY¶
  DECLARE FUNCTION Seek& LIBRARY¶
  DECLARE FUNCTION AllocMem& LIBRARY¶
  DECLARE FUNCTION AllocRaster& LIBRARY¶
¶
REM **** OPEN LIBRARIES ***********************¶
  LIBRARY "dos.library"¶
  LIBRARY "exec.library"¶
  LIBRARY "graphics.library"¶
¶
REM **** ERROR TRAPPING ***********¶
```

```
    ON ERROR GOTO errorcheck¶
  ¶
REM **** INPUT THE FILENAME ******************¶
nameinput:  ¶
    ¶


REM **** FREE MEMORY FROM THE BASIC-WINDOW   *******¶
REM **** OPEN NEW WINDOW AND MINISCREEN *******¶
  WINDOW CLOSE WINDOW(0)¶
  SCREEN 1,320,31,1,1¶
  WINDOW 1,"FAST-GFX-CONVERTER",,0,1¶
  PALETTE 0,0,0,0¶
  PALETTE 1,1,0,0¶
  FOR i=1 TO 4¶
    MENU i,0,0,""¶
  NEXT¶
  PRINT "IFF-ILBM-Picture:"¶
  LINE INPUT filename$¶
  PRINT "Fast-GFX-Picture:"¶
  LINE INPUT target$¶
  PRINT "Name of the Loader:"¶
  LINE INPUT loader$¶
  CHDIR "df0:"¶
  ¶
REM **** OPEN IFF-DATA FILE ********************¶
  file$=filename$+CHR$(0)¶
  handle&=xOpen&(SADD(file$),1005)¶
  IF handle&=0 THEN ERROR 255¶
  ¶
REM **** CREATE INPUT-BUFFER ****************¶
  buffer&=AllocMem&(160,65537&)¶
  IF buffer&=0 THEN ERROR 254¶
  colorbuffer&=buffer&+96¶
  ¶
REM **** GET AND TEST CHUNK-FORM *********¶
  r&=xRead&(handle&,buffer&,12)¶
  IF PEEKL(buffer&)<>1179603533& THEN ERROR 253¶
  IF PEEKL(buffer&+8)<>1229734477& THEN ERROR 252¶
  bmhdflag%=0¶
  flag%=0¶
  ¶
REM **** GET CHUNK NAME + CHUNK LENGTH ***********¶
  WHILE flag%<>1¶
    r&=xRead&(handle&,buffer&,8)¶
    IF r&<8 THEN flag%=1:GOTO whileend¶
  ¶
    length&=PEEKL(buffer&+4)¶
  ¶
REM **** BMHD-CHUNK? (CVL("BMHD")) **************¶
    IF PEEKL(buffer&)=1112361028& THEN¶
  ¶
      r&=xRead&(handle&,buffer&,length&)¶
  ¶
      pwidth%=PEEKW(buffer&)        :REM * PICTUREWIDTH¶
      pheight%=PEEKW(buffer&+2)     :REM * PICTUREHEIGHT¶
```

```
        pdepth%=PEEK(buffer&+8)        :REM * PICTUREDEPTH¶
        packed%=PEEK(buffer&+10)       :REM * PACK-STATUS¶
        swidth%=PEEKW(buffer&+16)      :REM * SCREENWIDTH¶
        sheight%=PEEKW(buffer&+18)     :REM * SCREENHEIGHT¶
    ¶
        bytes%=(pwidth%-1)\8+1¶
        sbytes%=(swidth%-1)\8+1¶
        colmax%=2^pdepth%¶
        IF colmax%>32 THEN colmax%=32¶
        IF pwidth%<321 THEN mode%=1 ELSE mode%=2¶
        IF pheight%>256 THEN mode%=mode%+2¶
        IF pdepth%=6 THEN extraplane%=1 ELSE extraplane%=0¶
    ¶
REM **** NEW SCREEN PARAMETERS ****************¶
        WINDOW CLOSE 1¶
        SCREEN CLOSE 1¶
        SCREEN 1,pwidth%,pheight%,pdepth%-
extraplane%,mode%¶

        WINDOW 1,,,0,1¶
    ¶
REM **** DETERMINE SCREEN-DATA *****************¶
        picscreen&=PEEKL(WINDOW(7)+46)¶
        viewport&=picscreen&+44¶
        rastport&=picscreen&+84¶
        colormap&=PEEKL(viewport&+4)¶
        colors&=PEEKL(colormap&+4)¶
        bmap&=PEEKL(rastport&+4)¶
    ¶
REM **** HALFBRIGHT OR HOLD-AND-MODIFY ? ******¶
        IF extraplane%=1 THEN¶
    ¶
REM **** MAKE 6TH BITPLANE ******¶
        plane6&=AllocRaster&(swidth%,sheight%)¶
        IF plane6&=0 THEN ERROR 251¶
    ¶
REM **** AND ADD IT TO THE DATA STRUCTURE *****¶
        POKE bmap&+5,6¶
        POKEL bmap&+28,plane6&¶
    ¶
        END IF¶
    ¶
        bmhdflag%=1¶
    ¶
REM **** CMAP-CHUNK (SET EACH COLOR: R,G,B) ***¶
    ELSEIF PEEKL(buffer&)=1129136464& THEN¶
    ¶
        IF (length& OR 1)=1 THEN length&=length&+1¶
        r&=xRead&(handle&,buffer&,length&)¶
    ¶
        FOR i%=0 TO colmax%-1¶
    ¶
REM **** CONVERT TO THE FORM FOR THE   ***¶
REM **** THE HARDWARE-REGISTERS        ***¶
        POKE colorbuffer&+i%*2,PEEK(buffer&+i%*3)/16¶
        greenblue%=PEEK(buffer&+i%*3+1)¶
```

49

```
                greenblue%=greenblue%+PEEK(buffer&+i%*3+2)/16¶
                POKE colorbuffer&+i%*2+1,greenblue%¶
        ¶
        NEXT¶
        ¶
REM **** CAMG-CHUNK = VIEWMODE (ie. HAM or LACE) ***¶
        ELSEIF PEEKL(buffer&)=1128353095& THEN¶
        ¶
            r&=xRead&(handle&,buffer&,length&)¶
        ¶
            viewmode&=PEEKL(buffer&)¶
REM **** BODY-CHUNK = BITMAPS, LINE FOR LINE ******¶
        ELSEIF PEEKL(buffer&)=1112491097& THEN¶
¶
REM **** DOES THE SCREEN EXIST AT ALL? *******¶
            IF bmhdflag%=0 THEN ERROR 250¶
        ¶
REM **** IS THIS LINE PACKED? *******¶
            IF packed%=1 THEN¶
¶
REM **** THEN UNPACK IT!!! *********¶
                FOR y%=0 TO pheight%-1¶
                  FOR z%=0 TO pdepth%-1¶
                    ad&=PEEKL(bmap&+8+4*z%)+y%*sbytes%¶
                    count%=0¶
                    WHILE count%<bytes%¶
                      r&=xRead&(handle&,buffer&,1)¶
                      code%=PEEK(buffer&)¶
                      IF code%>128 THEN¶
                        r&=xRead&(handle&,buffer&,1)¶
                        value%=PEEK(buffer&)¶
                        endbyte%=count%+257-code%¶
                        FOR x%=count% TO endbyte%¶
                          POKE ad&+x%,value%¶
                        NEXT¶
                        count%=endbyte%¶
                      ELSEIF code%<128 THEN¶
                        r&=xRead&(handle&,ad&+count%,code%+1)¶
                        count%=count%+code%+1¶
                      END IF¶
                    WEND¶
                  NEXT z%,y%¶
        ¶
REM **** OR PERHAPS NOT PACKED? *****¶
            ELSEIF packed%=0 THEN¶
¶
REM **** FILL IN THE BITMAPS WITH THE DOS-COMMAND READ *¶
                FOR y%=0 TO pheight%-1¶
                  FOR z%=0 TO pdepth%-1¶
                    ad&=PEEKL(bmap&+8+4*z%)+y%*sbytes%¶
                    r&=xRead&(handle&,ad&,bytes%)¶
                  NEXT z%,y%¶
        ¶
REM **** CODING-METHOD UNKNOWN? ****¶
            ELSE¶
        ¶
```

```
            ERROR 249¶
  ¶
      END IF¶
  ¶
    ELSE¶
                    ¶
REM **** WE DO NOT HAVE TO BE ABLE TO CHUNK. ******¶
REM **** SHIFT DATA FILE POINTER  ******¶
      IF (length& OR 1)=1 THEN length&=length&+1¶
      now&=Seek&(handle&,length&,0)¶
  ¶
      END IF¶
¶
REM **** END THE SUBROUTINE *******************¶
whileend:¶
¶
  WEND¶
¶
REM **** LOAD COLOR AND CLOSE FILE ****¶
  IF bmhdflag%=0 THEN ERROR 248¶
  CALL LoadRGB4(viewport&,colorbuffer&,colmax%)¶
  CALL xClose(handle&)¶
¶
REM **** VIEW MODE GOTTEN? THEN ALSO STORE *¶
  IF viewmode&<>0 THEN¶
    POKEW viewport&+32,viewmode&¶
  END IF¶
¶
REM **** OPEN DESTINATION DATA FILE *************¶
  file$=target$+CHR$(0)¶
  handle&=xOpen&(SADD(file$),1005)¶
  IF handle&=0 THEN¶
    handle&=xOpen&(SADD(file$),1006)¶
  END IF¶
¶
REM ********************************************¶
REM **** SO YOU CAN REMOVE A GRAPHIC       *****¶
REM **** FROM MEMORY VERY QUICKLY          *****¶
¶
  bitmap&=sbytes%*pheight%   :REM ONE LARGE BITPLANE¶
¶
  FOR i%=0 TO pdepth%-1¶
    ad&=PEEKL(PEEKL(WINDOW(8)+4)+8+4*i%)¶
    w&=xWrite&(handle&,ad&,bitmap&)¶
  NEXT¶
¶
  w&=xWrite&(handle&,colorbuffer&,64)¶
¶
REM **** CLOSE DATA FILE, AND FREE BUFFER *****¶
  CALL xClose(handle&)¶
  CALL FreeMem(buffer&,160)¶
¶
REM ********************************************¶
REM **** GENERATES BASIC-PROGRAM (ASCII-FORMAT) *¶
  OPEN loader$ FOR OUTPUT AS 1¶
¶
```

```
     PRINT#1,"' ##################";CHR$(10);¶
     PRINT#1,"' # Fast-Gfx Loader #";CHR$(10);¶
     PRINT#1,"' #----------------#";CHR$(10);¶
     PRINT#1,"' # ";CHR$(169);"'87 S. Maelger #";CHR$(10);¶
     PRINT#1,"' ##################";CHR$(10);¶
     PRINT#1,CHR$(10);¶
¶
REM **** DECLARE THE ROM-ROUTINES ******¶
     PRINT#1,"DECLARE FUNCTION xOpen& LIBRARY";CHR$(10);¶
     PRINT#1,"DECLARE FUNCTION xRead& LIBRARY";CHR$(10);¶
     PRINT#1,"DECLARE FUNCTION AllocMem& LIBRARY";CHR$(10);¶
¶
REM **** FOR THE CASE OF H.A.M. OR HALFBRIGHT ****¶
     IF pdepth%=6 THEN¶
¶
        PRINT#1,"DECLARE FUNCTION AllocRaster& LIBRARY";¶
           PRINT#1,CHR$(10);¶
¶
     END IF¶
¶
REM **** OPEN NEEDED LIBRARIES ********************¶
     PRINT#1,CHR$(10);¶
     PRINT#1,"LIBRARY ";CHR$(34);"dos.library";CHR$(34);¶
        PRINT#1,CHR$(10);¶
     PRINT#1,"LIBRARY ";CHR$(34);"exec.library";CHR$(34);¶
        PRINT#1,CHR$(10);¶
     PRINT#1,"LIBRARY
";CHR$(34);"graphics.library";CHR$(34);¶
        PRINT#1,CHR$(10);¶
     PRINT#1,CHR$(10);¶
¶
REM **** RESERVE MEMORY FOR PALETTE ******¶
     PRINT#1,"b&=AllocMem&(64,65537&)";CHR$(10);¶
     PRINT#1,"IF b&=0 THEN ERROR 7";CHR$(10);¶
¶
REM **** OPEN PICTURE-DATA FILE ******************¶
     PRINT#1,"file$=";CHR$(34);target$;CHR$(34);
"+CHR$(0)";¶
        PRINT#1,CHR$(10);¶
     PRINT#1,"h&=xOpen&(SADD(file$),1005)";CHR$(10);¶
¶
REM **** CREATE SCREEN **********************¶
     PRINT#1,"WINDOW CLOSE WINDOW(0)";CHR$(10);¶
     PRINT#1,"SCREEN 1,";MID$(STR$(swidth%),2);",";¶
        PRINT#1,MID$(STR$(pheight%),2);",";¶
        PRINT#1,MID$(STR$(pdepth%-extraplane%),2);",";¶
        PRINT#1,MID$(STR$(mode%),2);CHR$(10);¶
     PRINT#1,"WINDOW 1,,,0,1";CHR$(10);¶
     PRINT#1,"viewport&=PEEKL(WINDOW(7)+46)+44";CHR$(10);¶
¶
REM **** SET ALL COLORS TO ZERO ************¶
     lcm$="CALL LoadRGB4(viewport&,b&,"¶
     lcm$=lcm$+MID$(STR$(colmax%),2)+")"+CHR$(10)¶
     PRINT#1,lcm$;¶
¶
REM **** IS HAM OR HALFBRIGHT ON, 6 PLANES ********¶
```

```
   IF tiefe%=6 THEN¶
¶
    PRINT#1,"n&=AllocRaster&(";¶
      PRINT#1,MID$(STR$(swidth%),2);",";¶
      PRINT#1,MID$(STR$(pheight%),2);")";CHR$(10);¶
    PRINT#1,"IF n&=0 THEN ERROR 7";CHR$(10);¶

PRINT#1,"bmap&=PEEKL(PEEKL(WINDOW(7)+46)+88)";CHR$(10);¶
    PRINT#1,"POKE bmap&+5,6";CHR$(10);¶
    PRINT#1,"POKEL bmap&+28,n&";CHR$(10);¶
    PRINT#1,"POKEL viewport&+32,PEEKL(viewport&+32)OR
2^";¶
¶
REM **** AND SET VIEWMODE ****************¶
    IF (viewmode& OR 2^7)=2^7 THEN¶
¶
REM **** SET HALFBRIGHT-BIT ******************¶
      PRINT#1,"7";¶
¶
    ELSE¶
¶
REM **** SET HOLD-AND-MODIFY - BIT ***********¶
      PRINT#1,"11";¶
¶
    END IF¶
¶
      PRINT#1,CHR$(10);¶
¶
   END IF¶
¶
REM **** AND NOW THE MAIN ROUTINE ****************¶
  PRINT#1,"FOR i%=0 TO";STR$(pdepth%-1);CHR$(10);¶
  PRINT#1,"
ad&=PEEKL(PEEKL(WINDOW(8)+4)+8+4*i%)";CHR$(10);¶
  PRINT#1,"   r&=xRead&(h&,ad&,";¶
    PRINT#1,MID$(STR$(bitmap&),2);"&)";CHR$(10);¶
  PRINT#1,"NEXT";CHR$(10);¶
¶
REM **** GET PALETTE (ALREADY IN THE RIGHT FORM)¶
  PRINT#1,"r&=xRead&(h&,b&,64)";CHR$(10);    ¶
¶
REM **** CLOSE THE FILE AGAIN ****************¶
  PRINT#1,"CALL xClose(h&)";CHR$(10);¶
¶
REM **** SET COLOR TABLE **************¶
  PRINT#1,lcm$;¶
¶
REM **** FREE COLOR BUFFER AGAIN ****¶
  PRINT#1,"CALL FreeMem(b&,64)";CHR$(10);¶
¶
REM **** CLOSE LIBRARIES AGAIN ************¶
  PRINT#1,"LIBRARY CLOSE";CHR$(10);¶
¶
REM **** WAIT FOR MOUSE-CLICK ****************¶
  PRINT#1,"WHILE MOUSE(0)<>0:WEND";CHR$(10);¶
  PRINT#1,"WHILE MOUSE(0)=0:WEND";CHR$(10);¶
```

53

```
¶
REM **** CLOSE SCREEN AND BASIC-WINDOW  *****¶
REM **** TURN WORKBENCH-SCREEN ON AGAIN *****¶
  PRINT#1,"WINDOW CLOSE 1";CHR$(10);¶
  PRINT#1,"SCREEN CLOSE 1";CHR$(10);¶
  PRINT#1,"WINDOW 1,";CHR$(34);"OK";CHR$(34);¶
    PRINT#1,",(0,11)-(310,185),0,-1";¶
    PRINT#1,CHR$(10);CHR$(10);¶
¶
  CLOSE 1¶
¶
REM **** BACK TO THE WORKBENCH *****************¶
  WINDOW CLOSE 1¶
  SCREEN CLOSE 1¶
  WINDOW 1,,,0,-1¶
  PRINT "Creating Loader-Icon"¶
¶
REM **** DATA FOR SPECIAL-ICON IMAGE *******¶
  RESTORE icondata¶
¶
  file$=loader$+".info"+CHR$(0)¶
¶
  a$=""¶
  FOR i%=1 TO 486¶
    READ b$¶
    a$=a$+CHR$(VAL("&H"+b$))¶
  NEXT¶
¶
REM **** AND WRITE THE ICON DATA-FILE ****¶
REM **** TO DISK    (MODE=OLDFILE)    ****¶
  h&=xOpen&(SADD(file$),1005)¶
  w&=xWrite&(h&,SADD(a$),498)¶
¶
  CALL xClose(h&)¶
¶
REM **** PERHAPS STILL ANOTHER PICTURE ???
*****************¶
  CLS¶
  PRINT "Another Picture (y/n)? >";¶
¶
pause:¶
¶
  a$=INKEY$¶
  IF a$<>"y" AND a$<>"n" GOTO pause¶
¶
  PRINT UCASE$(a$)¶
  IF a$="y" GOTO nameinput¶
¶
REM **** WERE DONE... *****************¶
  LIBRARY CLOSE¶
  MENU RESET¶
  END¶
¶
REM **** ERROR-TRAPPING *******************¶
errorcheck: ¶
¶
  n%=ERR¶
¶
  IF n%=255 THEN¶
    PRINT "Picture not found"¶
    GOTO rerun¶
  ELSEIF n%=254 THEN¶
    PRINT "Not enough Memory!"¶
    GOTO rerun¶
  ELSEIF n%=253 OR n%=252 THEN¶
    PRINT "Not IFF-ILBM-Picture!"¶
    GOTO rerun¶
```

```
      ELSEIF n%=251 THEN¶
         PRINT "Can Not Open 6th Plane."¶
         GOTO rerun¶
      ELSEIF n%=250 THEN¶
         PRINT "Not BMHD-Chunk form BODY!"¶
         GOTO rerun¶
      ELSEIF n%=249 THEN¶
         PRINT "Unknown Crunch-Algorithm."¶
         GOTO rerun¶
      ELSEIF n%=248 THEN¶
         PRINT "No more to view."¶
         GOTO rerun¶
¶
      ELSE¶
         CLOSE¶
         CALL xClose(handle&)¶
         CALL FreeMem(buffer&,160)¶
         LIBRARY CLOSE¶
         MENU RESET¶
         ON ERROR GOTO 0¶
         ERROR n%¶
         STOP¶
¶
      END IF¶
¶
      STOP¶
¶
rerun:¶
¶
      IF n%<>255 THEN¶
         CALL xClose(handle&)¶
         IF n%<>254 THEN CALL FreeMem(buffer&,160)¶
      END IF¶
¶
      BEEP¶
      LIBRARY CLOSE¶
      RUN¶
¶
icondata:¶
DATA E3,10,0,1,0,0,0,0,0,0,0,0,0,0,2E,0,1F,0,5,0,3,0,1¶
DATA 0,1,BD,A0,0,0,0,0,0,0,0,0,0,0,0,0,0,0,0,0,0,0,0¶
DATA 0,0,0,4,0,0,0,F2,98,0,0,0,0,80,0,0,0,80,0,0,0,0¶
DATA 0,0,0,0,0,0,0,0,0,10,0,0,0,0,0,0,0,2E,0,1F,0,2,0¶
DATA 2,B1,E0,3,0,0,0,0,0,0,0,0,0,0,3,FF,FF,FF,FF,0¶
DATA 3,0,0,0,3,0,2,0,0,0,1,0,2,0,0,0,1,0,2,7,80,0,1¶
DATA 0,2,1,F8,0,1,0,2,0,3F,C0,1,0,2,3,FC,0,1,0,2,0¶
DATA 1F,C0,1,0,2,0,1,FE,1,0,2,0,0,1F,F1,0,2,0,0,FF,1¶
DATA 0,3,0,1F,FE,3,0,3,FF,FF,FF,FF,0,0,0,6A,BF,F0,0¶
DATA 0,0,0,7,FE,0,0,0,0,0,FF,80,7F,EF,FF,FD,FF,F8,7F¶
DATA EF,FF,FD,E0,38,7F,EF,FF,FD,FF,F8,0,0,0,0,0,0,0¶
DATA 0,0,0,0,0,0,0,0,0,0,0,0,3E,7C,F9,B0,0,0,20,40¶
DATA 80,A0,0,0,3C,4C,F0,40,0,0,20,44,80,A0,0,0,20,7C¶
DATA 81,B0,0,0,0,0,0,0,0,0,0,0,0,3,FF,FF,FF,FF,0¶
DATA 4,0,0,0,0,80,4,FF,FF,FF,FC,80,5,FF,FF,FF,FE,80¶
DATA 5,FF,FF,FF,FE,80,5,FF,FF,FF,FE,80,5,FF,FF,FF,FE¶
DATA 80,5,FF,FF,FF,FE,80,5,FF,FF,FF,FE,80,5,FF,FF,FF¶
DATA FE,80,5,FF,FF,FF,FE,80,5,FF,FF,FF,FE,80,5,FF,FF¶
DATA FF,FE,80,4,FF,FF,FF,FC,80,4,0,3,FF,80,80,7,FF¶
DATA 95,7F,FF,80,1,FF,FF,FF,FE,0,7F,FF,FF,FF,FF,F8¶
DATA 80,10,0,2,FF,84,80,10,0,2,7F,C4,B0,10,0,2,0,4¶
DATA 7F,FF,FF,FF,FF,FC,38,0,0,0,38,30,0,0,0,0,18,0¶
DATA 0,0,0,0,0,0,0,0,0,0,0,0,0,0,0,0,0,0,0,0,0,0,0¶
DATA 0,0,0,0,0,0,0,0,0,0,0,0,0,0,0,0,0,0,0,0,C,3A,41¶
DATA 6D,69,67,61,42,41,53,49,43,0¶
```

3.2.5 IFF brushes as objects

If you own a high-quality paint program like *DeluxePaint®*, you can actually use it as an object editor. You can create sprites and bobs with this program.

The program in this section lets you convert any IFF graphic into an object file. The only requirement is that the graphic cannot be too large for an object string.

This graphic object can be activated and moved. Since there are no special techniques used for storing the background, too many bitplanes can cause a flickering effect.

```
' #####################################
' #  Use DPaint as Object-Editor with #
' #-----------------------------------#
' # B R U S H - T R A N S F O R M E R #
' #-----------------------------------#
' #       (W) 1987 by Stefan Maelger   #
' #####################################
'
  CLEAR,30000&
  DIM r(31),g(31),b(31)

nameinput:
  PRINT "Brush-File Name (and Path): ";
  LINE INPUT brush$
  PRINT
  PRINT "Object-Data File (and Path): ";
  LINE INPUT objectfile$
  PRINT
  PRINT "Create Color-Data File? (Y/N) ";
pause:
  a$=LEFT$(UCASE$(INKEY$+CHR$(0)),1)
  IF a$="N" THEN
    PRINT "NO!"
  ELSEIF a$="Y" THEN
    PRINT "OK."
    colorflag%=1
    PRINT
    PRINT "Color-Data File Name (and Path): ";
    LINE INPUT colorfile$
  ELSE
    GOTO pause
  END IF
  PRINT

  OPEN brush$ FOR INPUT AS 1
  a$=INPUT$(4,1)
  IF a$<>"FORM" THEN CLOSE 1:RUN
```

56

```
    a$=INPUT$(4,1)¶
    a$=INPUT$(4,1)¶
    IF a$<>"ILBM" THEN CLOSE 1:RUN¶
¶
getchunk:¶
    a$=INPUT$(4,1)¶
¶
  IF a$="BMHD" THEN¶
    PRINT "BMHD-Chunk found."¶
    PRINT ¶
    a$=INPUT$(4,1)¶
    bwidth%=ASC(INPUT$(1,1)+CHR$(0))*256¶
    bwidth%=bwidth%+ASC(INPUT$(1,1)+CHR$(0))¶
    PRINT "Image width :";bwidth%;" Pixels"¶
    IF bwidth%>320 THEN¶
      PRINT "It is too wide."¶
      BEEP¶
      CLOSE 1¶
      RUN¶
    END IF¶
    bheight%=ASC(INPUT$(1,1)+CHR$(0))*256¶
    bheight%=bheight%+ASC(INPUT$(1,1)+CHR$(0))¶
    PRINT "Image height:";bheight%;" Pixels"¶
    IF bheight%>200 THEN¶
      PRINT "It is too high."¶
      BEEP¶
      CLOSE 1¶
      RUN¶
    END IF¶
    a$=INPUT$(4,1)¶
    planes%=ASC(INPUT$(1,1))¶
    PRINT "Image Depth :";planes%;" Planes"¶
    IF planes%>5 THEN¶
      PRINT "Too many Planes!"¶
      BEEP¶
      CLOSE 1¶
      RUN¶
    ELSEIF planes%*((bwidth%-1)\16+1)*2*bheight%>32000
THEN¶
      PRINT "Too many Bytes for the Object-String!"¶
      BEEP¶
      CLOSE 1¶
      RUN¶
    END IF ¶
    a$=INPUT$(1,1)¶
    packed%=ASC(INPUT$(1,1)+CHR$(0))¶
    IF packed%=0 THEN¶
      PRINT "Pack status: NOT packed."¶
    ELSEIF packed%=1 THEN¶
      PRINT "Pack status: ByteRun1-Algorithm."¶
    ELSE¶
      PRINT "Pack status: Unknown method"¶
      BEEP¶
      CLOSE 1¶
      RUN¶
    END IF¶
```

```
                      a$=INPUT$(9,1)¶
                      Status%=Status%+1¶
                      PRINT¶
                      PRINT   ¶
            ¶
            ELSEIF a$="CMAP" THEN¶
                      PRINT "CMAP-Chunk found."¶
                      a$=INPUT$(3,1)¶
                      l%=ASC(INPUT$(1,1))¶
                      colors%=l%\3¶
                      PRINT colors%;"Colors found"¶
                      FOR i%=0 TO colors%-1¶
                        r(i%)=ASC(INPUT$(1,1)+CHR$(0))/255¶
                        g(i%)=ASC(INPUT$(1,1)+CHR$(0))/255¶
                        b(i%)=ASC(INPUT$(1,1)+CHR$(0))/255¶
                      NEXT¶
                      Status%=Status%+2¶
                      PRINT ¶
                      PRINT ¶
            ¶
            ELSEIF a$="BODY" THEN¶
                      PRINT "BODY-Chunk found."¶
                      PRINT ¶
                      a$=INPUT$(4,1)¶
                      bytes%=(bwidth%-1)\8+1¶
                      bmap%=bytes%*bheight%¶
                      obj$=STRING$(bytes%*bheight%*planes%,0)¶
                      FOR i%=0 TO bheight%-1¶
                        PRINT "Getting lines";i%+1¶
                        FOR j%=0 TO planes%-1¶
                          IF packed%=0 THEN¶
                            FOR k%=1 TO bytes%¶
                              a$=LEFT$(INPUT$(1,1)+CHR$(0),1)¶
                              MID$(obj$,j%*bmap%+i%*bytes%+k%,1)=a$¶
                            NEXT¶
                          ELSE¶
                            pointer%=1¶
                            WHILE pointer%<bytes%+1¶
                              a%=ASC(INPUT$(1,1)+CHR$(0))¶
                              IF a%<128 THEN¶
                                FOR k%=pointer% TO pointer%+a%¶
                                  a$=LEFT$(INPUT$(1,1)+CHR$(0),1)¶
                                  MID$(obj$,j%*bmap%+i%*bytes%+k%,1)=a$¶
                                NEXT¶
                                pointer%=pointer%+a%+1¶
                              ELSEIF a%>128 THEN¶
                                a$=LEFT$(INPUT$(1,1)+CHR$(0),1)¶
                                FOR k%=pointer% TO pointer%+257-a%¶
                                  MID$(obj$,j%*bmap%+i%*bytes%+k%,1)=a$¶
                                NEXT¶
                                pointer%=pointer%+256-a%¶
                              END IF¶
                            WEND¶
                          END IF¶
                        NEXT¶
                      NEXT¶
```

```
      Status%=Status%+4¶
¶
  ELSE¶
    PRINT a$;" found."¶
    a=CVL(INPUT$(4,1))/4¶
    FOR i%=1 TO a¶
      a$=INPUT$(4,1)¶
    NEXT¶
    GOTO getchunk¶
      ¶
  END IF¶
¶
checkstatus:¶
  IF Status%<7 GOTO getchunk¶
¶
  CLOSE 1¶
  PRINT ¶
¶
  PRINT "OK, Creating Object."¶
  ob$=""¶
  FOR i%=0 TO 10¶
    ob$=ob$+CHR$(0)¶
  NEXT¶
  ob$=ob$+CHR$(planes%)+CHR$(0)+CHR$(0)¶
  ob$=ob$+MKI$(bwidth%)+CHR$(0)+CHR$(0)¶
  ob$=ob$+MKI$(bheight%)+CHR$(0)+CHR$(24)¶
  ob$=ob$+CHR$(0)+CHR$(3)+CHR$(0)+CHR$(0)¶
  ob$=ob$+obj$¶
  PRINT ¶
¶
  PRINT "Create Object-Data File as ";CHR$(34);¶
  PRINT objectfile$;CHR$(34)¶
  PRINT ¶
¶
  OPEN objectfile$ FOR OUTPUT AS 2¶
    PRINT#2,ob$;¶
  CLOSE 2¶
  PRINT "Object stored."¶
¶
  IF colorflag%=1 THEN¶
    PRINT ¶
    PRINT "Creating Color-Data File:"¶
    OPEN colorfile$ FOR OUTPUT AS 3¶
      PRINT#3,CHR$(planes%);¶
      PRINT " Byte 1 = Number of Bitplanes"¶
      FOR i%=0 TO 2^planes%-1¶
        PRINT "Byte";i%*3+2;"= red   (";i%;")*255"¶
        PRINT#3,CHR$(r(i%)*255);¶
        PRINT "Byte";i%*3+3;"= green(";i%;")*255"¶
        PRINT#3,CHR$(g(i%)*255);¶
        PRINT "Byte";i%*3+4;"= blue (";i%;")*255"¶
        PRINT#3,CHR$(b(i%)*255);¶
      NEXT¶
    CLOSE 3¶
  END IF¶
¶
```

```
SCREEN 1,320,200,planes%,1¶
WINDOW 2,,,0,1¶
FOR i%=0 TO 2^planes%-1¶
  PALETTE i%,r(i%),g(i%),b(i%) ¶
NEXT¶
¶
OBJECT.SHAPE 1,ob$¶
OBJECT.PLANES 1,2^planes%-1,0¶
¶
FOR i=0 TO 300 STEP .1¶
  OBJECT.X 1,i¶
  OBJECT.Y 1,(i\2) ¶
  OBJECT.ON¶
NEXT¶
¶
WINDOW CLOSE 2¶
SCREEN CLOSE 1¶
¶
RUN¶
```

Variables

status	status of chunks read
a	help variable
b	array, blue scales of a color
bmap	size of BOB bitplane in bytes
bwidth	width of BOB in pixels
brush	name of IFF-ILBM file
bytes	width of BOB in bytes
colorfile	color file name
colors	number of IFF file colors stored
g	array, green scales of a color
packed	pack status0=not packed;1=byterun 1
bheight	height of BOB in pixels
i	loop variable
j	loop variable
k	loop variable
l	loop variable
ob	object string
obj	image string
objectfile	file stored in ob$
planes	bitplane depth of BOB
pointer	counter variable for bytes read from a line
r	array, red scale of a color

Color file data (optional)

Byte 1=	number of bitplanes in the object
Byte 2=	red scale of background color * 255
Byte 3=	green scale of background color * 255
Byte 4=	blue scale of background color * 255
Byte 5=	red scale of 1st color * 255
Byte 6=	green scale of 1st color * 255
Byte 7=	blue scale of 1st color * 255

IFF structure

Now a few words about IFF-ILBM-format. A file in this format has several adjacently stored files called chunks. Every chunk has the following design:

1	Chunk name	=	4-byte-long string (e.g., "BODY")
2	Chunk length	=	4-byte integer (i.e., LONG format)
3	Chunk data	=	#chunk-long bytes

The header chunk which begins every IFF file has a similar design:

1	Filetype	=	"FORM" (IFF file header)
2	File length	=	Long value
3	Data type	=	"ILBM" (interleaved bitmaps)

The most important chunks:

BMHD chunk

1	long	=	"BMHD" (bitmap header chunk)
2	long	=	chunk length
3	word	=	graphic width in pixels
4	word	=	graphic height in pixels
5	word	=	X-position of graphic
6	word	=	Y-position of graphic
7	byte	=	number of bitplanes on screen
8	byte	=	masking
9	byte	=	crunch type
10	byte	=	??
11	word	=	transparent color
12	byte	=	X-aspect
13	byte	=	Y-aspect
14	word	=	screen width in pixels
15	word	=	screen height in pixels

CMAP chunk

1	long	=	"CMAP" (ColorMap)
2	long	=	chunk length
3	byte	=	color 0 red value *255
4	byte	=	color 0 green value *255
5	byte	=	color 0 blue value *255
6	byte	=	color 1 red value *255

CRNG chunk (DeLuxe Paint)

1	long	=	"CRNG" (ColorCycle chunk-4 times)
2	long	=	chunk length
3	word	=	always 0 (at this time)
4	word	=	speed
5	word	=	active/inactive
6	byte	=	lower color
7	byte	=	upper color

CCRT chunk (Graphic-raft)

1	long	=	"CCRT" (ColorCycle chunk from Graphicraft)
2	long	=	chunk length
3	word	=	direction
4	byte	=	starting color
5	byte	=	ending color
6	long	=	seconds
7	long	=	microseconds

BODY	1	long =	"BODY" (Bitmaps)
chunk	2	long =	chunk length
	3	=	1st line of 1st bitplane (for eventual packing - see BMHD above)
			1st line of 2nd bitplane
			1st line of 3nd bitplane
			2nd line of 1st bitplane...

ByteRun1-Crunch Algorithm

There is never more than one line of a bitplane packed at a time. This packing can occur in line order. The coding consists of one code byte. If this byte has a value larger than 128, then the next byte repeats with a value at least 3 times more (e.g., 129 results in the next byte at 258 more). Since FOR/NEXT loops require a starting value for loop variables, this construct must begin with the value 1, listed as follows:

```
FOR i=startvalue TO startvalue+258-codebyte-1
```

Or as shown above, `257-codebyte`. The second coding applies to codebytes less then 128. Here the next `codebyte+1` byte is not used. In short, you could say that the first and second coding types use a maximum of 128 bytes. Since the width of a 640*x screen only requires 80 bytes, then one line of one bitplane only requires one coding.

3.2.6   Another floodfill

The Amiga has the ability to execute complicated area filling at a rate of one million pixels per second in any color. The AmigaBASIC PAINT command performs this task. This command has one disadvantage in its current form: It can only fill an area that is bordered by only one predetermined color. This limits anyone who might want to use this in their own applications (e.g., drawing programs). A solution might be to set up parameters with the PAINT command that uses any color for the floodfill border. A routine like this exists in the operating system. Since the graphics library handles it as one of its own routines, the program stays in memory and doesn't disappear when the Workbench reboots.

The routine is called Flood and can be called from AmigaBASIC as follows:

```
CALL Flood&(Rastport,Mode,x,y)
```

Here is a SUB routine that uses Flood:

```
REM ##############################¶
REM # F L O O D F I L L  Amiga  #¶
REM #----------------------------#¶
REM #  PAINT until to any        #¶
REM #  other color if found      #¶
```

```
REM #----------------------------#¶
REM # (W) 1987 by Stefan Maelger #¶
REM ##############################¶
¶
LIBRARY "graphics.library"¶
¶
SCREEN 1,640,255,2,2¶
WINDOW 2,"FLOODFILL",,0,1¶
¶
LOCATE 2,2¶
PRINT "Floodfill-Demo"¶
¶
CIRCLE (200,80),150,2¶
CIRCLE (400,80),150,3¶
¶
FLOODFILL 200,80,1¶
FLOODFILL 300,80,1¶
FLOODFILL 400,80,1¶
¶
LIBRARY CLOSE¶
¶
LOCATE 4,2¶
PRINT "PRESS ANY KEY"¶
¶
WHILE INKEY$=""¶
WEND¶
¶
STOP¶
¶
SUB FLOODFILL(x%,y%,fcolor%) STATIC¶
  PSET (0,0),0¶
  PAINT (0,0),0¶
  COLOR fcolor%¶
  rastport&=WINDOW(8)¶
  ToAnyColorMode%=1¶
  CALL Flood&(rastport&,ToAnyColorMode%,x%,y%)¶
END SUB¶
```

Initializing this routine is as simple as calling PAINT.

3.2.7 Window manipulation

You already know that windows can do a lot. This section shows you a
few extra ideas for working with windows in AmigaBASIC.

3.2.7.1 Borderless BASIC windows

An Amiga expert published a long program listing in a recent magazine. This listing looked up a bitmap address and erased the border bit
by bit—it took more than a minute to execute. Here's an easier way to
get the same result:

```
' ####################################¶
' # BORDERLESS for AmigaBASIC-Windows #¶
' #-----------------------------------#¶
' #      (W) 1987 by Stefan Maelger    #¶
' ####################################¶
'¶
  LIBRARY "intuition.library"¶
  CLS¶
  PRINT "Here is a Default Window with a Border-"¶
  PRINT¶
  pause 2¶
  PRINT "And Without a Border (Frame)-"¶
  PRINT¶
  PRINT "Press any Key to Restore Default Window"¶
¶
¶
  killborder¶
¶
  waitkey¶
  remake¶
  LIBRARY CLOSE¶
  END¶
¶
¶
SUB remake STATIC¶
  WINDOW CLOSE 1¶
  WINDOW 1¶
END SUB¶
¶
SUB pause(seconds%) STATIC¶
  t=TIMER+seconds%¶
  WHILE t>TIMER¶
  WEND¶
END SUB¶
¶
SUB waitkey STATIC¶
  WHILE INKEY$=""¶
  WEND¶
END SUB¶
¶
SUB killborder STATIC¶
  borderless&   =2^11¶
  gimmezerozero&=2^10¶
  window.base&=WINDOW(7)¶
  window.modi&=window.base&+24¶
  Mode&=PEEKL(window.modi&)¶
  Mode&=Mode& AND(2^26-1-gimmezerozero&)¶
  Mode&=Mode& OR borderless&¶
  POKEL window.modi&,Mode&¶
  CALL RefreshWindowFrame(window.base&)¶
END SUB¶
```

3.2.7.2   Gadgets on, gadgets off

This program removes and adds gadgets to windows.

```
' ####################################¶
' # GADGETon/off in AmigaBASIC-Windows #¶
' #-----------------------------------#¶
' #      (W) 1987 by Stefan Maelger    #¶
' ####################################¶
```

```
'¶
LIBRARY "intuition.library"¶
¶
  PRINT "Make all the Gadgets disappear!"¶
  SaveGadgetPointer GadgetStore&¶
  pause 5¶
  UnlinkGadgets¶
  pause 10¶
  PRINT "And now bring them back again."¶
  pause 5¶
  SetGadgets GadgetStore&¶
  LIBRARY CLOSE¶
  WINDOW CLOSE 1¶
  WINDOW 1¶
  END¶
¶
SUB pause(seconds%) STATIC¶
  t=TIMER+seconds%¶
  WHILE t>TIMER¶
  WEND¶
END SUB¶
¶
SUB SaveGadgetPointer(Pointer&) STATIC¶
  window.base&   =WINDOW(7)¶
  gadget.pointer&=window.base&+62¶
  Pointer&=PEEKL(gadget.pointer&)¶
END SUB¶
¶
SUB UnlinkGadgets STATIC¶
  window.base&   =WINDOW(7)¶
  gadget.pointer&=window.base&+62¶
  POKEL gadget.pointer&,0¶
  CALL RefreshWindowFrame(window.base&)¶
END SUB¶
¶
SUB SetGadgets(Pointer&) STATIC¶
  window.base&   =WINDOW(7)¶
  gadget.pointer&=window.base&+62¶
  POKEL gadget.pointer&,Pointer&¶
  CALL RefreshWindowFrame(window.base&)¶
END SUB¶
```

3.2.7.3   DrawBorder

Imagine that you want to draw a border from Intuition. You must first know the structure of the border, and the address of a border structure for the DrawBorder routine to execute. Here's the structure:

1st word   horizontal spacing from X-coordinate called by the routine (defines only one form and can be drawn in any spacing)
2nd word   vertical spacing of Y-coordinate
3rd byte   Character color (from BASIC)
4th byte   Background color
5th byte   Character mode (JAM1=0)
6th byte   Number of X/Y coordinate pairs
7th long   Coordinate table address
8th long   Address of next structure or value of 0

The 7th part of the structure needs a coordinate table consisting of words. These words contain the X-coordinate and the Y-coordinate of one pixel. One pixel requires four bytes (two words) of memory.

When you call the routine with the Window Rastport instead of the Border Rastport (WINDOW(8)), you can draw any complex structure you wish in the **BASIC** window. There is one problem with this: The window's character cursor appears after the last pixel of the last structure. A PRINT command starts output at this position. AmigaBASIC uses the cursor position as the starting place for PRINT. Be careful with your use of the PRINT statement after calling DrawBorder.

```
' ####################################¶
' #   DRAWBORDER  - The Border Drawer   #¶
' #       (W) 1987 by Stefan Maelger    #¶
' ####################################¶
'¶
LIBRARY "intuition.library"¶
¶
PRINT "Putting the Coordinate-String Together"¶
¶
bwidth%=PEEKW(WINDOW(7)+8)-1¶
bheight%=PEEKW(WINDOW(7)+10)-1¶
xleft%=0¶
ytop%=0¶
xy$=MKI$(xleft%)+MKI$(ytop%)¶
xy$=xy$+MKI$(xleft%)+MKI$(bheight%)¶
xy$=xy$+MKI$(bwidth%)+MKI$(bheight%)¶
xy$=xy$+MKI$(bwidth%)+MKI$(ytop%)¶
Pairs%=4¶
xOffset%=0¶
yOffset%=0¶
bcolor%=0¶
¶
PRINT "Draw the border"¶
¶
Setborder xy$,Pairs%,bcolor%,xOffset%,yOffset%¶
¶
FOR i%=3 TO 1 STEP -1¶
   PRINT "Wait for a few seconds"¶
   t=TIMER+10:WHILE t>TIMER:WEND¶
   PRINT "Drawing in Color";i%¶
   Setborder xy$,Pairs%,i%,xOffset%,yOffset%¶
NEXT¶
¶
LIBRARY CLOSE¶
END¶
¶
SUB Setborder(xy$,number%,bcolor%,x%,y%) STATIC¶
   window.base&=WINDOW(7)¶
   borderrastport&=PEEKL(window.base&+58)¶
   IF borderrastport&=0 THEN EXIT SUB¶
   a$=MKI$(0)             'Horizontal Distance¶
   a$=a$+MKI$(0)          'Vertical Distance¶
   a$=a$+CHR$(bcolor%)    'Drawing Color¶
   a$=a$+CHR$(0)          'Background (unused)¶
   a$=a$+CHR$(0)          'Mode: JAM1¶
   a$=a$+CHR$(number%)    'Number of x-y-Pairs¶
   a$=a$+MKL$(SADD(xy$))  'Pointer to Coordinate¶
   a$=a$+MKL$(0)          'Pointer to Next Structure¶
   CALL DrawBorder(borderrastport&,SADD(a$),x%,y%)¶
   ' --- Last Parameters are relative X- and Y-
Coordinates¶
END SUB¶
```

3.2.7.4   ChangeBorderColor

The next routine can change a window's border color, including the title bar. The entire process occurs in the form of a SUB command.

```
' ####################################¶
' #   CHANGE BORDER COLOR             #¶
' #----------------------------------#¶
' #       (W) 1987 by Stefan Maelger  #¶
' ####################################¶
'¶
LIBRARY "intuition.library"¶
¶
PRINT "Have you ever been disturbed that the"¶
PRINT "drawing color in which borders are always"¶
PRINT "drawn is in color register 0 and that the"¶
PRINT "background is always register 1?"¶
PRINT¶
PRINT "We can change the colors defined"¶
PRINT "in the Window command itself!"¶
¶
LOCATE 10,1:PRINT "Foreground"¶
LOCATE 13,1:PRINT "Background"¶
t=TIMER+15:WHILE t>TIMER:WEND
FOR i=0 TO 3
   LINE (i*30,136)-STEP(30,20),i,bf¶
   LINE (i*30,136)-STEP(30,20),1,b¶
NEXT¶
¶
FOR b%=0 TO 3¶
  FOR f%=0 TO 3¶
     ChangeBorderColor f%,b%¶
     LOCATE 10,14:PRINT f%¶
     LOCATE 13,14:PRINT b%¶
     t=TIMER+5¶
     WHILE t>TIMER¶
     WEND¶
NEXT f%,b%¶
¶
ChangeBorderColor 1,0¶
¶
LIBRARY CLOSE¶
END¶
¶
SUB CHangeBorderColor(DetailPen%,BlockPen%) STATIC¶
 window.base&=WINDOW(7)¶
 Detail.pen& =window.base&+98¶
 Block.pen&  =window.base&+99¶
 POKE Detail.Pen&,Detail.Pen%¶
 POKE BlockPen&,BlockPen%¶
 CALL RefreshWindowFrame(window.base&)¶
END SUB¶
```

3.2.7.5   Monocolor Workbench

This program supplies you with an additional 16K of memory by setting up a single bitplane for color on the Workbench. A monocolor Workbench speeds up the screen editing of BASIC programs.

```
' #####################################¶
' #           MONOCOLOR WORKBENCH        #¶
' #-------------------------------------#¶
' #      (W) 1987 by Stefan Maelger      #¶
' #####################################¶
'¶
LIBRARY "intuition.library"¶
LIBRARY "graphics.library"¶
¶
Setplanes 1¶
¶
LIBRARY CLOSE¶
SYSTEM¶
¶
SUB Setplanes(planes%) STATIC¶
  IF planes%<1 OR planes%>6 THEN EXIT SUB¶
  rastport&       =WINDOW(8)¶
  bitmaps&        =PEEKL(rastport&+4)¶
  current.planes%=PEEK(bitmaps&+5)¶
  window.base&    =WINDOW(7)¶
  screen.base&    =PEEKL(window.base&+46)¶
  screen.width%   =PEEKW(screen.base&+12)¶
  screen.height%  =PEEKW(screen.base&+14)¶
  IF current.planes%>planes% THEN¶
    POKE bitmaps&+5,planes%¶
    FOR kill.plane%=current.planes% TO planes%+1 STEP -1¶

      plane.ad&=PEEKL(bitmaps&+4+4*kill.plane%)¶
      CALL
FreeRaster(plane.ad&,screen.width%,screen.height%)¶
      CALL RemakeDisplay¶
      CALL RefreshWindowFrame(WINDOW(7))¶
      CLS¶
    NEXT   ¶
  END IF¶
END SUB       ¶
```

3.2.7.6   PlaneCreator and HAM-Halfbrite

You've seen an example of how FreeRaster can free a bitplane from memory. You can also insert other bitplanes, if you know the addresses of these new bitplanes. The programmers of AmigaBASIC skipped over support for the Hold-and-Modify (HAM) and Halfbrite modes. These modes require six bitplanes, and must be accessed using the LIBRARY command (they cannot be used through AmigaBASIC commands). Here is a multi-purpose program, which lets you switch between modes and insert additional bitplanes.

This program displays all 4096 colors available to AmigaBASIC in the
AmigaBASIC window. Pressing a mouse key displays the 64 colors
contained in Halfbrite mode.

```
' ###########################################¶
' #HAM  P L A N E C R E A T O R  HALFBRIGHT #¶
' #         (W) 1987 by Stefan Maelger      #¶
' ###########################################¶
DECLARE FUNCTION AllocMem& LIBRARY¶
LIBRARY "exec.library"¶
LIBRARY "intuition.library"¶
SCREEN 1,320,200,1,1          :REM *** just ONE Plane¶
WINDOW 1,"What a wonderful feeling",,,1¶
PALETTE 0,0,0,0¶
PALETTE 1,1,1,1¶
FOR i%=2 TO 6¶
  CreateNewPlane¶
  LOCATE 1,1¶
  PRINT "I have";i%;"Planes";¶
  FOR j%=1 TO i%¶
    PRINT "!";¶
  NEXT¶
  PRINT¶
  PRINT "Press left Mouse-Button"¶
  Wait.for.the.Click.of.the.Left.MouseButton¶
NEXT ¶
HAM¶
FOR green=0 TO 15¶
  blue=0¶
  red=0¶
  LINE (0,green*10)-STEP(0,9),0¶
  LINE (1,green*10)-STEP(0,9),green+48¶
  FOR x=0 TO 7¶
    FOR red=1 TO 15¶
      LINE(x*32+red+1,green*10)-STEP(0,9),red+32¶
    NEXT red¶
    blue=blue+1¶
    LINE(x*32+17,green*10)-STEP(0,9),blue+16¶
    FOR red=14 TO 0 STEP -1¶
      LINE(x*32+17+15-red,green*10)-STEP(0,9),red+32¶
    NEXT red¶
    blue=blue+1¶
    IF blue<16 THEN LINE(x*32+33,green*10)-
STEP(0,9),blue+16¶
  NEXT x¶
NEXT green¶
Wait.for.the.Click.of.the.Left.MouseButton¶
CLS¶
HB¶
FOR i%=0 TO 3¶
  FOR j%=0 TO 15¶
    LINE (j%*18,i%*45)-STEP(18,45),i%*16+j%,bf¶
    LINE (j%*18,i%*45)-STEP(18,45),1,b¶
  NEXT¶
NEXT¶
Wait.for.the.Click.of.the.Left.MouseButton¶
WINDOW 1,"What a wonderful feeling",,,-1¶
SCREEN CLOSE 1¶
LIBRARY CLOSE¶
END¶
SUB CreateNewPlane STATIC¶
  bitmap&=PEEKL(WINDOW(7)+46)+184¶
  bitplane&=PEEKW(bitmap&)*PEEKW(bitmap&+2)¶
  wdepth%=PEEK(bitmap&+5) ¶
  IF wdepth%>5 THEN EXIT SUB¶
  newplane&=AllocMem&(bitplane&,65538&)¶
```

```
    IF newplane&=0 THEN ERROR 7¶
    POKEL bitmap&+8+wdepth%*4,newplane&¶
    POKE bitmap&+5,wdepth%+1¶
    IF wdepth%<5 THEN CALL RemakeDisplay¶
END SUB¶
SUB HAM STATIC¶
   viewmode&=PEEKL(WINDOW(7)+46)+76¶
   POKEW viewmode&,2^11¶
   CALL RemakeDisplay¶
END SUB¶
SUB HB STATIC¶
   viewmode&=PEEKL(WINDOW(7)+46)+76¶
   POKEW viewmode&,2^7¶
   CALL RemakeDisplay¶
END SUB¶
SUB Wait.for.the.Click.of.the.Left.MouseButton STATIC¶
   WHILE MOUSE(0)<>0¶
   WEND¶
   WHILE MOUSE(0)=0¶
   WEND¶
END SUB¶
```

You can now draw with colors from 0 to 63. The Amiga normally doesn't support this mode or the setup of the screens. If you want to work in these modes, there are some details you must know.

Let's begin with the Halfbrite mode. Here are a total of 32 colors (0 to 31), spread over the course of 5 planes. The PALETTE command initializes these colors, as well as those for Hold-And-Modify mode. The colors in Halfbrite mode (32 to 63) correspond directly to the colors 0 to 31. In other words, color number 33 is half as bright as color 1 (33-32=1). This equation applies to the other colors as well. You should be careful about the color selection with the PALETTE command. The following calculation returns the RGB proportions of Halfbrite colors:

$$\text{Proportion}(x)=\text{INT}(\text{Proportion}(x-32)*15/2)/15$$

This equation uses INT with the slashes (x/y is the same as INT(x/y) here). A PALETTE command for Halfbrite colors would look like this:

$$\text{PALETTE } 1,15/15,12/15,11/15$$

The command above assigns color 33 the values 7/15, 6/15, 5/15. Now try assigning the values 14/15, 13/15, 10/15 to another color–it should be another color altogether, but the result is two equal halfbrite colors. Just one reminder: PALETTE doesn't allow colors over 31.

HAM poses even more problems. Colors 0-15 are usable here. When you set a pixel in one of these colors, a point always appears in this color.

Colors 16-31 are another matter. First the RGB value of the pixel is set to the left of the pixel to be drawn (Hold), and then the blue proportion is changed (Modify). The equation for setting the new blue portion is:

$$\text{new\_blue\_portion} = (\text{color}-16)/15$$

Colors 32-47 change the red portion:

```
new_red_portion = (color-32)/15
```

Colors 48-63 modify the green portion of the color:

```
new_green_portion = (color-48)/15
```

You see, this way you can set up the desired color using not more than 3 pixels for one "color."

3.2.7.7   The coordinate problem

The pixel with the coordinates 0,0 lies below the title bar and to the right of the left border. Most programmers would expect 0,0 to be at the upper left corner of the screen. This can pose problems if you want to place an untitled window directly over the title bar of a standard window (e.g., the **BASIC** window).

What you want is a window eight pixels higher than normal. You must enter the WINDOW command as follows:

```
WINDOW 2,, (0,0) - (311,-2),16,-1
```

The Y-coordinate moves from 0 to -2. This causes a system error, though. The first coordinate set (0,0) interprets correctly; the second coordinate pair views the Y-value as false at best, since the interpreter reads the relative coordinates of the standard **BASIC** window. You could also try making a window with the following:

```
WINDOW 2,, (0,0) - (311,8),16,-1
```

This gives you a window 18 pixels high. In this case, you need a window the height of the title bar (10 pixels), to re-establish the screen coordinate system (8-10=-2).

If you only need to cover the title bar of the standard window, you'll need the following coordinate sets:

y2=10   height of the new window
y2=y2-10   subtract height of the title bar in proportion to the coordinates
y2=y2-4   subtract the top and bottom borders of the new window

The result:

```
WINDOW 2,, (0,0) - (311,-4),16,-1
```

3.3 Fade-in and fade-out

Fading is the term used to describe gradual increases or decreases For example, when a song on a record ends by decreasing in volume instead of ending, this is a *fade-out*. A graphic fade-out occurs when a scene in a movie gradually drops to blackness. A *fade-in* is the opposite action.

You can create some really interesting effects using fading. For example, you can fade text in or out, or change graphic colors constantly ("cycle"). One program helps you do all this.

3.3.1 Basic fading

Like the other programs in this book, these fade programs are simply an example. You can install these routines into your own programs, and adapt them to your own uses.

This first program shows the basic idea. It shows you how to change the screen from black to any color on the palette, and return this color gradually to black:

```
' Fading-In and Out of colored areas¶
'¶
'    by Wgb in June '87¶
'¶
¶
Variables:¶
¶
  DEFINT a-z¶
¶
  In=1¶
  Out=-1¶
  Number=7¶
¶
  DIM SHARED Red!(Number),Green!(Number),Blue!(Number)¶
¶
MainProgram:¶
¶
  GOSUB CreateColorScreen¶
¶
  Fading:¶
¶
    GOSUB SetColors¶
    CALL Fade (0,7,16,In)¶
    CALL Fade (0,7,16,Out)¶
¶
  GOTO Fading¶
¶
END¶
¶
¶
SetColors:¶
```

```
¶
FOR i=1 TO Number¶
    Red!(i)=RND¶
    Green!(i)=RND¶
    Blue!(i)=RND¶
NEXT i¶
¶
RETURN¶
¶
CreateColorScreen:¶
¶
SCREEN 2,640,256,3,2¶
WINDOW 1,"Color Test",(0,0)-(623,200),0,2¶
¶
FOR i=0 TO Number¶
    PALETTE i,0,0,0¶
NEXT i¶
¶
SWidth=640/Number¶
FOR j=0 TO 20¶
    FOR i=1 TO Number¶
        x=RND*600 ¶
        y=RND*150¶
        LINE (x,y)-(x+SWidth,y+SWidth/2),i,bf¶
    NEXT i¶
NEXT j¶
¶
RETURN¶
¶
SUB Fade (Start,Number,NumSteps,Mode) STATIC¶
¶
StartState=0 : EndState=NumSteps¶
IF Mode=-1 THEN¶
    StartState=NumSteps : EndState=0¶
END IF¶
FOR j=StartState TO EndState STEP Mode¶
    Factor!=j/NumSteps¶
    FOR i=Start TO Start+Number¶
        PALETTE
i,Red!(i)*Factor!,Green!(i)*Factor!,Blue!(i)*Factor!¶
        NEXT i¶
NEXT j¶
¶
END SUB¶
```

Arrays

Blue	blue scale array
Green	green scale array
Red	red scale array

Variables

StartState	starting state of colors
Number	number of colors (in SUB: number of faded colors)
SWidth	width of sample area
EndState	ending state of colors
Factor	color scale at current time
In	fadein pointer
Mode	mode: fade in or fade out
Out	fadeout pointer
NumSteps	number of steps for process
Start	first color number
i,j	floating variables

x,y	coordinates for sample field

Program description

The program defines a function which allows the fading in or fading out of any color on the palette. Combined color groups can be faded as well. First, two variables are set up for the type of fading required. You can only use the variable names once numbers are assigned to them. Next, 7 colors are set as the resolution (e.g., the background). Every color is defined by an array, which accesses the individual subroutine. These arrays contain the color values used in the fading process.

The `CreateColorScreen` subroutine opens a new screen for demonstration purposes. It uses the color depths set above. The output window shows colored rectangles.

The main section of the program branches to a subroutine which fills the color arrays with "random" numbers. The main subroutine is then called twice. It gives the number of the first color and the increment needed for fading. Then it indicates whether the fade should be into the desired color or out to black. The ending point determines the individual increments.

Now on to the routine itself. The starting value is set depending upon the pointer setting—either 0 for black, or the value taken from `NumSteps` for "full color" display. The loop used to move through the increments is computed through `Factor` and sets the next color up from black through the `PALETTE` command contained in an inner loop. This loop repeats until either the full brightness or blackness is reached.

3.3.2   Fade-over

This is a variation on the above program. Instead of fading to and from black, however, this program fades to and from the starting and ending colors set by you.

```
' Fade-From one Color to Another¶
'¶
' by Wgb in June '87¶
'¶
¶
Variables:¶
¶
  DEFINT a-z¶
¶
  Number=7¶
¶
  DIM SHARED
Red!(Number,1),Green!(Number,1),Blue!(Number,1) ¶
MainProgram:¶
  ¶
  GOSUB CreateColorScreen¶
  ¶
```

```
Fading:¶
¶
  GOSUB SetColors¶
  CALL Fade (0,7,8)¶
¶
GOTO Fading¶
¶
END¶
¶
¶
SetColors:¶
¶
  FOR i=1 TO Number¶
      Red!(i,0)=Red!(i,1)¶
      Green!(i,0)=Green!(i,1)¶
      Blue!(i,0)=Blue!(i,1)¶
      Red!(i,1)=RND¶
      Green!(i,1)=RND¶
      Blue!(i,1)=RND¶
  NEXT i¶
¶
RETURN¶
¶
CreateColorScreen:¶
¶
  SCREEN 2,640,256,3,2¶
  WINDOW 1,"Color Test",(0,0)-(623,200),0,2¶
  FOR i=0 TO Number¶
      PALETTE i,0,0,0¶
  NEXT i¶
¶
  SWidth=640/Number¶
  FOR j=0 TO 20¶
      FOR i=1 TO Number¶
          x=RND*600 ¶
          y=RND*150¶
          LINE (x,y)-(x+SWidth,y+SWidth/2),i,bf¶
      NEXT i¶
  NEXT j¶
¶
RETURN¶
¶
SUB Fade (Start,Number,NumSteps) STATIC¶
¶
  FOR j=0 TO NumSteps¶
      FOR i=Start TO Start+Number¶
          Rdiff!=(Red!(i,1)-Red!(i,0))/NumSteps*j¶
          Gdiff!=(Green!(i,1)-Green!(i,0))/NumSteps*j¶
          Bdiff!=(Blue!(i,1)-Blue!(i,0))/NumSteps*j¶
          PALETTE
i,Red!(i,0)+Rdiff!,Green!(i,0)+Gdiff!,Blue!(i,0)+Bdiff!¶

      NEXT i¶
  NEXT j¶
¶
END SUB¶
```

Program description

The basic structure of the earlier fade program remains, but some fine-tuning has been done here. The variable definitions no longer require the pointer In and pointer Out for fading to new colors. This is also why the main program call to the fade routine is missing; the program goes to the new color setting for the fade.

The color arrays have an identifier which shows whether the starting color (0) or ending color (1) is set. Reaching the new color value copies the last new value in the starting value register, and redefines the ending value. The program can then tell the current status, even though no reading function exists.

The fading subroutine now goes in any increment of color change. The difference is divided by the step value and multiplied by the number in the already set NumSteps. The result is added to the individual values of the RGB colors. When the outermost loop executes, the new color is on the screen.

3.3.3   Fading RGB color scales

This last fading option originates from the program in Section 3.3.1. PALETTE commands let you fade RGB colors individually. This means that you can start a screen in red, fade it to green, then end by fading to blue.

```
' Fading-In and Out of Colored Areas¶
'¶
' by Wgb in June '87¶
'¶
¶
Variables:¶
¶
 DEFINT a-z¶
¶
 In=1¶
 Out=-1¶
 Number=7¶
¶
 DIM SHARED Red!(Number),Green!(Number),Blue!(Number)¶
¶
MainProgram:¶
 ¶
 GOSUB CreateColorScreen¶
 ¶
 Fading:¶
 ¶
  GOSUB SetColors¶
  CALL Fade (0,7,16,In)¶
  CALL Fade (0,7,16,Out)¶
  ¶
 GOTO Fading¶
 ¶
END¶
 ¶
 ¶
SetColors:¶
```

```
¶
 FOR i=1 TO Number¶
     Rer!(i)=RND¶
     Green!(i)=RND¶
     Blue!(i)=RND¶
 NEXT i¶
 ¶
RETURN¶
¶
CreateColorScreen:¶
 ¶
 SCREEN 2,640,256,3,2¶
 WINDOW 1,"Color Test",(0,0)-(623,200),0,2¶
 ¶
 FOR i=0 TO Number¶
     PALETTE i,0,0,0¶
 NEXT i¶
 ¶
 SWidth=640/Number¶
 FOR j=0 TO 20¶
     FOR i=1 TO Number¶
         x=RND*600 ¶
         y=RND*150¶
         LINE (x,y)-(x+SWidth,y+SWidth/2),i,bf¶
     NEXT i¶
 NEXT j¶
 ¶
RETURN¶
 ¶
SUB Fade (Start,Number,NumSteps,Mode) STATIC¶
 ¶
 NumSteps=NumSteps/2¶
 StartState=0 : EndState=NumSteps¶
 IF Mode=-1 THEN¶
     StartState=NumSteps : EndState=0¶
 END IF¶
 StartAt=StartState/NumSteps¶
 EndAt=EndState/NumSteps¶
 FOR j=StartState TO EndState STEP Mode¶
     Factor!=j/NumSteps¶
     FOR i=Start TO Start+Number¶
         PALETTE i,Red!(i)*Factor!,Green!(i)*StartAt,
Blue!(i)*StartAt¶
     NEXT i¶
 NEXT j¶
 FOR j=StartState TO EndState STEP Mode¶
     Factor!=j/NumSteps¶
     FOR i=Start TO Start+Number¶
         PALETTE i,Red!(i)*EndAt,Green!(i)*Factor!,
Blue!(i)*StartAt¶
     NEXT i¶
 NEXT j¶
 FOR j=StartState TO EndState STEP Mode¶
     Factor!=j/NumSteps¶
     FOR i=Start TO Start+Number¶
```

```
        PALETTE i,Red!(i)*EndAt,Green!(i)*EndAt,
Blue!(i)*Factor!¶
    NEXT i¶
  NEXT j¶
  ¶
END SUB¶
```

Program
description

The first section of this listing is identical to the first program up until
the subroutine. Use `Copy` and `Paste` from the `Edit` pulldown menu
to copy the first section from the program in Section 3.3.1.

First the `SUB` routine divides the increment number in half. This sets
all the programs to about the same "speed setting." Then the same loop
executes three times (it executes three times longer). The program looks
for the starting value of the fade loop. Whether you start with black or
with the color, the mouse pointer is set by this value.

Since the `PALETTE` instruction uses all color values, you must set the
starting value of the red color scale in the first loop, and the other color
scales in the other two loops. The other loops bring the program to the
end value, as already handled by the red scale. This is computed by the
`SUB` routine at the start under two factors (`StartAt` and `EndAt`). All
other routines run similar to those in the first fade program.

3.4   Fast vector graphics

Vector graphics are the displayed outlines of objects on the screen, rather than the complete objects. This speeds up display, since the computation time is minimized for complicated graphics, and the computer is limited to the corner point and the resulting outline.

3.4.1   Model grids

Working with three-dimensional objects requires storing the corner point as three-dimensional coordinates. First a compound specification must be set up, after which the coordinate triplets are combined.

Once you have all this data, you must project the space on the screen followed by an area. The following program selects a central spot on the screen plane. All objects here are based upon a single vanishing point perspective.

Since the plane of your screen is set by its Z-coordinate, this value is uninteresting for all points. The grid network comes from this setup.

To find the X- and Y-coordinates on the screen, a space must be provided for the 3-D object. Furthermore, this space must have a point set as the vanishing point. The Z-value lies between the object and the vanishing point on the screen plane. Now draw a line to the vanishing point from every corner of our object. When you intersect these lines with the screen plane, you'll find the desired X- and Y-values for these corner points, and their positions on the screen.

The illustration on the next page shows a cross section of the Y- and Z-coordinates.

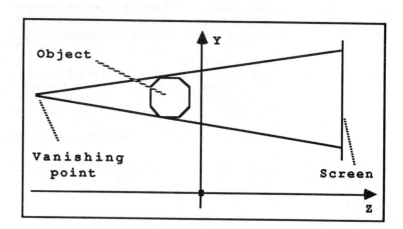

**Three-
dimensional
grid**

How should you design a program that reproduces the illustration
above? The most important factor is setting up the corner point data.
You can place this data in DATA statements without much trouble.
First, though, the corner point coordinates must be on hand in the
compound specification, which can also go into DATA statements.

When the program identifies all spatial coordinates, it can begin
calculating the screen coordinates. The following line formula is used in
three-dimensional space computation:

3D Line formula

$$
\begin{matrix}
X \\
Y \\
Z
\end{matrix}
\quad = \quad
\begin{matrix}
px \\
py \\
pz
\end{matrix}
\quad +1* \quad
\begin{matrix}
dx \\
dy \\
dz
\end{matrix}
$$

You must remember the following when using the above formula: The
desired screen coordinates are called X and Y. You figured out the Z-
coordinate above. The P-coordinate belongs to the point used as part of
the multiplication. All that remains is the D-value. This is the
difference of individual point coordinate subtracted from the vanishing
point (px-vx, py-vy, pz-vz).

```
' 3D Vector-Graphics I¶
'¶
' © 8.5.1987 Wgb¶
' ¶
¶
Variables:¶
¶
 RESTORE CubeData¶
 DEFINT B,C¶
¶
 MaxPoints=25   ' Maximum Number of Object Points¶
```

```
ZCoord=-25      ' Z-Coordinates of Screen¶
NumPoints=0     ' Number of Object Points¶
Connections=0 ' Number of Connections¶
¶
OPTION BASE 1¶
DIM P(MaxPoints,3)      ' Spatial Coordinates¶
DIM B(MaxPoints,2)      ' Screen Coordinates¶
DIM C(MaxPoints*1.8,2) ' Connecting Instructions¶
DIM D(3)               ' Difference¶
¶
DIM F(3)               ' Vanishing Point (x,y,z)¶
¶
F(1)=-70               ' Vanishing Point x¶
F(2)=-50               ' y¶
F(3)=240               ' z¶
¶
MainProgram:¶
¶
PRINT "Vanishing Point (x,y,z): ";F(1)","F(2)","F(3)¶
¶
GetPoint:¶
¶
CBase=NumPoints         ' Base for Connections¶
¶
Loop:¶
¶
READ px,py,pz¶
IF px<>255 THEN ¶
  NumPoints=NumPoints+1 ¶
  P(NumPoints,1)=px¶
  P(NumPoints,2)=py*-1¶
  P(NumPoints,3)=pz¶
  GOTO Loop¶
END IF¶
        ¶
GetConnection:¶
¶
READ v1,v2¶
IF v1<>255 THEN¶
  Connections=Connections+1¶
  C(Connections,1)=CBase+v1¶
  C(Connections,2)=CBase+v2¶
  GOTO GetConnection¶
END IF¶
¶
READ Last¶
IF Last<>0 THEN GOTO GetPoint¶
¶
¶
CalculatePicture:¶
¶
FOR i=1 TO NumPoints¶
   FOR j=1 TO 3¶
      D(j)=F(j)-P(i,j)¶
   NEXT j¶
   lambda=(ZCoord-P(i,3))/D(3)¶
```

```
      B(i,1)=P(i,1)+lambda*D(1) ¶
      B(i,2)=P(i,2)+lambda*D(2) ¶
   NEXT i¶
¶
   CreatePicture:¶
¶
   FOR i=1 TO Connections¶
      x1=B(C(i,1),1)+50¶
      x2=B(C(i,2),1)+50¶
      y1=B(C(i,1),2)+100¶
      y2=B(C(i,2),2)+100 ¶
      LINE (x1,y1)-(x2,y2) ¶
   NEXT i¶
¶
END¶
¶
¶
CubeData:¶
¶
   REM   x,y,z¶
   DATA   32, 20, 20¶
   DATA  -32, 20, 20¶
   DATA  -32,-20, 20¶
   DATA   32,-20, 20¶
   DATA   32, 20,-20¶
   DATA  -32, 20,-20¶
   DATA  -32,-20,-20¶
   DATA   32,-20,-20¶
   DATA 255,0,0¶
¶
   REM   p1,p2¶
   DATA 1,2¶
   DATA 2,3¶
   DATA 3,4¶
   DATA 4,1¶
   DATA 1,5¶
   DATA 5,6¶
   DATA 6,7¶
   DATA 7,8¶
   DATA 8,5¶
   DATA 4,8¶
   DATA 3,7¶
   DATA 2,6¶
   DATA 255,0,1¶
¶
PyramidData:¶
¶
   DATA -32, 25,-20¶
   DATA  32, 25,-20¶
   DATA  32, 25, 20¶
   DATA -32, 25, 20¶
   DATA   0, 65,  0¶
   DATA 255,0,0¶
¶
   DATA 1,2¶
   DATA 2,3¶
   DATA 3,4¶
   DATA 4,1¶
   DATA 5,1¶
   DATA 5,2¶
   DATA 5,3¶
   DATA 5,4¶
   DATA 255,0,0¶
```

Arrays	P()	spatial coordinates
	B()	int, screen coordinates
	D()	differences from the illustration
	F()	vanishing point coordinates
	C()	int, connection specifications for all objects

Variables	Last	value read, equals 0 when program ends
	CBase	object connection identifier
	NumPoints	number of points to be drawn
	MaxPoints	maximum number of object points
	Connections	number of connections
	ZCoord	Z-coordinate of screen plane
	i,j	floating variables
	lambda	coordinate calculation factor
	px,py,pz	coordinates of one point in space
	v1	first point of a connection
	v2	second point of a connection
	x1,y1	screen coordinates for output (1st point)
	x2,y2	screen coordinates for connection (2nd point)

Program description

First, the variable definition sets the DATA pointer to the beginning of the pixel data. In this particular case, the coordinates are a cube. Then all variables starting with B or C are set up as integers. You'll see why soon. Since the arrays for the points can be dimensioned later on, the program sets the maximum number of points to be stored in the MaxPoints variable. Also, the screen plane's position in space appears through the Z-coordinate. Then the number of points and connections to be read are set to null.

Now follow the dimensioning of necessary variable arrays. These are the P array, into which the point coordinates are stored (an index of 3), then the B array which holds the later screen coordinates for every spatial point. Also, the C array always contains two point numbers which indicate which points should be connected with one another. The last array, D, shows the differences between point computations.

The F array contains the vanishing point position, holding an index for automatic computations (Fpx,Fpy,Fpz).

The next line displays the vanishing point coordinates. Then the point reading routine follows. This routine first sets the CBase pointer to the first number of the point to be read. It works with several objects, so all you need is to enter a coordinate for the first point of the next object later. The loop reads spatial coordinates and checks these coordinates for a px value of 255. This marker reads all the points of an object. The connection specification follows next. If not, new points are entered into the table, and new coordinates are read.

The loop for reading connections works in much the same way. It reads the number of points to be connected. Then the loop ends. Otherwise, the two numbers are entered in the array. Finally, a number is read from the data that indicates whether another object follows. This occurs when the value is unequal to zero.

When both loops end, the program computes the screen points of the objects. This occurs in a loop which goes through the list point by point and computes all screen values.

Once the difference between the vanishing point value and the current point goes in the D array, the program computes the lambda factor. Next, the program sets the equations up for the X- and Y-values.

The grid display follows. A loop executes for setting up all connections, and sets up all the necessary point coordinates. A previously set point cannot be used in this, since it cannot exchange connections. Since the object next to the null point was defined, you must move the screen center to make it visible. This redraws it line by line.

3.4.2 Moving grid models

Movement is just a shifting of a standing screen. You can program the display and easily change the spatial coordinates of any graphic. Unfortunately, the movement is far too slow for practical use.

For faster movement on the screen, all values must be computed before the movement. Also, you have to rely on an operating system routine for drawing lines, instead of the multiple LINE commands.

3.4.3 Moving with operating system routines

The developers of the Amiga operating system thought a lot about applications that would later run on this super computer. Vector graphics were probably part of the plan for future expansion. These make real-time graphics possible under certain conditions. This next routine places all points into a list. This routine is the best option for us, although a faster method exists. It lets you draw a grid network. Then you enter the corner point for your spatial coordinates to be projected on the screen later on. The corner point moves within the space, while retaining the original corner coordinates. The routine loses little time, since the program computes all movements before the scenes and places these computations into an array.

Now comes the first problem. The routine waits for a list of screen coordinates connected in a given sequence. There is an advantage and a disadvantage to this process. For one, not every coordinate pair is stored, and for another the figure must be designed in such a way that a constant line can be drawn. If not, those sections considered unnecessary are skipped. However, flat objects can be drawn with just an endless line.

To adapt this to the operating system, you must change the connection specification. Enter the corners of the object and the number of corners instead of the coordinate pairs.

When the program has this data, it can start its calculations. First the object is moved in space by the screen coordinates. Then the new graphic transfer occurs. This section enters the available screen values in a long list, for later use by the operating system.

If the list is complete, the program branches to the display loop. Here all scenes execute, and a corresponding pointer points to the data list for the current scene. Then these values transfer to the display routine. The color changes to the background to clear the screen, and the program redraws the object at its new location on the screen. When all graphics have been displayed, the program branches to the beginning of display, and starts the process again.

```
' 3D Vector Graphics  V¶
'¶
' Faster by using¶
' The PolyDraw Routine¶
'¶
' by Wgb in June '87¶
'¶
¶
LIBRARY "graphics.library"¶
RESTORE¶
OPTION BASE 1¶
¶
Variables:¶
¶
 DEFINT B,C,G¶
¶
 READ MaxPoints      ' Number of Object Points¶
 READ Connections    ' Number of Connections¶
 ZCoord=25           ' Z-Coordinate in Screen Plane¶
 Scenes=50           ' Number of Scenes¶
¶
 DIM P(MaxPoints,3)          ' Spatial Coordinates¶
 DIM B(Scenes,MaxPoints,2)   ' Screen Coordinates¶
 DIM G(Connections*2*Scenes)¶
 DIM C(Connections)          ' Connection Rules¶
 DIM D(3)                    ' Difference¶
¶
 DIM F(3)        ' Vanishing Point (x,y,z)¶
¶
 F(1)=-70        ' Vanishing Point x¶
 F(2)=-50        ' y ¶
 F(3)=180        ' z¶
```

```
¶
PRINT "Vanishing Point (x,y,z): ";F(1)","F(2)","F(3)¶
¶
GetPoint:¶
RESTORE PyramidData    ' Object ¶
¶
FOR i=1 TO MaxPoints¶
   READ px,py,pz¶
     P(i,1)=px¶
     P(i,2)=py*-1      ' Transfer to other Coordinate
System¶
     P(i,3)=pz¶
NEXT i¶
        ¶
GetConnection:¶
¶
 FOR i=1 TO Connections¶
   READ C(i)¶
 NEXT i¶
¶
PreCalculatePicture:¶
¶
 FOR sz=1 TO Scenes¶
    FOR i=1 TO MaxPoints¶
       FOR j=1 TO 3¶
          D(j)=F(j)-P(i,j)¶
       NEXT j¶
       P(i,3)=P(i,3)+3¶
       P(i,2)=P(i,2)-2¶
       P(i,1)=P(i,1)+2¶
       Lambda=(ZCoord-P(i,3))/D(3)¶
       B(sz,i,1)=P(i,1)+Lambda*D(1)+200¶
       B(sz,i,2)=P(i,2)+Lambda*D(2)+200¶
    NEXT i¶
 NEXT sz¶
¶
GraphicTransfer:¶
¶
 FOR j=0 TO Scenes-1¶
    FOR i=1 TO Connections*2 STEP 2¶
       G(i+j*Connections*2)=B(j+1,C(i/2+.5),1)¶
       G(i+1+j*Connections*2)=B(j+1,C(i/2+.5),2)¶
    NEXT i¶
 NEXT j¶
¶
ConstructScreen:¶
  ¶
 FOR i=0 TO Scenes-1¶
    Pointer=Connections*2*i¶
    FOR j=1 TO 0 STEP-1¶
       COLOR j¶
       CALL Move(WINDOW(8),G(1+Pointer),G(2+Pointer))¶
       CALL PolyDraw(WINDOW(8),Connections-
VARPTR(G(3+Pointer)))¶
    NEXT j¶
 NEXT i¶
```

```
¶
GOTO ConstructScreen¶
¶
¶
GraphicData:¶
¶
 DATA 5,10¶
 ' MaxPoints,Connections¶
¶
PyramidData:¶
¶
 DATA -32, 25,-20¶
 DATA  32, 25,-20¶
 DATA  32, 25, 20¶
 DATA -32, 25, 20¶
 DATA   0, 65,  0¶
¶
PointConnections:¶
 ¶
 DATA 2,1,5,4,3,5,2,3,4,1¶
 ¶
 DATA 4,1¶
```

Arrays	B()	screen coordinates
	D()	differences from the illustration
	F()	vanishing point coordinates
	G()	coordinates of all scenes
	P()	spatial coordinates
	C()	connection specifications
Variables	Lambda	coordinate calculation factor
	Pointer	pointer to coordinate list of one scene
	MaxPoints	maximum number of object points
	Scenes	number of scenes to be computed
	Connections	number of connections
	ZCoord	Z-coordinate of screen plane
	i,j	floating variables
	px,py,pz	spatial coordinates of corner point
	sz	loop pointer for scenes

Program description

Before the variable definition, the program opens the graphics library. This supplies the graphic routines needed for the grid network. Then all variables beginning with B, C or G are declared as integers. This allows the integer variable character to be left off these variables. The grid network display uses the new G array, into which all coordinates are stored in their proper sequences. Each set consists of a 2-byte integer for the X-coordinate and a 2-byte integer for the Y-coordinate.

The new features of this program are the point and connection loops. These work from established values placed at the beginning of the program in DATA statements. If you leave off the end marker, the program runs somewhat faster. The connection array is defined as one dimensional, instead of as a string of characters.

After the computation, the data must be converted to a form that the operating system can handle. The `PolyDraw` routine places a table at the X- and Y-values stated as integer values. In addition, the table must list how many elements are used. The table can be fairly long. This table doesn't need a pointer to the end of data. You place the graphic data for all scenes into one array, and move the routine to the address of the first element of the next scene. The next input is the number of corner points required. The rest of the `PolyDraw` program should speak for itself.

The display occurs in a new loop. It corresponds to the number of scenes executed. This loop first computes the pointer to the first element to display on the grid network. The second loop executes twice. It draws the network, sets the graphic cursor to the starting point and executes your drawing in the `PolyDraw` routine. The second run of the loop sets the floating variables from 1 to 0, and sets the drawing color to the background color through the `COLOR` command. The Amiga draws the grid network in the background color, erasing the net. This process repeats as long as there are scenes available for plotting, then the display loop exits.

3.4.4   3-D graphics for 3-D glasses

While experimenting with the multiple-point system and random 3-D production, this idea came up for making a graphic you can view with 3-D glasses. You've seen these glasses; one lens is red and the other lens is usually green (sometimes blue).

This program works under the same principle as 3-D movies. Since you have two eyes, you're actually viewing two different graphics. These two graphics appear to merge into one when you look at the screen through 3-D glasses. The red lens blocks red light and shows you every other color. The green lens blocks green light and allows other colors to show through. The problem in most cases is that some colors are combinations of red and green. This means that some objects cannot be viewed the way you want them seen through the 3-D glasses. If you use simple colors with 3-D glass viewing, the effect is dramatic.

This 3-D graphic is based on the grid network used in the previous programs. The programming principle circles around having one vanishing point for each eye. Since both eyes are set fairly close to one another, the vanishing points must be set close together as well. In this case, two graphics are drawn with horizontally shifted vanishing points. One graphic is drawn in red, and the other in green. All overlapping areas appear in brown (the color you get when you combine a red light and green light).

To make use of this program comfortable, the slider from Chapter 4 has been integrated into this program (see section 4.1.1). You can change the degrees of red, green and blue to suit your 3-D glasses. You can even change the locations of the vanishing points for an optimal 3-D effect. When you are satisfied with your settings, press a key to see the result. You can use these values in this program or in your own 3-D programming.

```
' 3D Vector Graphics for Red-Green Glasses ¶
'¶
' © 24.5.1987 Wgb¶
' ¶
¶
LIBRARY "graphics.library"¶
¶
RESTORE CubeData¶
DEFINT B,C¶
OPTION BASE 1¶
¶
Variables:¶
¶
MaxPoints=25      ' Maximum Number of Object Points¶
ZCoord=-25        ' Z-coordinates of Screen Plane¶
NumPoints=0       ' Number of Object Points¶
Connections=0     ' Number of Connections¶
¶
NumClicks=0¶
MaxClicks=20¶
¶
DIM SHARED ClickTable(MaxClicks,4)¶
DIM SHARED ClickValue(MaxClicks)¶
DIM SHARED ClickID(MaxClicks)¶
¶
DIM P(MaxPoints,3)        ' Spatial Coordinates¶
DIM B(2,MaxPoints,2)      ' Screen Coordinates¶
DIM C(MaxPoints*1.8,2)    ' Connection Rules¶
DIM D(3)                  ' Difference¶
DIM F(2,3)                ' Vanishing Point (x,y,z)¶
¶
F(1,1)=-40                ' 1st Vanishing Point x¶
F(1,2)=-50                ' y¶
F(1,3)=240                ' z¶
¶
F(2,1)=-80                ' 2nd Vanishing Point x¶
F(2,2)=-50                ' y¶
F(2,3)=240                ' z¶
¶
DisplayText:¶
¶
CLS¶
LOCATE 1,40¶
PRINT "Vanishing Point 1 (x,y,z) :"¶
```

```
LOCATE 2,40¶
PRINT "Vanishing Point 2 (x,y,z) :"¶
GOSUB DisplayCoordinates¶
¶
SetColors:¶
PALETTE 0,.6,.55,.4      ' Background = bright-beige¶
PALETTE 1,.4,.35,0       ' Neutral Color = Dark Brown ¶
PALETTE 2,.7,0,0         ' Red 70%¶
PALETTE 3,0,.65,0        ' Green 65%¶
¶
SliderControl:¶
¶
Text$="Red"             ¶
DefMove 40!,8!,100!,70!,2!¶
Text$="Green"¶
DefMove 45!,8!,100!,65!,2!¶
Text$="Brown"¶
DefMove 50!,8!,100!,40!,2!¶
¶
Text$="VPoint1"¶
DefMove 60!,8!,100!,40!,2!¶
Text$="VPoint2"¶
DefMove 65!,8!,100!,80!,2!¶
¶
¶
GetPoint:¶
CBase=NumPoints         ' Base for Connections¶
¶
Loop:¶
READ px,py,pz¶
IF px<>255 THEN ¶
  NumPoints=NumPoints+1 ¶
  P(NumPoints,1)=px¶
  P(NumPoints,2)=py*-1¶
  P(NumPoints,3)=pz¶
  GOTO Loop¶
END IF¶
        ¶
GetConnections:¶
READ v1,v2¶
IF v1<>255 THEN¶
  Connections= Connections+1¶
  C(Connections,1)=CBase+v1¶
  C(Connections,2)=CBase+v2¶
  GOTO GetConnections¶
END IF¶
¶
READ Last¶
IF Last<>0 THEN GOTO GetPoint¶
¶
¶
CalculateScreen:¶
FOR k=1 TO 2               ' 2 Vanishing Points¶
  FOR i=1 TO NumPoints ' All Points¶
    FOR j=1 TO 3          ' Difference for x,y,z¶
      D(j)=F(k,j)-P(i,j)¶
```

```
         NEXT j¶
         lambda=(ZCoord-P(i,3))/D(3)¶
         B(k,i,1)=P(i,1)+lambda*D(1)¶
         B(k,i,2)=P(i,2)+lambda*D(2)¶
      NEXT i¶
   NEXT k¶
¶
¶
DrawScreen:¶
LINE (0,0)-(300,200),0,bf    ' Clear Area¶
FOR j=1 TO 2¶
   COLOR 1+j¶
   IF j=2 THEN CALL SetDrMd&(WINDOW(8),7)¶
      FOR i=1 TO Connections¶
      x1=B(j,C(i,1),1)+100¶
      x2=B(j,C(i,2),1)+100¶
      y1=B(j,C(i,1),2)+70¶
      y2=B(j,C(i,2),2)+70 ¶
      LINE (x1,y1)-(x2,y2)¶
   NEXT i¶
NEXT j¶
¶
CALL SetDrMd&(WINDOW(8),1)¶
COLOR 1¶
¶
Interrupt:¶
¶
ON MOUSE GOSUB CheckTable¶
ON TIMER (.5) GOSUB ColorSet¶
¶
TIMER ON¶
MOUSE ON¶
¶
Pause:¶
IF ClickValue(4)*-1<>F(1,1) THEN¶
   F(1,1)=ClickValue(4)*-1¶
   ReDraw:¶
   GOSUB DisplayCoordinates¶
   GOTO CalculateScreen¶
END IF¶
IF ClickValue(5)*-1<>F(2,1) THEN¶
   F(2,1)=ClickValue(5)*-1¶
   GOTO ReDraw¶
END IF¶
IF INKEY$="" THEN GOTO Pause¶
¶
OBJECT.OFF¶
TIMER OFF¶
MOUSE OFF¶
LOCATE 15,1¶
PRINT "Red Value :";ClickValue(1);"%"¶
PRINT "Green Value:";ClickValue(2);"%"¶
PRINT "Brown Value from :"¶
PRINT ClickValue(3);"% Red and "ClickValue(3)*.875;"%
Green"¶
PRINT "Vanishing Point Value's X-Coordinate:"¶
```

```
PRINT "V1 ";ClickValue(4)*-1;" and V2 ";ClickValue(5)*-1¶
END¶
¶
¶
DisplayCoordinates:¶
¶
LOCATE 1,63¶
PRINT F(1,1)","F(1,2)","F(1,3)¶
LOCATE 2,63¶
PRINT F(2,1)","F(2,2)","F(2,3)¶
RETURN¶
¶
CheckTable:¶
¶
IF NumClicks=0 THEN RETURN¶
¶
FOR i=1 TO NumClicks¶
    mstat=MOUSE(0)¶
    mx=MOUSE(1)-6¶
    my=MOUSE(2)¶
    IF mx>=ClickTable(i,1) THEN¶
      IF my>=ClickTable(i,2) THEN¶
        IF mx<=ClickTable(i,3) THEN¶
          IF my<=ClickTable(i,4) THEN¶
             ¶
             ClickValue(i)=(my-ClickTable(i,2))¶
             OBJECT.Y i,ClickTable(i,2)+ClickValue(i)+12¶
             ¶
          END IF¶
        END IF¶
      END IF¶
    END IF¶
NEXT i¶
IF MOUSE(0)=-1 THEN CheckTable¶
RETURN¶
¶
ColorSet:¶
 Red=ClickValue(1)/100¶
 Green=ClickValue(2)/100¶
 DrawColor=ClickValue(3)/100¶
 PALETTE 2,Red,0,0¶
 PALETTE 3,0,Green,0¶
 PALETTE 1,DrawColor,(COLOR*.875),0¶
RETURN¶
¶
¶
SUB DefMove (sx,sy,yd,po,mo) STATIC¶
   SHARED NumClicks¶
   ¶
x=sx*8    'Coordinates for Line *10 at 60 Drawing Color¶
 ¶
y=sy*8¶
 ¶
LINE (x,y)-(x+20,y+8+yd),,B¶
 ¶
'Extras desired?¶
```

```
¶
IF mo AND 1 THEN   ' Scale¶
¶
   FOR sk=y TO y+yd+8 STEP (yd+8)/16 '16 Units¶
      LINE (x,sk)-(x+2,sk)¶
      LINE (x+20,sk)-(x+18,sk)¶
   NEXT sk¶
¶
END IF¶
¶
IF mo AND 2 THEN    ' Text¶
¶
   SHARED Text$¶
   sy=sy-LEN(Text$)¶
   FOR txt=1 TO LEN(Text$)¶
      LOCATE sy+txt,sx+2¶
      PRINT MID$(Text$,txt,1)¶
   NEXT txt¶
¶
END IF¶
¶
'Enter Click Value in Table ¶
¶
NumClicks=NumClicks+1¶
ClickTable(NumClicks,1)=x¶
ClickTable(NumClicks,2)=y¶
ClickTable(NumClicks,3)=x+20¶
ClickTable(NumClicks,4)=y+yd¶
ClickID(NumClicks)=1            '1 set for Slider¶
ClickValue(NumClicks)=po        'Beginning Value defined by
the User¶
¶
OPEN "df0:4. User-Friendliness/Slider2" FOR INPUT AS
NumClicks¶
OBJECT.SHAPE NumClicks,INPUT$(LOF(NumClicks),NumClicks)¶
CLOSE NumClicks¶
OBJECT.X NumClicks,x-1¶
OBJECT.Y
umClicks,ClickTable(NumClicks,2)+ClickValue(NumClicks)+12
¶
OBJECT.ON NumClicks¶
¶
END SUB¶
¶
CubeData:¶
REM  x,y,z¶
DATA  32, 20, 20¶
DATA -32, 20, 20¶
DATA -32,-20, 20¶
DATA  32,-20, 20¶
DATA  32, 20,-20¶
DATA -32, 20,-20¶
DATA -32,-20,-20¶
DATA  32,-20,-20¶
DATA 255,0,0¶
¶
```

```
REM   p1,p2¶
DATA 1,2¶
DATA 2,3¶
DATA 3,4¶
DATA 4,1¶
DATA 1,5¶
DATA 5,6¶
DATA 6,7¶
DATA 7,8¶
DATA 8,5¶
DATA 4,8¶
DATA 3,7¶
DATA 2,6¶
DATA 255,0,1¶
¶
PyramidData:¶
DATA -32, 25,-20¶
DATA  32, 25,-20¶
DATA  32, 25, 20¶
DATA -32, 25, 20¶
DATA   0, 65,  0¶
DATA 255,0,0¶
¶
DATA 1,2¶
DATA 2,3¶
DATA 3,4¶
DATA 4,1¶
DATA 5,1¶
DATA 5,2¶
DATA 5,3¶
DATA 5,4¶
DATA 255,0,0¶
```

Arrays		
	B	screen coordinates
	D	differences from the coordinate computation
	F	vanishing point coordinates (both graphics)
	ClickID	identifier for slider
	ClickTable	slider coordinates
	ClickValue	value of a slider
	P	spatial coordinates
	C	compound specification

Variables

NumClickes	number of defined click arrays
Last	value read, equals 0 when program ends
Green	value for green
CBase	object connection identifier
NumPoints	number of points to be drawn
MaxPoints	maximum number of object points
Red	value for red
Text	text output for slider definition
Connections	number of connections
ZCoord	Z-coordinates of screen plane
DrawColor	drawing color for "Brown"
i,j,k	floating variables
lambda	coordinate calculation factor
mo	mode parameters for slider extras
mstat	mouse status
mx,my	mouse coordinates
po	slider starting position
px,py,pz	coordinates of one point in space
sk	floating variable scaling
sx,sy	text output coordinates
txt	text output floating variable
v1,v2	combination points
x,y	slider positions
x1,y1	screen coordinates for output (1st point)
x2,y2	screen coordinates for connection (2nd point)
yd	slider status

*Program
description*

First the graphics library opens, which contains the important graphic routines. The DATA pointer then moves to the needed data, and all arrays beginning with B or C are defined as integers. Base array indices are set to 1. The variables here have similar functions to those in the earlier programs. The slider arrays and variables are new, and most of the variables used before have been changed slightly.

The array containing the vanishing point has an additional index on it. This corresponds to the number of vanishing points, and makes later development easier. This index lets you put up to 40 pixels as vanishing points. This index is ideal for spacing between projection surfaces and vanishing points.

A new method must be used for setting the vanishing points. This new value is set in a subroutine.

The color setting is new as well. All four colors are available; the background can prevent the proper effect if you select the wrong color. The other three colors need no explanation.

The slider definitions follow. The values of the first three sliders affect the colors. The last two sliders make it possible for you to set the vanishing points in horizontal directions.

The point and connection reader routines act as normal. Only the computation of the graphic has a slight change to it. The loop counts from one vanishing point to the next. This counter also depends on the screen coordinates as an index.

Before screen display, the screen clears. Both vanishing points appear in their respective colors. When the grid for the second point is drawn, the program goes into a new character mode (see the table in Chapter 4 for the modes). When you draw with the second color, any overlapping between this color and red lines change to brown. At the end of the loop, the character mode returns to normal status, and the drawing color returns to 1.

A mouse and time interrupt activate. The first interrupt reads the sliders. The second interrupt resets the colors when you change them. The wait loop checks the program for one vanishing point or two vanishing points. If there are two, the value transfers over, and the screen is recalculated.

The system waits for a keypress. When this occurs, the program turns all objects, sliders, mouse and time readers off, and displays all established values on the screen.

3.5 The Amiga fonts

There are two sources of fonts on the Amiga:

1)   ROM font which resides in the Amiga

2   Disk-resident fonts contained in the `fonts` directory of the
        Workbench diskette.

The following program lets you access character sets through the `SUB`
command `FontSet` which gives you access to both ROM and RAM
character sets. This is called as follows:

```
DiskFont "name",height%
```

To tell which character sets are on the Workbench diskette under which
names, enter a directory command, e.g.:

```
FILES "SYS:fonts"
```

Along with these character sets, you can also access the ROM character
set `topaz` in 8- and 9-point sizes. It is extremely important that you
enter the name `topaz` in lowercase characters, since the `OpenFont()`
function is very picky. It will not read entries like `Topaz` or `TOPAZ` as
the ROM character set `topaz`. Instead, it loads the 11-point disk font
`Topaz`.

```
'############################¶
'#                          #¶
'#  Program: Set TextFont   #¶
'#  Author:  tob            #¶
'#  Date:    12/8/87        #¶
'#  Version: 1.0            #¶
'#                          #¶
'############################¶
¶
DECLARE FUNCTION OpenDiskFont& LIBRARY¶
DECLARE FUNCTION OpenFont& LIBRARY¶
¶
LIBRARY "diskfont.library"¶
LIBRARY "graphics.library"¶
¶
demo:   ' Demonstration of SetFont Command¶
        LOCATE 4,1¶
        FontSet "Sapphire", 19¶
        PRINT "This is Sapphire 19 Points"¶
        FontSet "Diamond", 20¶
        PRINT "...another TextFont..."¶
        FontSet "Garnet", 16¶
```

```
        PRINT "...and yet another!  Amiga has still
more!"¶
        FontSet "ruby", 12¶
        PRINT "However this should be enough to
demonstrate the point!"¶
        FontSet "topaz", 8¶
        ¶
        LIBRARY CLOSE¶
        END¶
¶
SUB FontSet (FontName$, FontHeight%) STATIC¶
    f.old&      = PEEKL(WINDOW(8)+52)¶
    f.pref%     = 0¶
    FontName0$  = FontName$ + ".font" + CHR$(0)¶
    tAttr&(0)   = SADD(FontName0$)¶
    tAttr&(1)   = FontHeight%*2^16 + f.pref%¶
    f.new&      = OpenFont&(VARPTR(tAttr&(0)))¶
    f.check%    = PEEKW(WINDOW(8) + 60)¶
    ¶
    IF f.new& = 0 THEN¶
      f.new& = OpenDiskFont&(VARPTR(tAttr&(0)))¶
    ELSEIF f.check% <> FontHeight% THEN¶
      CALL CloseFont(f.new&)¶
      f.new& = OpenDiskFont&(VARPTR(tAttr&(0)))¶
    END IF¶
¶
    IF f.new& <> 0 THEN¶
      CALL CloseFont(f.old&)¶
      CALL SetFont(WINDOW(8), f.new&)¶
    ELSEIF UCASE$(FontName$) = "UNDO" THEN¶
      CALL CloseFont(f.old&)¶
      CALL SetFont(original&)¶
    ELSE¶
      BEEP¶
    END IF¶
END SUB¶
```

Variables   FontName$ character set name
               FontName0$ like FontName$, except it ends with CHR$(0)
               FontHeight% height of the font in pixels
               f.old&   address of previously active character set
               f.prefs%   preference bits
               tAttr&()   text attribute structure; variable array used as memory
               f.new&   address of newly opened character set
               f.check%   current height of new character set

*Program
description*

In order to open a character set, a TextAttr structure must be filled
out. This is stored in the tAttr& array. The address at the beginning
of this field (taken from VARPTR) calls the graphic routine
OpenFont(). This looks for a character set matching the parameters
stated in the TextAttr structure. The normal fonts are the ROM font
topaz in 8-point and 9-point, but when other fonts are still open,
these fonts can be accessed by OpenFont(). OpenFont() is so
flexible that if it can't find a font that matches the given parameters, it
loads the font most similar to the desired font. This means that the font
loaded may not be the one you want. The check% variable checks the
height of the found font, and compares it with the height found in
FontHeight%. If the two are unequal, the opened font closes and
OpenFont() looks for another font on diskette.

If, on the other hand, the program finds a font (f.old&<>0),
CloseFont() closes the currently active font, and activates the new
font with SetFont(). Otherwise the Amiga emits a warning beep
and returns to the old font.

3.6   Fast and easy PRINT

The weakest command in AmigaBASIC is PRINT. This command has three disadvantages to it: Slow execution, no word wrap and no editing capabilities.

Let's take these one at a time. PRINT executes very slowly: An entire page of text can take several seconds to display in a window. In addition, PRINT doesn't know when it reaches the end of a screen line: Long strings of characters go past the right border of the window, instead of "wrapping around" to the next screen line. Finally, PRINT displays text and nothing more. PRINT cannot execute editor commands that might exist, such as CLEAR SCREEN, CURSOR UP, INSERT LINE, etc.

Since PRINT is one of the most frequently used commands in Amiga-BASIC, here is a program that solves all of these problems. The solution is a simple one: The program activates the internal system's Console Device. This system component handles text input and output. Once active, Console Device handles all the tasks that PRINT can't handle: Fast text display, adaptation to window size, and a number of editor commands.

Unfortunately, it's not that easy to adapt Console Device for your own purposes, since it must be treated as an I/O device. A number of Exec functions are necessary. However, once initialized, you have a PRINT command of much larger dimensions. With this new command's help, your program runs faster, and editor commands make programming easier.

The following program consists of the SUB programs CreatePort, RemovePort, CreateStdIO, RemoveStdIO, OpenConsole, CloseConsole, SystemOn, SystemOff and ConPrint:

```
'###########################¶
'#                          #¶
'# Program: Console Device  #¶
'# Author:  tob             #¶
'# Date:    04/08/87        #¶
'# Version: 1.0             #¶
'#                          #¶
'###########################¶
¶
DECLARE FUNCTION OpenDevice% LIBRARY¶
DECLARE FUNCTION AllocMem& LIBRARY¶
DECLARE FUNCTION AllocSignal% LIBRARY¶
DECLARE FUNCTION FindTask& LIBRARY¶
DECLARE FUNCTION DoIO& LIBRARY¶
```

```
¶
LIBRARY "exec.library"¶
¶
init:  '* Control-Sequence definitions¶
       C1$ = CHR$(155) 'Control Sequence Introducer¶
       C2$ = CHR$(8)   'Backspace¶
       C3$ = CHR$(10)  'Line Feed¶
       C4$ = CHR$(11)  'VTab¶
       C5$ = CHR$(12)  'Form Feed¶
       C6$ = CHR$(13)  'CR¶
       C7$ = CHR$(14)  'SHIFT IN¶
       C8$ = CHR$(15)  'SHIFT OUT¶
       C9$ = CHR$(155) + "1E" 'RETURN¶
¶
demo:  '* Demonstration¶
       ConPrint C1$+"20CA Good Day to You!"+C9$¶
       ConPrint "It had been a normal day so far, but
while on the way to the barn we saw a very big bear!"¶
¶
SystemOff¶
¶
SUB ConPrint (text$) STATIC¶
    SHARED c.io&¶
    IF c.io& = 0 THEN : SystemOn¶
    POKEL c.io& + 36, LEN(text$)¶
    POKEL c.io& + 40, SADD(text$)¶
    e& = DoIO&(c.io&)¶
END SUB¶
¶
SUB SystemOff STATIC¶
    SHARED c.io&¶
    CloseConsole c.io&¶
END SUB¶
¶
SUB SystemOn STATIC¶
    SHARED c.io&, c.c$¶
    OpenConsole c.io&¶
    POKEW c.io& + 28, 3¶
END SUB¶
¶
SUB OpenConsole (result&) STATIC¶
    CreatePort "basic.con", 0, c.port&¶
    IF c.port& = 0 THEN ERROR 255¶
    CreateStdIO c.port&, c.io&¶
    POKEL c.io& + 36, 124¶
    POKEL c.io& + 40, WINDOW(7)¶
    dev$ = "console.device" + CHR$(0)¶
    c.error% = OpenDevice%(SADD(dev$), 0, c.io&, 0)¶
    IF c.error% <> 0 THEN ERROR 255¶
    result& = c.io&¶
END SUB¶
¶
SUB CloseConsole (io&) STATIC¶
    port& = PEEKL(io& + 14)¶
    CALL CloseDevice(io&)¶
    RemovePort port&¶
```

```
        RemoveStdIO io&¶
END SUB¶
¶
SUB CreateStdIO (port&, result&) STATIC¶
        opt& = 2^16¶
        result& = AllocMem&(48, opt&)¶
        IF result& = 0 THEN ERROR 7¶
        POKE result& + 8, 5¶
        POKEL result& + 14, port&¶
        POKEW result& + 18, 50¶
END SUB¶
¶
SUB RemoveStdIO (io&) STATIC¶
        IF io& <> 0 THEN¶
          CALL FreeMem(io&, 48)¶
        END IF¶
END SUB¶
¶
SUB CreatePort (port$, pri%, result&) STATIC¶
        opt& = 2^16¶
        byte& = 38 + LEN(port$)¶
        port& = AllocMem&(byte&, opt&)¶
        IF port& = 0 THEN ERROR 7¶
        POKEW port&, byte&¶
        port& = port& + 2¶
        sigBit% = AllocSignal%(-1)¶
        IF sigBit% = -1 THEN¶
          CALL FreeMem(port&, byte&)¶
          ERROR 7¶
        END IF¶
        sigTask& = FindTask& (0)¶
        ¶
        POKE  port& + 8 , 4¶
        POKE  port& + 9 , pri%¶
        POKEL port& + 10, port& + 34¶
        POKE  port& + 15, sigBit%¶
        POKEL port& + 16, sigTask&¶
        POKEL port& + 20, port& + 24¶
        POKEL port& + 28, port& + 20¶
        FOR loop% = 1 TO LEN(port$)¶
          char% = ASC(MID$(port$, loop%, 1))¶
          POKE port& + 33 + loop%, char%¶
        NEXT loop%¶
        CALL AddPort(port&)¶
        result& = port&¶
END SUB¶
¶
SUB RemovePort (port&) STATIC¶
        byte&  = PEEKW(port& - 2)¶
        sigBit% = PEEK (port& + 15)¶
        CALL RemPort(port&)¶
        CALL FreeSignal(sigBit%)¶
        CALL FreeMem(port& - 2, byte&)¶
END SUB¶
```

As you can see, you can use the new ConPrint much the same as you used the normal PRINT:

ConPrint "displayed text"

However, ConPrint works much faster than PRINT. Also, long lines of text are tailored to fit the width of the window. If the text is longer than the window is wide, the text wraps around to the next window line. You also have the following editor sequences available:

C1$	CSI (Control Sequence Introducer)
C2$	Backspace (1 character to the left)
C3$	Linefeed (1 line down)
C4$	VTab (one line up)
C5$	Formfeed (clear screen)
C6$	CR (start of next line)
C7$	SHIFT IN (caps)
C8$	SHIFT OUT (normal)
C9$	RETURN (end of line)

These are the simplest editor text sequences. You add them to text strings using the plus sign character (<+>). For example:

ConPrint "Hello, Worker!"+C9$

Console Device can do a lot more. The following editor sequences begin immediately after the control sequence introducer (C1$). The editor sequences are as follows:

C1$ +	Definition
"[n]@"	Insert [n] characters in this line
"[n]A"	Cursor [n] lines up
"[n]B"	Cursor [n] lines down
"[n]C"	Cursor [n] characters right
"[n]D"	Cursor [n] characters left
"[n]E"	Cursor [n] characters down + to start of line
"[n]F"	Cursor [n] characters up + to start of line
"[n];[n]H"	Cursor to line [n], column [n]
"J"	Clear screen from current cursor position
"K"	Delete line at current cursor position
"L"	Insert line
"M"	Delete line
"[n]P"	Delete character to right of cursor
"[n]S"	Scroll [n] lines up
"[n]T"	Scroll [n] lines down
"20h"	Set mode
"20l"	Reset mode
"[n];[n];[n]m"	Graphic mode
	Style:
	0=normal
	1=bold
	3=italic
	4=underline
	7=reverse
	Foreground color:
	30-37
	Background color:
	40-47
"[n]t"	Window height in raster lines
"[n]u"	Line length in pixels
"[n]x"	Indent [n] characters
"[n]y"	[n] lines spacing from top border

3.7 Multitasking INPUT

The INKEY$, LINE INPUT and INPUT commands are Amiga-BASIC's ways of accepting user input. These commands do their best, but that isn't enough sometimes. For example, try using LINE INPUT to ask for a street address. If the user makes a mistake, he can only correct it by pressing the <Backspace> key until he erases the error, and retyping the rest of the entry. LINE INPUT and INPUT support no cursor movement, and have no editing facilities like Undo, Insert or Delete. This is fine if you prefer to avoid user-friendliness, but programs should be made as friendly to the user as possible.

This input programming can create problems: Try to design a screen mask around LINE INPUT. It can't be done: LINE INPUT doesn't allow length limits to input, so it accepts any number of characters. This could move the cursor past the mask, destroying the screen mask and other input areas. Also, this input doesn't provide margin for error in the next input. For example, an address file program asks you for the city. You enter <Grand Rapids MI> and press the <RETURN> key. The next input asks for the state—but you've already entered the state name. Another major problem with LINE INPUT is that you cannot freely choose data fields in a mask, so mistakes are unavoidable. The only way to check for errors is to have the program ask, "IS ALL DATA CORRECT (Y/N)?" If there are errors, the user has to enter the data all over again.

Now that you have heard about the disadvantages, here is an alternative program that solves these difficulties. Here's how it works. You create a screen mask into which you place all the necessary data fields with the MField command. You can start your fields at any point on the screen using X- and Y-coordinates. You can also set your fields to any length up to a maximum of your screen's width. Finally, you can specify whether the system should accept a normal (alphanumeric) input or just numeric input. In this last case, the Amiga accepts numbers and ignores all other input.

The MField command syntax:

```
MField nr%, x%, y%, wid%, max%, nam$, typ$
```

nr%	field number (0-40)
x%, y%	starting coordinates of field
wid%	field width in characters
max%	maximum input length
nam$	field name (e.g., STREET)
typ$	"S" = alphanumeric input
	"VAR" = numbers only

This method lets you set up your screen mask freely. Every MField command draws an orange border around the entry and displays the field name on the screen.

Immediately after the screen mask appears, the user can begin text or numeric input. Clicking on the desired field with the mouse calls an orange cursor. The user's entry appears in that field. The Amiga supports this new input control 100%.

The user has editor commands available in this input system. Like LINE INPUT, MField uses the <DEL> key and the <BACKSPACE> key. These delete characters to the left or to the right of the current cursor position. The cursor keys move the cursor to the left or right. Text inserted at the current cursor position moves the remaining text to the right. Pressing <SHIFT> and a cursor key moves the cursor to the beginning or end of the text. The <Right Amiga><Q> key combination acts as the <UNDO> function, restoring the previous input. If the user enters more text than provided for in the field, the text scrolls to the left and the right edge opens up space for the new letters. That is, until you reach the maximum input length. You see, you can even enter text longer than the field window.

The Check command lets you view data in the individual fields. You can search for fields and remove the ones you don't want anymore:

        Check nr%, text$, mode%

nr%   field number
text$ field contents
mode%   1 = display
                0 = display and remove field

The following program demonstrates the options offered by these powerful and user-friendly commands:

```
'#####################¶
'#                   #¶
'# Program: NewInput #¶
'# Author:  tob      #¶
'# Date:    11/08/87 #¶
'# Version: 2.0      #¶
'#                   #¶
'#####################¶
¶
DECLARE FUNCTION AllocMem& LIBRARY¶
DECLARE FUNCTION AddGadget% LIBRARY¶
¶
LIBRARY "exec.library"¶
LIBRARY "intuition.library"¶
LIBRARY "graphics.library"¶
¶
var:    '* variables¶
        DIM SHARED reg&(40,1) ¶
```

```
¶
demo:    '* Demonstration of NewInput by Building a Mask¶
         CLS¶
         PRINT TAB(20); "Personnel Screen"¶
         ¶
         '* Build Field Masks¶
         MField 1,    5, 30, 35, 40, "First Name ", "S"¶
         MField 2,    5, 45, 35, 50, "Last Name  ", "S"¶
         MField 3,    5, 60,  7,  7, "Street      ", "VAR"¶
         MField 4, 165, 60, 26, 40, "",            "S"¶
         MField 5,    5, 75, 30, 30, "City, State", "S"¶
         MField 6, 340, 75,  6, 11, "Zip.",        "S"¶
         ¶
         LOCATE 15,20¶
         PRINT "When finished, please press RETURN!"¶
         LINE INPUT pause$¶
         ¶
         '* Evaluate Field¶
         Check 1, First$,     0¶
         Check 2, Last$,      0¶
         Check 3, Number$,    0¶
         Check 4, Street$,    0¶
         Check 5, CityState$, 0¶
         Check 6, Zip$,       0¶
         ¶
         CLS¶
         PRINT "...the following is the data you input"¶
         PRINT "which can now be used in other routines:"¶
         PRINT¶
         PRINT "Last and First Name: "; Last$;", ";
First$¶
         PRINT¶
         PRINT "Address:"¶
         PRINT " ";Number$;" ";Street$¶
         PRINT " ";CityState$;"   ";Zip$¶
         ¶
         FOR t% = 1 TO 10000¶
         NEXT t%¶
         ¶
         '* Simultaneous Evaluation¶
         CLS¶
         MField 1, 30, 40, 10, 40, "Test field.  Enter
some text. ", "S"¶
         ¶
         WHILE INKEY$ = ""¶
           Check 1, test$, 1¶
           LOCATE 1,1¶
           PRINT "Current Contents: ";test$;" "¶
         WEND¶
         ¶
         Check 1, test$, 0¶
         LOCATE 9,1¶
         PRINT "Final results: ";test$¶
         ¶
         LIBRARY CLOSE¶
         END¶
```

```
¶
SUB MField (nr%, x%, y%, wid%, max%, nam$, typ$) STATIC¶
SHARED Er%¶
colB%  = 3¶
typ$   = UCASE$ (typ$)¶
l%     = LEN(nam$)¶
IF reg&(nr%, 0) = 0 THEN¶
  mem& = 82 + 2*max% + 20¶
  opt& = 2^16¶
  add& = AllocMem&(mem&, opt&)¶
  IF add& = 0 THEN¶
    Er% = 1¶
    EXIT SUB¶
  ELSE¶
    Er% = 0¶
  END IF¶
  POKEL add&, mem&¶
  ¶
  IF typ$ = "VAR" THEN¶
    typ% = &H802¶
  ELSE¶
    typ% = 2¶
  END IF¶
  ¶
  chx% = PEEKW (WINDOW(8) + 58)¶
  chy% = PEEKW (WINDOW(8) + 60)¶
  FWidth% = wid% * chx%¶
  FHeight% = chy%¶
  ¶
  CALL Move(WINDOW(8), x% - 1, y% - 1 + chy%)¶
  PRINT nam$;¶
  ¶
  x% = x% + l% * chx%¶
  str& = add& + 4¶
  inf& = str& + 44¶
  bf1& = str& + 82¶
  bf2& = bf1& + max%¶
  ¶
  '* Initialization of Structure¶
  POKEW str& + 4 , x%¶
  POKEW str& + 6 , y%¶
  POKEW str& + 8 , FWidth%¶
  POKEW str& + 10, FHeight%¶
  POKEW str& + 14, typ%¶
  POKEW str& + 16, 4¶
  POKEL str& + 34, inf&¶
  POKEL inf&      , bf1&¶
  POKEL inf& + 4 , bf2&¶
  POKEW inf& + 10, max%¶
  ¶
  '* Add Gadgets¶
  reg&(nr%, 0) = add&¶
  p% = AddGadget%(WINDOW(7), str&, 65535&)¶
  LINE (x%-2, y%-2) - (x% + FWidth%, y% + FHeight% +
1), colB%, b¶
  CALL OnGadget(str&, WINDOW(7), 0)¶
```

```
            END IF¶
    END SUB¶
    ¶
    SUB Check (nr%, NewText$, md%) STATIC¶
        count%   = 0¶
        NewText$ = ""¶
        IF reg&(nr%, 0) <> 0 THEN¶
          add&  = reg&(nr%, 0)¶
          str&  = add& + 4¶
          bfl&  = str& + 82¶
          x%   = PEEKW (str& + 4)¶
          y%   = PEEKW (str& + 6)¶
          w%   = PEEKW (str& + 8)¶
          h%   = PEEKW (str& + 10)¶
          typ% = PEEKW (str& + 14)¶
          ¶
          in% = PEEK (bfl&)¶
          WHILE in% <> 0¶
            NewText$ = NewText$ + CHR$(in%)¶
            count% = count% + 1¶
            in% = PEEK (bfl& + count%)¶
          WEND¶
          ¶
          IF md% = 0 THEN¶
            CALL RemoveGadget (WINDOW(7), str&)¶
            size& = PEEKL (add&)¶
            CALL FreeMem(add&, size&)¶
            LINE (x%-2, y%-2) - (x% + w%, y% + h% + 1), 0,
bf¶
            reg&(nr%, 0) = 0¶
          END IF¶
        END IF¶
    END SUB¶
```

Variables		
	reg&()	gadget starting address storage
	nr%	field number (0-40)
	x%,y%	field coordinates
	wid%	field lengths in characters
	max%	maximum input length
	nam$	field name (prompt)
	typ$	field type ("S"=string, "VAR"=numbers)
	colB%	border color
	l%	prompt length
	mem&	size of necessary memory block
	opt&	memory options; 2^{16} = CLEAR_MEMORY
	add&	starting address of memory block; 0=error
	Er%	=1; OUT_OF_MEMORY flag
	typ%	$802 = "VAR", 2 = "S"
	chx%, chy%	width and height of active character set
	FWidth%	data field width
	FHeight%	data field height
	str&	starting address of gadget block
	inf&	starting address of StrInfo block
	bfl&	starting address of input buffer

bf2&	starting address of Undo buffer
p%	position at which new gadget should be inserted
w%, h%	like FWidth% and FHeight%
in%	ASCII code of character read by bf1&
NewText$	text from text buffer
count%	counter
md%	0=remove gadget; 1=read input only
size&	size of free memory

Program description

This program uses an element of the Intuition library known as a *gadget*. Gadgets are elements accessible to the mouse pointer. They perform such functions as allowing size changes and movment of windows. One of these gadgets, the *string gadget*, allows text input.

The "MField" SUB initializes a gadget data structure with the corresponding parameters, into which your values integrate. This data structure takes the active gadgets listed by AddGadget() and places them in your output window.

The "Check" SUB reads the data structure field containing the current input. "Check" transfers this input to the variable NewText$ and returns the system to the main program. If mode=0, then Remove-Gadget() takes the gadget from the system list.

These are the main components of the SUBs. After these actions, "MField" displays a prompt at the data field's beginning. Move() allows cursor movement in either the X- or Y-directions, and text display through PRINT. "MField" also draws a border around the data field. You can easily select data fields with the mouse pointer.

This sample program creates a mask of 6 fields. You can define up to 40 fields if you wish, or even increase the number of fields using the DIM SHARED statement.

After defining the mask, the Amiga waits for the user to press the <RETURN> key at the end of an entry. The user has plenty of time to enter data in the fields, or click gadgets. If you press <RETURN> for an empty set of data fields, the program continues. "Check" places input into the appropriate variables. If md%=0, the program removes the gadgets (this happens before the program can exit). The Amiga displays the data, and a second example begins.

This test should show field control during input. This is done by Check with md%=1. This way, a menu can be displayed as soon as the user writes data in a previously set data field. Check with md%=0 deletes the gadget at the end. The current output changes to a blank space for input (" "). The BACKSPACE command redraws the screen when input isn't appearing fast enough.

4
User-
friendliness

4.   User-friendliness

A few years ago, the term "user-friendly" didn't exist in computing. The user had to type in exactly what he wanted the computer to do. If he entered the data incorrectly, the computer returned an error message (if the user was lucky). The manual was a necessity for the user to survive computing.

As computers became more common in the home, software and hardware designers helped shape the technology that brought about user-friendly interfaces between the computer and user. Intuition is the Amiga's user interface, using windows, icons and the mouse as user input.

User-friendly program design is important to the developer, and even more important to the user. Most users prefer a program that makes operation simple and clear, without having to even pick up a manual. In addition, user-friendly programs are more attractive to the consumer, and may mean more profits for the developer.

This chapter shows you how you can make your programs as user-friendly as possible. This sort of programming focuses on input, selection and control. Often an icon or other self-expanatory graphic helps the user to understand program operation better. In any case, most programming for user response should be mouse-based, and not just for starting and quitting the program. Here are some easily implemented functions that you can include in your own programs.

4.1 Other input

Since not everything can be done by menus, there must be some alternative forms of access. To see a few of these other forms, put your Workbench diskette in your disk drive and open the main directory. Double-click the Preferences icon. Preferences contains user-defined parameters. When you turn on the Amiga, the Workbench diskette defines these parameters as it loads.

The Preferences screen contains *sliders* which let you set the colors. The time and date gadgets in this screen have sliders which you click on to change the hour, day, etc. There are also selectors that you click for changing from 60 characters per line to 80 characters per line. Also, this screen has many gadgets that you can click for saving or cancelling your changes. The Change Printer screen uses many table gadgets for selecting printer options.

4.1.1 Sliders

Sliders are just one kind of input element. You can have a slider represent any value within a range of numbers. You have already seen a practical application of sliders in color assignment. The color sliders in Preferences can handle any values between 0 and 15. You could write three INPUT commands to read numbers for color input, but the sliders are much easier to use: All you do is move a slider left to decrease the amount of that color, and right to increase the amount of that color.

Before you look at the sample program below, there are a few facts you should know about sliders:

Sliders must have their size and position in the window set. In addition, you must establish the scaling or the text that must appear.

The organization of a slider is very important. When you are clear about the coordinates and the orientation of the slider, then the slider can appear on the screen. Simply drawing the slider isn't enough. The program should be programmed so that the click of the left mouse key changes the slider's setting. This data could be placed in an indexed array, particularly when multiple sliders are used in one program.

The above items can all be accomplished with a SUB program which places the data into corresponding variable arrays. The first slider is defined from this data.

The second point to consider is mouse reading. This occurs through an interrupt routine which checks for a pressed left mouse button while the pointer is within a specific range. If this is the case, the correspond-ing slider knob (loaded as a bob) moves to the new position.

```
' Definition of a Horizontal Slider Controller¶
' with x Positioning¶
' ---------------------------------------------------------¶
¶
Variables:¶
¶
  DEFINT a-z¶
  FileName$="Slider2"¶
  Text$="Blue Value"¶
¶
  NumClicks=0¶
  MaxClicks=20¶
¶
  DIM SHARED ClickTable(MaxClicks,3)¶
  DIM SHARED ClickValue(MaxClicks)¶
  DIM SHARED ClickID(MaxClicks)¶
¶
Main:¶
¶
  ON MOUSE GOSUB CheckTable¶
  ON TIMER (.5) GOSUB ColorSet¶
  TIMER ON¶
¶
  DefMoveScale 13,6,100,16,0      'with Nothing¶
  DefMoveScale 13,8,100,16,1      'with Scaling¶
  DefMoveScale 13,10,100,60,2     'with Text¶
¶
  LINE (157,100)-(477,120),2,bf¶
  LOCATE 1,1¶
  PRINT "Slider Controls:"¶
  PRINT "1st Control => Red value, without Enhancements"¶

  PRINT "2nd Control => Green value, with Scaling (16
Units)"¶
  PRINT "3rd Control => Blue value, with Text ahead of the
Slider"¶
  PRINT " (Any Key = End)"¶
¶
  WHILE INKEY$=""¶
    SLEEP¶
  WEND¶
¶
  OBJECT.OFF¶
END¶
¶
¶
CheckTable:¶
¶
  IF NumClicks=0 THEN RETURN¶
¶
  FOR i=1 TO NumClicks¶
     mstat=MOUSE(0)¶
     mx=MOUSE(1)¶
     my=MOUSE(2)¶
     IF mx>=ClickTable(i,0) THEN¶
       IF my>=ClickTable(i,1) THEN¶
         IF mx<=ClickTable(i,2) THEN¶
           IF my<=ClickTable(i,3) THEN¶
             ¶
              IF ClickID(i)=1 THEN¶
                 ClickValue(i)=(mx-ClickTable(i,0))/4¶
                 SetSwitchScale i¶
```

115

```
                END IF¶
                   ¶
              END IF¶
             END IF¶
           END IF¶
         END IF¶
   NEXT i¶
   IF MOUSE(0)=-1 THEN CheckTable¶
 ¶
 RETURN¶
 ¶
 ' Set new Color¶
 ' --------------¶
 ¶
 ColorSet:¶
 ¶
  r!=ClickValue(1)/100¶
  g!=ClickValue(2)/100¶
  b!=ClickValue(3)/100¶
  PALETTE 2,r!,g!,b!¶
 ¶
 RETURN¶
 ¶
 ¶
 ' Define Slider-counter¶
 ' ---------------------¶
 ¶
 SUB DefMoveScale (sx,sy,xd,po,mo) STATIC¶
 ¶
  SHARED NumClicks,FileName$¶
    ¶
  x=sx*9    'Coordinate for Line¶
  y=sy*8¶
 ¶
  LINE (x,y)-(x+xd*4+20,y+12),,b¶
 ¶
  'Extras desired?¶
 ¶
  IF mo AND 1 THEN¶
     FOR sk=x TO x+xd*4+12 STEP (xd*4+20)/16 '16 Units¶
        LINE (sk,y)-(sk,y+2)¶
        LINE (sk,y+12)-(sk,y+10)¶
     NEXT sk¶
  END IF¶
 ¶
  IF mo AND 2 THEN¶
     SHARED Text$¶
     LOCATE sy+1,sx-LEN(Text$)-1¶
     PRINT Text$¶
  END IF¶
 ¶
  'ClickValue entry in Table¶
 ¶
  NumClicks=NumClicks+1¶
  ClickTable(NumClicks,0)=x+6¶
  ClickTable(NumClicks,1)=y¶
  ClickTable(NumClicks,2)=x+xd*4+6¶
  ClickTable(NumClicks,3)=y+12¶
  ClickID(NumClicks)=1   '1 as current setting for Slider¶

  ClickValue(NumClicks)=po 'Beginning value redefined by
 the User¶
  MOUSE ON¶
 ¶
  OPEN FileName$ FOR INPUT AS 1¶
   OBJECT.SHAPE NumClicks,INPUT$(LOF(1),1)¶
  CLOSE 1¶
   ¶
```

```
    OBJECT.Y NumClicks,y¶
    SetSwitchScale NumClicks¶
    OBJECT.ON NumClicks¶
    ¶
    END SUB¶
    ¶
    ' Set Slider-counter¶
    ' ------------------¶
    ¶
    SUB SetSwitchScale (Nr) STATIC¶
    ¶
      OBJECT.X Nr,ClickTable(Nr,0)+4*ClickValue(Nr)-1-6¶
      ¶
    END SUB¶
```

Arrays		
	ClickID	object identification
	ClickTable	coordinates of click range
	ClickValue	slider value

Variables		
	b	blue slider value
	NumClicks	previously defined click object
	MaxClick	possible number of click objects
	FileName	filename of bob used for slider
	Nr	SUB variable; number of set slider
	Text	text display in slider
	g	green slider value
	i	floating variable
	mo	SUB variable; slider position
	mstat	mouse status during reading
	mx, my	mouse coordinates
	po	SUB variable; slider position
	r	red slider value
	sk	floating variable scaling
	sx, sy	SUB variable; slider column coordinate
	x, y	coordinate scaling
	xd	SUB variable; slider width

Program description

First the bob's filename is assigned to a string variable so it can be changed later. The counters for the clickable area and the maximum number initialize, then the variable arrays initialize. Also, the text for the description of the last slider knob goes into a variable. The name corresponds to the subroutine which draws a slider.

The main section of the program reads the mouse through the CheckTable subroutine, and the color display appears after a half-second interrupt. Then the slider is set up according to the predefined parameters on the screen after calling the SUB routine containing these parameters. To observe the color changes, the program draws a colored box in the center of the window. Several lines of text appear on the screen explaining the individual sliders. This is done through PRINT statements. The program jumps to a loop which exits when any key is pressed which has a specific keycode. The slider bobs turn off and the program ends.

Subroutines

The first subroutine in the program, the `CheckTable` routine, tests for whether the mouse pointer lies within the slider area. This test occurs when a mouse button is pressed. Only then can the program continue. Here `ClickValue` computes the pointer coordinates, and the slider moves in the direction of the mouse pointer.

One brief but very important subroutine handles the position reading. This is the `ColorSet` routine, called every half second by the `TIMER` function. This routine sets the values in the array `ClickValue()` to the corresponding color values. Since the slider knobs are 100 pixels wide, the color value is divided into 16 sections.

`Define Slider-Counter:DefMoveScale` is the most important routine in this program. This routine is a `SUB` routine for easy access from the main program. The parameters appear in the main program after the command word, and must not be defined as variables beforehand. The routine itself computes the pixel positions of the box in which movement takes place. It indicates and tests for scaling within a mode. If so, a loop draws 16 divisions of color in the slider box, giving you 16 graduations of color. The second mode enables the slider text descriptions. You can use both modes at the same time if you wish. We suggest that you do not give the text as part of the parameters since the text is optional. Instead, define the text in the main program as a normal string variable, and declare it as a shared variable to the `SUB` routine.

Next the graphic generation occurs. Now the corner values of the boxes must be placed in a table. The program increments the number of previously defined sliders. Then the program stores the X- and Y-values, orientation and identifier for the sliders (more on this below). The most important data is the slider's position.

Next, you need an object to use as slider knobs. The following program creates a simple bob and places it on diskette for slider knob data.

```
RESTORE SliderData¶
datastring$=""¶
¶
FOR i=1 TO  130¶
   READ a$¶
   a$="&H"+a$¶
   datastring$=datastring$+CHR$(VAL(a$))¶
NEXT¶
¶
OPEN "Slider2" FOR OUTPUT AS 1¶
¶
  PRINT#1,datastring$;¶
¶
CLOSE 1¶
¶
¶
SliderData:¶
¶
 DATA 0,0,0,0,0,0,0,0,0,0,0,2,0,0,0,19,0,0,0,D¶
 DATA 0,38,0,3,0,0,0,0,0,0,1,FF,0,0,F,FF,E0,0,1F,FF¶
 DATA F0,0,3F,FF,F8,0,7F,FF,FC,0,7F,FF,FC,0,7F,FF¶
 DATA FC,0,3F,FFF8,0,1F,FF,F0,0,F,FF,E0,0,1,FF,0,0,0,0,0¶
```

```
DATA 0,0,0,0,0,0,0,0,0,0,0,0,0,0,0,0,0,0,0,0,0¶
DATA 0,0,0,0,0,0,0,0,0,0,0,0,0,0,0,0,0,0,0,0,0¶
DATA 0,0,0,0,0,0,0,0,0,0,0,0,0¶
```

Now the bob file can be opened and the program can set its Y-coordinates. A SUB routine sets the X-coordinates of the shifter position.

The value itself comes from the box position, multiplying the value contained in ClickValue by 4. This quadrupling is necessary since the shifter knob has more than 16 positions. The main disadvantage to this program is that you can't set a really precise color setting as you could with Preferences. The central point of the slider marks the value 7.

```
' Definition of a Vertical Slider Controller ¶
' with y Positioning¶
' ----------------------------------------------------------¶
¶
Variables:¶
¶
  DEFINT a-z¶
  FileName$="Slider2"¶
  Text$="Blue"¶
¶
  NumClicks=0¶
  MaxClicks=20¶
¶
  DIM SHARED ClickTable(MaxClicks,3)¶
  DIM SHARED ClickValue(MaxClicks)¶
  DIM SHARED ClickID(MaxClicks)¶
¶
Main:¶
¶
  ON MOUSE GOSUB CheckTable¶
  ON TIMER (.5) GOSUB ColorSet¶
  TIMER ON¶
¶
  DefMoveScale 12,6,100,16,0      'with Nothing¶
  DefMoveScale 16,6,100,0,1       'with Scaling¶
  DefMoveScale 20,6,100,100,2     'with Text¶
¶
  LINE (250,80)-(280,116),2,bf¶
¶
  LOCATE 1,27¶
  PRINT "Slider Controls:"¶
  LOCATE 3,27¶
  PRINT "1st Control => Red value,"¶
  PRINT TAB(40);"without Enhancements"¶
  PRINT TAB(27);"2nd Control => Green value,"¶
  PRINT TAB(40);"with Scaling (16 Units)"¶
  PRINT TAB(27);"3rd Control => Blue value,"¶
  PRINT TAB(40);"with Text above it"¶
¶
  WHILE INKEY$=""¶
    SLEEP¶
  WEND¶
¶
  OBJECT.OFF¶
END¶
  ¶
¶
CheckTable:¶
¶
  IF NumClicks=0 THEN RETURN¶
```

```
¶
FOR i=1 TO NumClicks¶
    mstat=MOUSE(0)¶
    mx=MOUSE(1)¶
    my=MOUSE(2)¶
    IF mx>=ClickTable(i,0) THEN¶
      IF my>=ClickTable(i,1) THEN¶
        IF mx<=ClickTable(i,2) THEN¶
          IF my<=ClickTable(i,3) THEN¶
            ¶
            IF ClickID(i)=2 THEN¶
              ClickValue(i)=(my-ClickTable(i,1))¶
              SetSwitchScale i¶
            END IF¶
            ¶
          END IF¶
        END IF¶
      END IF¶
    END IF¶
NEXT i¶
IF MOUSE(0)=-1 THEN CheckTable¶
¶
RETURN¶
¶
' Set new Color¶
' --------------¶
¶
ColorSet:¶
¶
 r!=ClickValue(1)/100¶
 g!=ClickValue(2)/100¶
 b!=ClickValue(3)/100¶
 PALETTE 2,r!,g!,b!¶
¶
RETURN¶
¶
¶
' Define Slider-counter¶
' ---------------------¶
¶
SUB DefMoveScale (sx,sy,yd,po,mo) STATIC¶
¶
 SHARED NumClicks,FileName$¶
   ¶
 x=sx*8    'Coordinates for Line *Draw 10 by 60¶
 y=sy*8¶
¶
 LINE (x,y)-(x+20,y+12+yd),,b¶
¶
 'Extras desired?¶
¶
 IF mo AND 1 THEN  ' Scales¶
   FOR sk=y TO y+yd+8 STEP (yd+12)/16 '16 Units¶
     LINE (x,sk)-(x+2,sk)¶
     LINE (x+20,sk)-(x+18,sk)¶
   NEXT sk¶
 END IF¶
¶
 IF mo AND 2 THEN    ' Text¶
   SHARED Text$¶
   sy=sy-LEN(Text$)-1¶
   FOR txt=1 TO LEN(Text$)¶
     LOCATE sy+txt,sx+2¶
     PRINT MID$(Text$,txt,1)¶
   NEXT txt¶
 END IF¶
¶
 'ClickValue entry in Table ¶
¶
 NumClicks=NumClicks+1¶
```

```
ClickTable(NumClicks,0)=x¶
ClickTable(NumClicks,1)=y+8¶
ClickTable(NumClicks,2)=x+20¶
ClickTable(NumClicks,3)=y+yd+8¶
ClickID(NumClicks)=2    '1 as current setting for Slider¶
ClickValue(NumClicks)=po¶
MOUSE ON¶
¶
OPEN FileName$ FOR INPUT AS 1¶
  OBJECT.SHAPE NumClicks,INPUT$(LOF(1),1)¶
CLOSE 1¶
¶
OBJECT.X NumClicks,x-1¶
SetSwitchScale NumClicks¶
OBJECT.ON NumClicks¶
¶
END SUB¶
¶
' Set Slider-counter¶
' --------------------¶
¶
SUB SetSwitchScale (Nr) STATIC¶
¶
OBJECT.Y Nr,ClickTable(Nr,1)+ClickValue(Nr)-8¶
¶
END SUB¶
```

***Program
description***

The second listing here is similar to the first. The major difference is that this program draws a vertical slider instead of a horizontal slider. The other sections of the program are identical to the earlier program: The color initialization, the mouse position reading and the main program are the same. If you wish, you can combine both programs with one another. You could have one window containing two different kinds of sliders. Copy the two SUB routines DefMove: and Set-Switch: of one type into the program containing the sliders of the other type. Finally, include the CheckTab loop from the other program.

The most practical method is to combine click areas with one another. The main section of the program contains a testing loop, and you could add more definitions for different fields and gadgets.

4.1.2   Table selection

The abovementioned sliders show how you can select one value in a given range. This range was *linear*, or an array of possible elements. There are many times when this form of selection doesn't work. Sometimes you need just a 10, not a 9.6. Or you may want a set of texts from which the user can select one text.

Tables perform this task. Most of these tables contain a number of values grouped under a certain category. Or tables may only contain two or three selections. The Text gadget in the **Preferences** window is a prime example of a table; it has only two options.

The first program should display all the elements of a table next to one another. Another displays the values under each other, something like the sliders.

To make the most of flexibility, the concrete elements of the table go into memory as strings, so you can use text as well as numbers.

The table definition is similar to that SUB routine that stores the corner pixel of the table in the ClickTable array (see Section 4.1.1). Again you have the power to combine this function with other functions such as the sliders. In this case, a few other values are stored: The elements of the table which can be used later as a response in the main program; and the program's storage of the maximum number of characters placed in a table. The last one lets the program know how far the mouse pointer should go near the upper left corner.

To display the prepared table, the subroutine must place all text into a box and center the text in this box as much as possible (it looks better this way). When the entire table appears, the main program can then wait for a keypress. This stops the program and tells you which table point was last looked for.

```
' Definition of a Click Table¶
' -----------------------------¶
¶
Variables:¶
¶
  DEFINT a-z¶
  MaxNum=2       ' a maximum of 3 Tables¶
  MaxEl=10       ' with a maximum of 11 Elements¶
  TabNum=0¶
  CharWid=8      ' CharacterWidth - 80 Width=8 ; 60 Width=10¶

¶
  DIM SHARED MaxLen(MaxNum)¶
  DIM SHARED ChoseTable$(MaxNum,MaxEl)¶
  DIM SHARED ClickTable(MaxNum,3)¶
  DIM SHARED ClickID(MaxNum)¶
  DIM SHARED ActEl(MaxNum)¶
  ¶
' -----------------------------¶
  ¶
Functions:¶
  ¶
  DECLARE FUNCTION Move& LIBRARY¶
  LIBRARY "graphics.library"¶
  ¶
Main:¶
  ¶
  PRINT "End Program by Pressing any Key."¶
  ¶
  RESTORE TableTest¶
  DefTabY "Table Test",10,5,3¶
  ¶
  ON MOUSE GOSUB CheckTable¶
  MOUSE ON¶
  ¶
  WHILE INKEY$=""¶
```

```
    SLEEP¶
   WEND¶
  ¶
   LOCATE 12,1¶
   PRINT "Item";ActEl(1);"was selected with a value of: ";¶

   PRINT ChoseTable$(1,ActEl(1))¶
  ¶
   MOUSE OFF¶
  END¶
  ¶
  '  ---------------------------¶
  ¶
  CheckTable:¶
  ¶
   IF TabNum=0 THEN RETURN¶
  ¶
   FOR loop=1 TO TabNum¶
      mx=MOUSE(1)¶
      my=MOUSE(2)¶
      IF mx>=ClickTable(loop,0) THEN¶
        IF my>=ClickTable(loop,1) THEN¶
          IF mx<=ClickTable(loop,2) THEN¶
            IF my<=ClickTable(loop,3) THEN¶
              ¶
              IF ClickID(loop)=3 THEN¶
                NumAct=INT((mx-ClickTable(loop,0)+
  MaxLen(TabNum))/MaxLen(TabNum))¶
                IF NumAct<>ActEl(loop) THEN MakeAct
  NumAct,loop¶
                              END IF¶
              ¶
              END IF¶
            END IF¶
          END IF¶
        END IF¶
   NEXT loop¶
  ¶
   IF MOUSE(0)=-1 THEN CheckTable¶
  ¶
  RETURN¶
  ¶
  ¶
  '  -------------------------------¶
  ¶
  SUB DefTabY(TableName$,x,y,NumAct) STATIC¶
  ¶
   SHARED TabNum,CharWid¶
  ¶
   TabNum=TabNum+1¶
   NumEl=1¶
  ¶
   loopread:¶
     READ ChoseTable$(TabNum,NumEl)¶
     IF ChoseTable$(TabNum,NumEl)<>"*" THEN¶
       l=LEN(ChoseTable$(TabNum,NumEl))*CharWid¶
       IF l>MaxLen(TabNum) THEN MaxLen(TabNum)=l¶
       NumEl=NumEl+1¶
       GOTO loopread¶
     END IF¶
  ¶
   NumElements(TabNum)=NumEl-1¶
  ¶
   xyPTAB x*CharWid,y*8¶
   PRINT TableName$¶
   ypos=y*8+10¶
  ¶
   FOR loop=1 TO NumElements(TabNum)¶
      xpos=x*CharWid+(loop-1)*(MaxLen(TabNum)+2)¶
```

123

```
      xtab=(MaxLen(TabNum)/CharWid-
LEN(ChoseTable$(TabNum,loop)))*CharWid/2¶
      xyPTAB xpos+xtab,ypos+8¶
      PRINT ChoseTable$(TabNum,loop)¶
      LINE (xpos-1,ypos)-(xpos+MaxLen(TabNum)+
1,ypos+10),1,b¶
 NEXT loop¶
¶
' Put Value in Table¶
¶
 ClickTable(TabNum,0)=x*CharWid¶
 ClickTable(TabNum,1)=y*8+11¶
 ClickTable(TabNum,2)=x*CharWid+(NumElements(TabNum)-
1)*(MaxLen(TabNum)+2)+MaxLen(TabNum)¶
 ClickTable(TabNum,3)=y*8+19¶
 ClickID(TabNum)=3                  'Click Table¶
 MaxLen(TabNum)=MaxLen(TabNum)+2¶
 IF NumAct>NumElements(TabNum) THEN ERROR¶
 MakeAct NumAct,TabNum ¶
¶
END SUB¶
¶
' ---------------------------¶
¶
SUB xyPTAB(x,y) STATIC¶
  e&=Move&(WINDOW(8),x,y)¶
END SUB¶
¶
' ---------------------------¶
¶
SUB SetDrawMode (mode) STATIC¶
 CALL SetDrMd&(WINDOW(8),mode)¶
END SUB¶
¶
' ---------------------------¶
¶
SUB MakeAct (NumAct,NumEl) STATIC¶
¶
 x=ClickTable(NumEl,0)¶
 y1=ClickTable(NumEl,1)¶
 y2=ClickTable(NumEl,3)¶
 z=ActEl(NumEl)¶
 SetDrawMode 2¶
¶
 IF z<>0 THEN¶
    LINE (x+(z-1)*MaxLen(NumEl),y1)-(x+z*MaxLen(NumEl)-
2,y2),,bf¶
 END IF¶
¶
 ActEl(NumEl)=NumAct¶
 LINE (x+(NumAct-1)*MaxLen(NumEl),y1)-
(x+NumAct*MaxLen(NumEl)-2,y2),,bf¶
 SetDrawMode 1¶
¶
END SUB¶
¶
' ---------------------------¶
¶
TableTest:¶
¶
 DATA "10"¶
 DATA "20"¶
 DATA "40"¶
 DATA "80"¶
 DATA "160"¶
 DATA "3200"¶
 DATA "64000"¶
 DATA "*"¶
```

Arrays

ChoseTable	table text
ClickID	object identification
ClickTable	coordinates of click range
ActEl	active element of a table
NumElements	number of elements of a table
MaxLen	maximum length of table text

Variables

MaxNum	maximum number of click fields
MaxEl	maximum number of table elements
TableName	SUB variable; table name
NumEl	SUB variable; number of elements in a table
CharWid	width of a character in pixels
NumAct	number of new active elements
l	text length
loop	loop counter variable
mx, my	mouse coordinates
x, y	SUB variable; table position
xpos	SUB variable; positioning variable
xtab	SUB variable; text tabulator
ypos	SUB variable; Y-position for table text

*Program
description*

After all variables receive integer definitions, the maximum number of tables becomes 2 (this program only uses 1). Each table can contain up to 10 elements. The program makes sure that no table was previously defined. The character width goes into a variable to ensure correct graphic output, then the arrays initialize.

Since the text output is no longer in 8x8 font size, the graphics.library file must set the pixel orientation below the PRINT position.

The DATA statements set the table definition through the READ pointer. Then the DATA branches to the parameters Name, xpos, ypos and the current elements.

The main program branches to the CheckTable routine when you press the left mouse button, then waits for a keypress. If you press a key, the last selected element on the table is displayed and the program ends.

The table definition routine is an interesting one. After the character width setup and the previously defined tables, a loop forces the program to read DATA statements until the program finds an asterisk (this marks the end of the DATA lines). Since this means that all DATA is in, the title appears and the vertical position is moved down. Another loop computes the X-position of every element, based on the maximum width of a box and the current text width. All points are placed one below the next. Last, the program enters the corner point in the known field, and activates a preset element.

125

Three very important subroutines follow. The first simplifies the use of the `Move&` function. The second routine changes the character mode. The third routine returns the currently active table point to normal and displays it in a new color. This display occurs through the character mode. When this is already active, it must first be deactivated, then the table points are reset and the corresponding element displayed. To avoid problems with output in the main program, the character mode returns to normal status.

The end of the listing contains the `DATA` statements with their numbers. These lines end with an asterisk (*).

Use the program below to create a vertical table:

```
' Definition of a Click Table¶
' ---------------------------¶
¶
Variables:¶
¶
 DEFINT a-z¶
 MaxNum=2      ' a maximum of 3 Tables¶
 MaxEl=10      ' with a maximum of 11 Elements¶
 TabNum=0¶
 CharWid=8     ' CharacterWidth - 80 Width=8 ; 60 Width=10¶
¶
 DIM SHARED MaxLen(MaxNum)¶
 DIM SHARED ChoseTable$(MaxNum,MaxEl)¶
 DIM SHARED ClickTable(MaxNum,3)¶
 DIM SHARED ClickID(MaxNum)¶
 DIM SHARED ActEl(MaxNum)¶
¶
' ---------------------------¶
¶
Functions:¶
¶
 DECLARE FUNCTION Move& LIBRARY¶
 LIBRARY "graphics.library"¶
¶
Main:¶
¶
 PRINT "End Program by Pressing any Key."¶
¶
 RESTORE TableTest¶
 DefTabY "Table Test",20,5,3¶
¶
 ON MOUSE GOSUB CheckTable¶
 MOUSE ON¶
¶
 WHILE INKEY$=""  ¶
  SLEEP¶
 WEND¶
¶
 LOCATE 18,1¶
 PRINT "Item";ActEl(1);"was selected containing the text: ".¶
 WRITE ChoseTable$(1,ActEl(1))¶
¶
 MOUSE OFF¶
END¶
¶
' ---------------------------¶
¶
CheckTable:¶
¶
```

```
      IF TabNum=0 THEN RETURN¶
      ¶
       FOR loop=1 TO TabNum¶
          mx=MOUSE(1)¶
          my=MOUSE(2)¶
          IF mx>=ClickTable(loop,0) THEN¶
            IF my>=ClickTable(loop,1) THEN¶
              IF mx<=ClickTable(loop,2) THEN¶
                IF my<=ClickTable(loop,3) THEN¶
                  ¶
                    IF ClickID(loop)=4 THEN¶
                      NumAct=INT((my-ClickTable(loop,1)+10)/10)¶

                      IF NumAct<>ActEl(loop) THEN MakeAct
NumAct,loop¶
                    END IF¶
                  ¶
                END IF¶
              END IF¶
            END IF¶
          END IF¶
       NEXT loop¶
      ¶
       IF MOUSE(0)=-1 THEN CheckTable¶
      ¶
RETURN¶
      ¶
      ¶
'  --------------------------------¶
      ¶
SUB DefTabY (TableName$,x,y,NumAct) STATIC¶
      ¶
       SHARED TabNum,CharWid¶
      ¶
       TabNum=TabNum+1¶
       NumEl=1¶
      ¶
       loopread:¶
        READ ChoseTable$(TabNum,NumEl)¶
        IF ChoseTable$(TabNum,NumEl)<>"*" THEN¶
          l=LEN(ChoseTable$(TabNum,NumEl))*CharWid¶
          IF l>MaxLen(TabNum) THEN MaxLen(TabNum)=l¶
          NumEl=NumEl+1¶
          GOTO loopread¶
        END IF¶
      ¶
       NumElements(TabNum)=NumEl-1¶
       xyPTAB x*CharWid,y*8¶
       PRINT TableName$¶
      ¶
       FOR loop=1 TO NumElements(TabNum)¶
          xpos=x*CharWid¶
          ypos=y*8+loop*10¶
          COLOR 1¶
          SetDrawMode 0¶
          xyPTAB xpos,ypos+8¶
          PRINT ChoseTable$(TabNum,loop)¶
          LINE (xpos-1,ypos)-(xpos+MaxLen(TabNum)+
1,ypos+10),1,b¶
       NEXT loop¶
      ¶
       ' Put Value in Table¶
      ¶
       ClickTable(TabNum,0)=x*CharWid¶
       ClickTable(TabNum,1)=y*8+11¶
       ClickTable(TabNum,2)=x*CharWid+MaxLen(TabNum)¶
       ClickTable(TabNum,3)=y*8+9+NumElements(TabNum)*10¶
       ClickID(TabNum)=4                    'Click Table¶
```

```
   IF NumAct>NumElements(TabNum) THEN ERROR¶
   MakeAct NumAct,TabNum ¶
   SetDrawMode 1¶
¶
END SUB¶
¶
' ----------------------------¶
¶
SUB xyPTAB(x,y) STATIC¶
   e&=Move&(WINDOW(8),x,y)¶
END SUB¶
¶
' ----------------------------¶
¶
SUB SetDrawMode (mode) STATIC¶
   CALL SetDrMd&(WINDOW(8),mode)¶
END SUB¶
¶
' ----------------------------¶
¶
SUB MakeAct (NumAct,NumEl) STATIC¶
¶
 x1=ClickTable(NumEl,0)¶
 y=ClickTable(NumEl,1)¶
 x2=ClickTable(NumEl,2)¶
 z=ActEl(NumEl)¶
 SetDrawMode 2¶
¶
 IF z<>0 THEN¶
   LINE (x1,y+(z-1)*10)-(x2,y+8+(z-1)*10),,bf¶
 END IF¶
¶
 ActEl(NumEl)=NumAct¶
 LINE (x1,y+(NumAct-1)*10)-(x2,y+8+(NumAct-1)*10),,bf¶
 SetDrawMode 1¶
¶
END SUB¶
¶
' ----------------------------¶
¶
TableTest:¶
 DATA "I will test"¶
 DATA "I will not test"¶
 DATA "I am not done yet"¶
 DATA "Nothing from Something"¶
 DATA "End"¶
 DATA "Longer Test for this Program"¶
 DATA "Still Another Line"¶
 DATA "*"¶
```

4.1.3   Scrolling tables

When a table contains more values than you can fit in a window, you
can adapt the table to scroll up or down. This saves space (X=36 and the
Y measurement depends on the maximum text length) and is very user-
friendly.

The basic idea of a scrolling table is that you display one section of the
table at a time. The other elements are either hidden above or below the

currently displayed selection. You can see the rest of these selections by clicking on one of two arrows. Click the arrow in the direction you want the table to scroll.

The way this program is constructed, you can combine these routines with very few changes. All you need is the subroutine in your own programs. You should bear in mind, however, that the arrays used here must be passed on to your own programs as well. This program ends when you press a key.

```
' Definition of a Click Table¶
' ---------------------------¶
¶
Variables:¶
¶
 DEFINT a-z¶
 MaxNum=2      ' a maximum of 3 Tables¶
 MaxEl=10      ' with a maximum of 11 Elements¶
 TabNum=0¶
 CharWid=8     ' CharacterWidth - 80 Width=8 ; 60 Width=10¶
¶
 DIM SHARED MaxLen(MaxNum)¶
 DIM SHARED ChoseTable$(MaxNum,MaxEl)¶
 DIM SHARED ClickTable(MaxNum,3)¶
 DIM SHARED ClickID(MaxNum)¶
 DIM SHARED ClickValue(MaxNum)¶
 DIM SHARED ActEl(MaxNum)¶
 DIM SHARED NumElements(MaxNum)¶
 ¶
' ---------------------------¶
¶
Functions:¶
¶
 DECLARE FUNCTION Move& LIBRARY¶
 LIBRARY "graphics.library"¶
¶
Main:¶
¶
 PRINT "End Program by Pressing any Key."¶
¶
 RESTORE TableTest¶
 DefTabScr "Scroll-Table",20,5,7,1¶
¶
 ON MOUSE GOSUB CheckTable¶
 MOUSE ON¶
¶
 WHILE INKEY$="" ¶
  SLEEP¶
 WEND¶
¶
 LOCATE 18,1¶
 PRINT "Item";ClickValue(1);"was selected containing the
text: ";¶
 WRITE ChoseTable$(1,ClickValue(1))¶
¶
 MOUSE OFF¶
END¶
¶
' ---------------------------¶
¶
CheckTable:¶
¶
 IF TabNum=0 THEN RETURN¶
¶
 FOR loop=1 TO TabNum¶
```

```
     mx=MOUSE(1)¶
     my=MOUSE(2)¶
     IF mx>=ClickTable(loop,0) THEN¶
       IF my>=ClickTable(loop,1) THEN¶
         IF mx<=ClickTable(loop,2) THEN¶
           IF my<=ClickTable(loop,3) THEN¶
             ¶
             IF ClickID(loop)=5 THEN¶
               IF my-ClickTable(loop,1)<18 THEN¶
                 IF ClickValue(loop)<NumElements(loop)
THEN¶
                   ClickValue(loop)=ClickValue(loop)+1¶
                 END IF¶
               ELSEIF ClickValue(loop)>1 THEN¶
                 ClickValue(loop)=ClickValue(loop)-1¶
               END IF¶
               DataOut loop,ClickValue(loop),
ClickTable(loop,0)+51,ClickTable(loop,1)¶
             END IF¶
             ¶
           END IF¶
         END IF¶
       END IF¶
     END IF¶
   NEXT loop¶
 ¶
 IF MOUSE(0)=-1 THEN CheckTable¶
 ¶
RETURN¶
 ¶
 ¶
' --------------------------------¶
 ¶
SUB DefTabScr (TableName$,x,y,MaxNum,NumAct) STATIC¶
 ¶
 SHARED TabNum,CharWid¶
 TabNum=TabNum+1¶
 ¶
 FOR i=1 TO MaxNum¶
   READ ChoseTable$(TabNum,i)¶
   l=LEN(ChoseTable$(TabNum,i))¶
   IF l>MaxLen(TabNum) THEN MaxLen(TabNum)=l¶
 NEXT i¶
 ¶
 NumElements(TabNum)=MaxNum¶
 ClickValue(TabNum)=NumAct¶
 MaxLen(TabNum)=MaxLen(TabNum)*CharWid¶
 ¶
 ' Output table¶
 ¶
 xyPTAB x*CharWid,y*8¶
 PRINT TableName$¶
 x1=x*CharWid : y1=y*8+6¶
 x2=x1+51¶
 LINE (x1,y1)-(x2+MaxLen(TabNum)+1,y1+36),1,b¶
 LINE (x2,y1)-(x2,y1+36),1¶
 LINE (x1,y1+18)-(x2,y1+18),1¶
 LINE (x2,y1+12)-(x2+MaxLen(TabNum)+1,y1+12),1¶
 LINE (x2,y1+24)-(x2+MaxLen(TabNum)+1,y1+24),1¶
 PSET (x1+17,y1+16)¶
 LINE -(x1+34,y1+16)¶
 LINE -(x1+34,y1+10)¶
 LINE -(x1+40,y1+10)¶
 LINE -(x1+25,y1+2)¶
 LINE -(x1+10,y1+10)¶
 LINE -(x1+17,y1+10)¶
 LINE -(x1+17,y1+16)¶
 PAINT (x1+18,y1+15),1,1¶
 ¶
```

```
                    PSET (x1+17,y1+20) ¶
                    LINE -(x1+34,y1+20) ¶
                    LINE -(x1+34,y1+26) ¶
                    LINE -(x1+40,y1+26) ¶
                    LINE -(x1+25,y1+34) ¶
                    LINE -(x1+10,y1+26) ¶
                    LINE -(x1+17,y1+26) ¶
                    LINE -(x1+17,y1+20) ¶
                    PAINT (x1+18,y1+21),1,1¶
                    ¶
                    DataOut TabNum,ClickValue(TabNum),x1+51,y1¶
                    ¶
                    ' Put Value in Table¶
                    ¶
                    ClickTable(TabNum,0)=x1¶
                    ClickTable(TabNum,1)=y1¶
                    ClickTable(TabNum,2)=x2¶
                    ClickTable(TabNum,3)=y1+36¶
                    ClickID(TabNum)=5                      'Scroll-Table¶
                    ¶
                  END SUB¶
                  ¶
                  SUB xyPTAB(x,y) STATIC¶
                    e&=Move&(WINDOW(8),x,y) ¶
                  END SUB¶
                  ¶
                  SUB SetDrawMode (mode) STATIC¶
                    CALL SetDrMd&(WINDOW(8),mode) ¶
                  END SUB¶
                  ¶
                  SUB DataOut (NumEl,start,x,y) STATIC¶
                    ¶
                    x=x+1¶
                    FOR loop=start-1 TO start+1¶
                      y1=y+12*(loop-start+2)-2¶
                      y2=y1+12-1 : x2=x+MaxLen(NumEl)-1¶
                      LINE (x,y1-9)-(x2,y2-10),0,bf¶
                      xyPTAB x,y1¶
                      PRINT ChoseTable$(NumEl,loop) ¶
                      IF loop=start THEN¶
                        SetDrawMode 2¶
                        LINE (x,y1-9)-(x2,y2-10),1,bf¶
                        SetDrawMode 1¶
                      END IF¶
                    NEXT loop¶
                    ¶
                  END SUB¶
                  ¶
                  TableTest:¶
                  ¶
                  DATA "I will test"¶
                  DATA "I will not test"¶
                  DATA "I am not done yet"¶
                  DATA "Nothing from Something"¶
                  DATA "End"¶
                  DATA "Longer Test for this Program"¶
                  DATA "Still Another Line"¶
```

Arrays

ChoseTable	table text
ClickID	object identification
ClickTable	coordinates of click range
ClickValue	number of selected elements
ActEl	active element of a table
NumElements	number of elements of a table
MaxLen	maximum length of table text

131

Variables

MaxNum	maximum number of click fields
MaxEl	maximum number of table elements
TableName	SUB variable; table name
NumEl	number of elements in a table
TabNum	number of defined tables
CharWid	pixel width of character
NumAct	number of new active elements
i	floating variable
l	text length
loop	floating variable
mode	mode set by SetDrawMode
mx, my	mouse coordinates
x, y	SUB variable; table position
x1, y1	character coordinates
x1, y1	character coordinates

Program description

All variables receive integer definitions. To properly display output, the character width in pixels is placed in a variable. Change that value when you want to use a different font. The program then dimensions all necessary arrays.

The graphics.library opens before the main program executes. This contains all the necessary graphic routines for display. Since one function is needed from it, it must be defined first.

The main program itself displays just a short bit of text, executes the routine that reads the data, and waits for a keypress. The selected value appears at the end, and the mouse reading routine turns off.

The CheckTable subroutine is different from those in the preceding programs. The coordinate checking is similar, but the kernel is modified. When a scroll table exists, it checks for a click in the upper or lower half of the range. If a click occurs in the upper end, and scrolling up is possible, the table scrolls up. If a click occurs in the lower end, and scrolling down is possible, the table scrolls down.

The tables number access and the character width is declared as SHARED. Then the number of tables increment, in order to define the new tables. The first loop of the subroutine reads all the elements of this table, and sets up the maximum number of characters. The correct width is computed from this, together with the element numbers in the preset arrays. The current point also sets up from this routine.

Next comes the graphic display. After the title, the table name appears, followed by the scroll arrows and three of the elements. LINE commands draw both boxes (can't get any simpler than that). Finally the coordinates of the clicking range are set into an array.

The subroutine demonstrates two new graphic functions: The Move command and the SetDrawMode routine.

4.2 Rubberbanding

Earlier in this chapter you learned about the most important elements of professional program design. You shouldn't be afraid of hunting for new ways to do things. Every new problem has a new solution.

This section discusses a function that you've used any number of times. The function is called *rubberbanding*. Rubberbanding occurs when you change the size of a window. Intuition lets you change a window's size by grabbing on to the sizing gadget at the lower right corner of most windows. This section, however, shows how to program rubberbanding in BASIC.

The trick lies in creating lines in complement mode instead of simply drawing lines. Complement mode allows you to move a line or set of lines around on the screen without redrawing the background.

You'd normally use rubberbanding for determining window size on the screen. However, this process also makes it easier to draw rectangles in graphic programs.

4.2.1 Rectangles in rubberbanding

This program serves no real purpose other than to show you how this function can be used in a program. You can adapt the mouse control techniques to your own applications.

When you start the program an empty window appears with a mouse pointer in it. Press and hold the left mouse button from any position in the window, and drag the pointer down and to the right. A rubberbanded rectangle appears, and changes size as you move the pointer. When you release the left mouse button, the rectangle stays on the screen and changes to character color 1.

```
' Drawing Rectangles with Rubberbanding¶
'¶
' by Wgb in June '87¶
'¶
¶
LIBRARY "graphics.library"¶
¶
ON MOUSE GOSUB SetPoint¶
MOUSE ON¶
¶
  WHILE INKEY$<>" "¶
    SLEEP¶
  WEND¶
```

```
¶
MOUSE OFF¶
END¶
¶
¶
SetPoint:¶
¶
 MStat=MOUSE(0)¶
 IF MStat<>-1 THEN RETURN¶
 ¶
 xStart=MOUSE(3)¶
 yStart=MOUSE(4)¶
 CALL SetDrMd&(WINDOW(8),2)¶
¶
 NewPosition:¶
 ¶
 mx=MOUSE(1)¶
 my=MOUSE(2)¶
 ¶
 LINE (xStart,yStart)-(mx,my),,b¶
 ¶
 WHILE MOUSE(0)=-1¶
   IF mx<>MOUSE(1) OR my<>MOUSE(2) THEN¶
     LINE (xStart,yStart)-(mx,my),,b¶
     GOTO NewPosition¶
   END IF¶
 WEND ¶
 ¶
 CALL SetDrMd&(WINDOW(8),1)¶
 LINE (xStart,yStart)-(mx,my),,b¶
 RETURN¶
 ¶
```

Variables

MStat	mouse status
mx, my	mouse coordinates
xStart	starting X-coordinate of rectangle
yStart	starting Y-coordinate of rectangle

Program description

The graphics.library opens. The program draws the guidelines in complement mode, and this library file transfers the necessary graphic routines to the program.

The SetPoint subroutine sets the mouse reading at the beginning of the program. The program waits for a keypress. When this occurs, the mouse reading routine turns off and ends.

The mouse reader is the central point of the program; take a good look at those program lines. The mouse status goes into a variable. When it notes that the user hasn't pressed the left mouse key, the subroutine exits. Otherwise, the program marks the pointer position as the starting value, and the drawing mode changes to complement mode. The routine then draws the rectangle and waits for the user to move the mouse. Following this, the program deletes the rectangle and redraws the rectangle to fit the new mouse position.

When the user releases the left mouse button, the program exits the loop. The program then returns to normal character mode, and the final rectangle is displayed.

4.2.2   Creating shapes

Rubberbanding can be used for much more than changing window sizes
and drawing rectangles. This program draws lines between two points
selected by the user. This routine also uses rubberbanding. When you
start the program and press the left mouse button, you'll see that two
pixels connected by a rubberband appear.

```
' Connections with Rubberbanding¶
'¶
' by Wgb in June '87¶
'¶
¶
LIBRARY "graphics.library"¶
¶
BaseGraphic:¶
¶
 LINE (100,180)-(540,180)¶
 ¶
 FOR i=100 TO 540 ¶
    x=(i-100)/2.444444¶
    y=SIN(x*3.1415/180)*100¶
    LINE -(i,180-y)¶
 NEXT i¶
 ¶
ON MOUSE GOSUB SetPoint¶
MOUSE ON¶
 ¶
 WHILE INKEY$<>" "¶
    SLEEP¶
 WEND¶
 ¶
MOUSE OFF¶
END¶
 ¶
 ¶
SetPoint:¶
 ¶
 MStat=MOUSE(0)¶
 IF MStat<>-1 THEN RETURN¶
 ¶
 CALL SetDrMd&(WINDOW(8),2)¶
 ¶
 NewPosition:¶
 ¶
 mx=MOUSE(1)¶
 CALL Connect(mx)¶
 ¶
 WHILE MOUSE(0)=-1¶
    IF mx<>MOUSE(1) THEN¶
       CALL Connect(mx)¶
       GOTO NewPosition¶
    END IF¶
 WEND ¶
 ¶
 CALL SetDrMd&(WINDOW(8),1)¶
 CALL Connect(mx)¶
 RETURN¶
 ¶
SUB Connect (x) STATIC¶
 ¶
 IF x<100 THEN x=100¶
 IF x>540 THEN x=540¶
```

```
¶
xw=(x-100)/2.444444¶
yw=SIN(xw*3.1415/180)*100¶
¶
LINE (100,180)-(x,180-yw)¶
LINE -(540,180)¶
PSET (x,180-yw)¶
¶
END SUB¶
¶
```

Variables

MStat	mouse status
i	floating variable
mx	mouse position
x, y	graphic coordinates
xw, yw	coordinates in SUB

Program description

The basic design is similar to the first listing. There is an additional routine for the banding based on a short sine equation, followed by the same delay loop.

The major changes appear in the SUB programs. The mouse control routine now checks the X-position of the pointer. This position controls the call of a subroutine. The routine then draws the connecting line, while reading the pointer's X-movement. Like the previous program, the old lines are deleted and redrawn at the new position.

Try the program out. The X-value goes into a specific range, since not every X-coordinate has a graphic equivalent. The program then computes the coordinates and draws the line.

4.2.3   Object positioning

This last routine came from the idea of a drawing program for two-dimensional grid graphics. When you draw multiple objects in such a program, you may find that you run out of room on the screen. The simplest way to move objects would be to select them with the mouse pointer and drag the objects to new screen locations. The following program performs a function similar to this. First it computes the corner point of a circle. Circles have no corners, but to make the coding simple, this program plots an imaginary corner point.

The circle is displayed as long as you press and hold the left mouse button; it disappears when you release the left mouse button.

```
' Objects with Rubberbanding¶
'¶
' by Wgb in June '87¶
'¶
¶
LIBRARY "graphics.library"¶
```

```
¶
ObjectDefinition:¶
 ¶
 DIM SHARED Ob%(10,1)¶
 Pi=3.141593¶
 ¶
 FOR i=0 TO 360 STEP 36¶
     x=COS(i*Pi/180)*30¶
     y=SIN(i*Pi/180)*15¶
     Ob%(i/36,0)=x¶
     Ob%(i/36,1)=y¶
 NEXT i¶
 ¶
  ¶
ON MOUSE GOSUB SetObject¶
MOUSE ON¶
 ¶
 WHILE INKEY$<>" "¶
   SLEEP¶
 WEND¶
 ¶
MOUSE OFF¶
END¶
 ¶
 ¶
SetObject:¶
 ¶
 MStat=MOUSE(0)¶
 IF MStat<>-1 THEN RETURN¶
 ¶
 CALL SetDrMd&(WINDOW(8),2)¶
 ¶
 NewPosition:¶
 ¶
 mx=MOUSE(1)¶
 my=MOUSE(2)¶
 CALL DrawObject(mx,my)¶
 ¶
 WHILE MOUSE(0)=-1¶
   IF mx<>MOUSE(1) OR my<>MOUSE(2) THEN¶
     CALL DrawObject(mx,my)¶
     GOTO NewPosition¶
   END IF¶
 WEND ¶
 ¶
 CALL SetDrMd&(WINDOW(8),1)¶
 CALL DrawObject(mx,my)¶
 ¶
RETURN¶
 ¶
SUB DrawObject(x,y) STATIC¶
 ¶
 PSET (Ob%(0,0)+x,Ob%(0,1)+y)¶
 ¶
 FOR i=1 TO 10¶
     LINE -(Ob%(i,0)+x,Ob%(i,1)+y) ¶
 NEXT i¶
 ¶
 LINE -(Ob%(10,0)+x,Ob%(10,1)+y)¶
 ¶
END SUB¶
```

Arrays	Ob	circle point array

Variables	MStat	mouse status
	Pi	3.141593
	i	floating variable
	mx, my	mouse coordinates
	x, y	circle coordinates

Program description

The graphics.library opens and the Ob% array reads the X- and Y-coordinates. A loop computes the 11-pixel offset from the circle's "corner" to the circle's border. The rest of the program should look familiar to you.

The most important changes occur in the mouse reader routine. If the left mouse button has not been depressed, the mouse reader branches back to the main program. If the user presses that button, the program sets the drawing mode and draws the object at the current position. Then the program goes into a delay loop again, and exits when you release the left mouse button. The program branches again to the point before the loop at which you change the mouse position, since the grid must be erased and the object drawn at its new position.

The subroutine for drawing the object takes the 11 coordinate pairs from the Ob% array. The first point is drawn, then the others, through LINE commands. All points drawn join to form a circle.

4.3   Status lines & animation

Invisible status lines are part of a new screen organization which offer you many new special effects. For example, it allows you to create a color bar that lets you move the entire screen up and down. This bar has its own foreground and background colors, and it can also contain movable text. With the same program, you can fill the screen background with a pattern or graphic, if you wish. This pattern stays intact, even when you use PRINT commands, draw or scroll. There's more: You can scroll your background independently of the foreground drawing.

You need only two applications for doing all this. Before listing the program, let's look at the individual SUB programs that perform these miracles. The first is CreateStatus. This command turns on the new screen organization. The next is Copy. This command copies the current screen contents in the background, where only colors 0 and 1 appear (only one bitplane is available in background memory). Once the screen contents are copied, a new background pattern appears. You can clear the "normal" screen with the CLS command; the background pattern stays on. The closing is the Move SUB program. This command scrolls the background pattern up or down. The command syntax needs two values:

    Move dir%,speed%

The dir% variable gives the number of pixels the background graphic should move. A positive value scrolls the graphic down; a negative number scrolls it up. The speed% variable sets the scrolling speed. 0 is the top speed; larger values slow the scrolling. Here's a sample call:

    Move 100, 40

This call moves the background 100 pixels down at a delay rate of 40.

As you'll see when you test the following programs, the Move command does more than just move the background. When you move the background graphic up or down, the opposite side of the page stays visible. The routine acts as an endless scroll routine, which can produce some very pretty effects. Try this version of the Move command:

    Move 0,0

This call appears to do nothing (moving the backgound graphic 0 pixels), but it has a special function: It clears the background graphic.

The EndStatus SUB reactivates the normal screen display. This command must be at the end of your programs to remove the

`CreateStatus` command's effects. Also, this command returns the entire user memory range.

```
'############################¶
'#                          #¶
'# Program: Dual BitMap     #¶
'# Author:  tob             #¶
'# Date:    May 8, 1987     #¶
'# Version: 2.0             #¶
'#                          #¶
'############################¶
¶
DECLARE FUNCTION AllocMem& LIBRARY¶
DECLARE FUNCTION BltBitMap% LIBRARY¶
¶
LIBRARY "graphics.library"¶
LIBRARY "intuition.library"¶
LIBRARY "exec.library"¶
¶
demo:   '* Open Screen¶
        SCREEN 1, 640, 240, 3, 2¶
        WINDOW 1,"DualBitmap",(0,0)-(610,217),1,1¶
        WINDOW OUTPUT 1¶
        ¶
        '* Draw Circle¶
        CreateStatus¶
        LINE (0,0) - (620,10),,bf¶
        Copy¶
        CLS¶
        ¶
        '* Color¶
        PALETTE 1,1,1,1¶
        PALETTE 4,1,0,0¶
        PALETTE 5,1,.5,.5¶
        ¶
        GOSUB text¶
        ¶
        '* Move Scroll Circle¶
        Move 166, 0¶
        PRINT "Please Press any Key.":PRINT" "¶
        WHILE INKEY$ = "": WEND¶
        Move 0,0¶
        ¶
        '* 2nd Experiment¶
        CLS¶
        CIRCLE (140,100), 120, 1¶
        CIRCLE (140,100), 100, 1¶
        CIRCLE (140,100),  80, 1¶
        CIRCLE (140,100),  50, 1¶
        CIRCLE (140,100),  25, 1¶
        PAINT  (250,100),   1, 1¶
        PAINT  (210,100),   1, 1¶
        PAINT  (140,100),   1, 1¶
        Copy¶
        CLS¶
        ¶
        '* Color¶
        PALETTE 0,0,0,1¶
        PALETTE 1,1,0,0¶
        PALETTE 4,0,1,1¶
        PALETTE 5,0,1,0¶
        ¶
        GOSUB text¶
        ¶
        LOCATE 22,1¶
PRINT "Please Press any Key."¶
        WHILE INKEY$ = ""¶
          Move -3, 0¶
        WEND¶
```

```
          ¶
          '* 3rd Experiment¶
          Move 0,0¶
          CLS¶
          WIDTH "scrn:", 85¶
          text$ = "* Amiga Tricks and Tips"¶
          FOR loop% = 1 TO 56¶
          LOCATE loop%,5¶
          PRINT text$¶
          NEXT loop%¶
          ¶
          Copy¶
          CLS¶
          ¶
          '* Color¶
          PALETTE 0,.1,.1,.8¶
          PALETTE 1,1,1,1¶
          PALETTE 4,.3,.3,.3¶
          PALETTE 5,1,1,1¶
          ¶
          GOSUB text¶
          ¶
          '* Animation¶
          WHILE INKEY$ = ""¶
            Move 1,0¶
          WEND¶
          ¶
          Move 0,0¶
          ¶
          EndStatus¶
          WINDOW 1,"Dual-Bitmap",,,-1¶
          SCREEN CLOSE 1¶
          ¶
          LIBRARY CLOSE¶
          END¶
text:     '* Print Text¶
          CLS¶
          LOCATE 5,1¶
          PRINT "This is the new 'Dual-Bitmap'."¶
          LOCATE 6,1¶
          PRINT "You can control two bitplanes,"¶
          LOCATE 7,1¶
          PRINT "one completely independent of"¶
          LOCATE 8,1¶
          PRINT "the display."¶
          LOCATE 9,1¶
          PRINT "The level helps"¶
          LOCATE 10,1¶
          PRINT "determine the color"¶
          LOCATE 11,1¶
          PRINT "registers using the bitplanes:"¶
          LOCATE 12,1¶
          PRINT "Level          Color register"¶
          LOCATE 13,1¶
          PRINT "------------------------------------"¶
          LOCATE 14,1¶
          PRINT "  1            not fuctional"¶
          LOCATE 15,1¶
          PRINT "  2            2, 3"¶
          LOCATE 16,1¶
          PRINT "  3            4, 5"¶
          LOCATE 17,1¶
          PRINT "  4            8, 9"¶
          LOCATE 18,1¶
          PRINT "  5            16, 17"¶
          RETURN¶
          ¶
SUB Copy STATIC¶
     SHARED bitmap&, bitmap2&¶
     l% = PEEK  (WINDOW(7) + 54)¶
```

```
        r% = PEEK   (WINDOW(7) + 56)¶
        u% = PEEK   (WINDOW(7) + 57)¶
        o% = PEEK   (WINDOW(7) + 55)¶
        w% = PEEKW  (WINDOW(7) + 8) - r% - l%¶
        h% = PEEKW  (WINDOW(7) + 10) - u% - o%¶
        x% = PEEKW  (WINDOW(7) + 4) + l%¶
        y% = PEEKW  (WINDOW(7) + 6) + o%¶
        ¶
        plc% = BltBitMap% (bitmap&, x%, y%, bitmap2&, x%, y%,
w%, h%, 200, 255, 0)¶
END SUB¶
¶
SUB Move (dir%, speed%) STATIC¶
        SHARED bitmap2&¶
        l% = PEEK   (WINDOW(7) + 54)¶
        r% = PEEK   (WINDOW(7) + 56)¶
        u% = PEEK   (WINDOW(7) + 57)¶
        o% = PEEK   (WINDOW(7) + 55)¶
        w% = PEEKW  (WINDOW(7) + 8) - r% - l%¶
        h% = PEEKW  (WINDOW(7) + 10) - u% - o%¶
        x% = PEEKW  (WINDOW(7) + 4) + l%¶
        y% = PEEKW  (WINDOW(7) + 6) + o%¶
¶
        spd% = 10*speed%¶
        u%   = y% + h% - 2¶
        IF dir% = 0 THEN¶
          bitplane& = PEEKL (bitmap2& + 8)¶
          m% = PEEKW (bitmap2&)¶
          n% = PEEKW (bitmap2& + 2)¶
          s& = (m%*n%)¶
          CALL BltClear(bitplane&, s&, 0)¶
          EXIT SUB¶
        END IF¶
        FOR z% = 1 TO ABS(dir%)¶
          IF dir% > 0 THEN¶
            plc% = BltBitMap% (bitmap2&, x%, u%, bitmap2&,
x%, y%, w%, 1, 200, 255, 0)¶
            plc% = BltBitMap% (bitmap2&, x%, y%, bitmap2&,
x%, y% + 1, w%, h% - 1, 200, 255, 0)¶
          ELSE¶
            plc% = BltBitMap% (bitmap2&, x%, y%, bitmap2&,
x%, u%, w%, 1, 200, 255, 0)¶
            plc% = BltBitMap% (bitmap2&, x%, y% + 1,
bitmap2&, x%, y%, w%, h% - 1, 200, 255, 0)¶
          END IF¶
          FOR del% = 1 TO spd%: NEXT del%¶
        NEXT z%¶
END SUB¶
¶
SUB EndStatus STATIC¶
        SHARED rasInfo&¶
        rasInfo2& = PEEKL (rasInfo&)¶
        bitmap&   = PEEKL (rasInfo& + 4)¶
        bitmap2&  = PEEKL (rasInfo2& + 4)¶
        level%    = PEEK  (bitmap& + 5)¶
        POKEL bitmap& + 8 + level%*4, PEEKL (bitmap2& + 8)¶

        POKE  bitmap& + 5, level% + 1¶
        POKEL rasInfo&, 0¶
        CALL FreeMem(rasInfo2&, 10)¶
        CALL FreeMem(bitmap2&, 40)¶
END SUB¶
¶
SUB CreateStatus STATIC¶
        SHARED rasInfo&, bitmap&, bitmap2&¶
        '* Get System Addresses¶
        wind& = WINDOW(7)¶
        rastport& = WINDOW(8)¶
        bitmap&   = PEEKL (rastport& + 4)¶
        level%    = PEEK  (bitmap& + 5)¶
```

142

```
    scr&       = PEEKL (wind& + 46)¶
    vp&        = PEEKL (scr& + 44)¶
    rasInfo&   = PEEK (vp& + 36)¶
    ¶
    IF level% < 2 THEN¶
      PRINT "A Screen with 2 levels is needed!"¶
      EXIT SUB¶
    END IF¶
    ¶
    '* Establish Structure¶
    opt&       = 2^1 + 2^16¶
    rasInfo2&  = AllocMem&(10, opt&)¶
    IF rasInfo2& = 0 THEN ERROR 7¶
    bitmap2&   = AllocMem& (40, opt&)¶
    IF bitmap2& = 0 THEN¶
      CALL FreeMem(rasInfo2&, 10)¶
      ERROR 7¶
    END IF¶
    ¶
    CALL CopyMem(rasInfo&, rasInfo2&, 10)¶
    CALL CopyMem(bitmap&, bitmap2&, 40)¶
    ¶
    POKE  bitmap&   + 5, level% - 1¶
    POKE  bitmap2&  + 5, 1¶
    POKEL bitmap2&  + 8, PEEKL (bitmap& + 4 + 4*level%)¶

    POKEL bitmap&   + 4 + 4*level%, 0¶
    POKEL rasInfo2& + 4, bitmap2&¶
    ¶
    POKEL rasInfo& , rasInfo2&¶
END SUB¶
```

Program description

Once you enter this program, be sure to save it to diskette <u>before</u> you try running it for the first time. The first experiment displays a red bar. It moves around the text page, and apparently can pass behind text in the window. The second experiment is similar. Transparent circles move around on the screen. The third experiment fills the background with a text pattern.

Now for the technical basics of what's going on here. The Amiga recognizes a special mode called the Dual Playfield mode. This mode can divide individual bitplanes in screen memory into two groups, and make these two groups independent of each other. These two groups are like independent screens; each one is visible through the other in the background. This graphic mode isn't used in these examples. Only one item is used which actually can be counted as Dual Playfield mode. The RasInfo data structure, which assigns a pointer in the viewport to the selected screen, lets you detach individual bitplanes from each other. The RasInfo structure connects one of its own bitmap structures contained in the disconnected bitmap.

The CreateStatus SUB reads the corresponding system addresses. Then it tests for a screen with a depth of 2 or more. If the screen has only one bitplane, the system can't use it. If two or more bitplanes are available, then the two Bitmap and RasInfo structures are set up (AllocMem() allocates the needed memory). The original bitplane takes on the named bitplane (incremented in depth by 1). The second bitmap receives a depth number of 1, and is inserted into the first bitmap. Finally, a pointer to the new bitmap must be inserted in the `RasInfo` structure.

The `Copy` SUB copies the contents of the first bitplane (colors 0 and 1) to the coupled bitplane (`bitplane2&`). Only window contents are copied. It would be simpler to just copy the entire screen contents, but then the window borders would be copied as well. Using the `Move` routine under these conditions would scroll the window borders as well as the background, and probably cause a system error. If you reduced the size of your window after the copy process, the background would keep its full size. You can avoid this by either not changing window size, or clearing the background with `Move 0,0`.

The `Move` SUB scrolls the background up or down. This affects the window contents only, nothing else. The system handles this as an endless scroll routine, which can scroll one line of pixels up or down at a time. Larger increments move through multiple looping.

Calling `Move 0,0` activates the `BitClear()` function, which clears the entire background (not just the window's contents). Any window section hidden beyond the edges of the screen is also cleared.

`EndStatus` restores the original bitmap and clears the dual structures.

Now that you have some background information on the program, let's take a closer look at the programming. When mixing bitplanes, the user doesn't have eight colors with a screen that has a depth of 3 planes (normally $2^3=8$). Instead, since two of those planes are merged, only four colors are available ($2^2=8$). However, you still get 8 colors in combination with the background. A screen with a depth of 3 appears in background memory with the color of color register 4. This command sets the color of the background graphic:

        PALETTE 4, 1, .6, .9

The combined color between background graphic and normal foreground drawing color comes from color register 5. This command sets the color shared by the background and normal foreground:

        PALETTE 5, 1, 1, .7

The color selections are up to you–you can get some nice effects. For example, you can combine the normal background and color register 4 to set a combined shade of red:

        PALETTE 0, 0, 0, 0
        PALETTE 4, 0, 0, 0
        PALETTE 5, 1, 0, 0

The result: The background is invisible. When the foreground color runs into the background (through PRINT, etc.), the text turns red.

Another is the transparent effect. Color register 4 must be assigned to different colors, like red. The best combined color should be a mixture of foreground color (register 1) and register 5:

```
PALETTE 1, 1, 1, 1  'White foreground color'
PALETTE 4, 1, 0, 0  'Red background graphic'
PALETTE 5, 1, .5, .5 'Combined pink color'
```

When you want to put a text or pattern in the background (see the third program above), make sure that the window height allows enough room for the entire graphic or text, without halving or splitting the material in the window. If this happens, when the line scrolls it reappears after scrolling as broken lines on the screen.

5
DOS routines

5.   DOS routines

The DOS, or *disk operating system*, is part of the internal operating system software of the Amiga. This DOS is essential to all communications between the Amiga and its disk drives.

Disk drives are important to the user and the Amiga, since diskettes are the Amiga's *mass storage media*. That is, you use diskettes for storing programs, files and other information. In fact, without diskettes, you wouldn't get past the startup icons (the KickStart icon in the Amiga 1000 and the Workbench icon in the Amiga 500 and 2000).

The Amiga Workbench diskette contains an additional library. This library, which has many machine language routines that perform complex disk functions, is called dos.library.

This chapter lists a number of disk utilities that access the dos.library program. You'll learn how to add program commentary, view diskettes for existing files and protect files from overwriting. In addition, you'll find out how you can rename diskettes, access a directory and more, all from AmigaBASIC.

5.1   Program comments

Any program or directory can have a comment of up to 80 characters connected to it. Often the program name itself doesn't give the user enough information about its purpose or use. Comments like "still under development!" or "written by Fred" or "Version 3.4" contain important information about the program in question. Subdirectories can be made more readable with comments like "This directory contains the .bmap files", "Business letters are stored here", or even "I wouldn't open this file if I were you".

The following program assigns comments to any file or directory. The comment appears on the screen if you access the file through the CLI's list command.

The command format is:

        SetComment "program name", "comment"

Here's an example of the command. This example puts a comment into the c directory of the Workbench diskette:

        SetComment "SYS:c", "CLI commands are in here"

```
'#######################¶
'#                      #¶
'# Program:SetComment   #¶
'# Author: tob          #¶
'# Date:   4.8.87       #¶
'# Version:1.0          #¶
'#                      #¶
'#######################¶
                        ¶
DECLARE FUNCTION SetComment% LIBRARY¶
LIBRARY "dos.library"¶
                     ¶
demo: '*Demonstrates commentary¶
      SetComment "program1", "SetDrMd()-Routines"¶
      ¶
      LIBRARY CLOSE¶
      END¶
      ¶
SUB SetComment (file$, comment$) STATIC¶
    file$ = file$ + CHR$(0)¶
    comment$ = comment$ + CHR$(0)¶
    suc% = SetComment%(SADD(file$), SADD(comment$))¶
    IF suc% = 0 THEN¶
       PRINT"SetComment unsuccessful."¶
       END IF¶
END SUB¶
    ¶
```

Variables   file$:   name of the desired file or directory
                    comment$:   comment
                    suc&:   error flag

Program   The necessary SetComment function is declared and the DOS library
description   opens. The filename (file$) and comment (comment$) are passed to
                    the SUB program. The two text strings terminate with zero bytes
                    (CHR$(0)) and the SetComment() function is called. When you
                    want to delete a comment, enter a null string (""). If DOS cannot
                    execute this command (file doesn't exist or is protected), then suc&
                    changes to 0 and an error message appears.

Note: If the desired file is in a different directory, you'll need to enter the entire
                    pathname in the command. For example, "Workbench:libs/gra-
                    phics.bmap".

5.2   CheckFile

Is a certain file on the diskette or isn't it? This question is important, since you can only open an existing file. Otherwise, an error message appears.

The following program can help you. The command syntax is:

        CheckFile "filename"

This command checks to see if the given file exists. If the file exists, it tells you the block number where the file lies. This allows you to quickly find a file with a disk monitor.

```
'#######################¶
'#                      #¶
'# Program:CheckFile    #¶
'# Author: tob          #¶
'# Date:   4.8.87       #¶
'# Version:1.0          #¶
'#                      #¶
'#######################¶
¶
DECLARE FUNCTION Lock& LIBRARY¶
LIBRARY "dos.library"¶
¶
demo: '*Demonstrates application¶
    LINE INPUT "File you want checked--->";file$¶
    CheckFile file$, block& ¶
    IF block& = 0 THEN¶
      PRINT "I can't find the file ";file$¶
        ELSE¶
        PRINT "Found the file ";file$¶
        PRINT "File header begins on the diskette¶
        PRINT "at block ";block&¶
    END IF¶
        ¶
    LIBRARY CLOSE¶
    END¶
        ¶
SUB CheckFile (file$, result&) STATIC¶
    file0$ = file$ + CHR$(0)¶
    a.read% = -2¶
    add& = Lock&(SADD(file0$), a.read%)¶
    IF add& <> 0 THEN¶
        result& = PEEKL(result&*4 + 4)¶
    ELSE¶
        result& = 0¶
    END IF¶
    CALL Unlock(add&)¶
    END SUB¶
        ¶
```

Variables	file$	name of desired file
	result&	result of search
	file0$	like file$, but terminated by null
	a.read%	ACCESS_READ, read only
	add&	file lock address

Program description

DOS uses the Lock function to "latch onto" a specific file or directory. A Lock data structure is set up which contains the special parameters for this file or directory.

The program uses Lock() to determine if a given file exists. Lock() sets the program name from file0$. If the file doesn't exist, then no Lock structure can be created and add& contains 0. If the file does exist, this variable contains the pointer from the data structure. This pointer is a BPTR type. It contains the longword offset instead of the starting address of the data block. Multiplying the BPTR value by four returns the correct starting address. Finally, the lock must be freed by Unlock() before you can view the file.

You may have been wondering about the a.read% variable. It contains the value -2, which stands for ACCESS_READ. This mode allows you to get the data structure of the file without blocking any other user access. In a multitasking system, another task may also be viewing the same file. There is no problem with this since all you are doing is reading the file. EXCLUSIVE_WRITE mode is useful when you want to write to a file, or change its contents in some way. Other tasks that try to access the file are sent a "FILE ALREADY OPEN" error message. If another task succeeded in writing to a file at the same time you were writing to it, the result could damage the file.

Here is the Lock data structure based on the BPTR:

```
+0   LONG   BPTR to the next block, else 0
+4   LONG   Block number of dir or file header
+8   LONG   Shared (-2) or exclusive access (-1)
+12  LONG   APTR to handler task ProcessID
+16  LONG   BPTR to the disk entry
```

Note:

You could use this program to check to see if the appropriate .bmap files are on a diskette before you use kernel command routines.

5.3   Protecting data

Has this happened to you? You write a program and save it to diskette. After you've saved it, you remember that yesterday you saved an even better program under the same name on this diskette. Saving the new program under the same name overwrote the old program.

Earlier versions of AmigaBASIC saved files without checking first to see if a file with the same name existed on the diskette. There is a cure for this problem, since you can easily "write-protect" programs on a diskette. Every program header has four bits which have the following meanings:

Bit 1:   DELETE
Bit 2:   EXECUTE
Bit 3:   WRITE
Bit 4:   READ

You can protect your program from accidental deletion or overwriting (DELETE), accidental starting (EXECUTE), modification (WRITE), and reading (READ). Earlier versions of DOS only checked the DELETE bit.

The following program creates the Protect command, which allows you to set any one of these four bits. You don't have to enter any bits or bytes; the command format is:

```
Protect "filename","read|write|execute|delete"
```

You can type <|> by holding <SHIFT> and pressing <\> (backslash).

You can specify the four file protection modes in any order. <|> characters must separate each mode word.

```
'#########################¶
'#                       #¶
'# Program:Protect       #¶
'# Author: tob           #¶
'# Date:    4.8.87        #¶
'# Version:1.0           #¶
'#                       #¶
'#########################¶
¶
DECLARE FUNCTION SetProtection% LIBRARY¶
LIBRARY "dos.library"¶
¶
demo: '*Demonstration¶
      Protect "prg1", "read|write|delete"¶
      ¶
      LIBRARY CLOSE¶
      END¶
      ¶
```

```
SUB Protect (file$, mask$) STATIC¶
    file0$ = file$ + CHR$(0)¶
    prot$(3) = "READ"¶
    prot$(2) = "WRITE"¶
    prot$(1) = "EXECUTE"¶
    prot$(0) = "DELETE"¶
    ¶
    FOR loop% = 1 TO LEN(mask$)¶
     byte$ = MID$(mask$,loop%,1)¶
     IF byte$ <> "|" THEN¶
       p$(count%) = p$(count%) + byte$¶
     ELSE¶
       count% = count% + 1¶
     END IF¶
    NEXT loop%¶
    ¶
    FOR loop1% = 3 TO 0 STEP -1¶
     FOR loop2% = 0 TO 3¶
      IF UCASE$(p$(loop2%)) = prot$(loop1%) THEN¶
       mask% = mask% + 2^loop1%¶
      END IF¶
     NEXT loop2%¶
    NEXT loop1%¶
    ¶
    suc% = SetProtection%(SADD(file0$),mask%)¶
    IF suc% = 0 THEN¶
       PRINT "No protection."¶
    END IF¶
END SUB¶
    ¶
```

Variables

file$	name of program you want changed
file0$	program name, terminated with null
mask$	mode mask, consisting of the modes read, write, execute and delete
prot$()	array containing names of protection modes
p$()	word memory for values read
byte$	one-byte character from mask
mask%	bit mask taken from the above mode mask
loop1%	loop variable
loop2%	another loop variable
suc&:	error flag from DOS routine; 0=error

Program description

First the program name in file$ must be converted (a nullbyte (CHR$(0)) must be added to the end of the filename). The string then transfers to the variable file0$. Finally the mode definition occurs at the prot$() array. These are later compared with the function call.

A loop goes through maske$ character by character. A <|> character signals the end of the word. The found words are stored in p$().

A second loop goes through the words. It actually involves two nested loops which compare each word with the keywords in prot$(). This permits you to list the attributes in any order in the function call. The protection bits described above are set and stored in mask%.

Protection then assigns the bits to the file. The protection bits in mask% are placed in the diskette's file header.

If problems occur (e.g., file not found, no diskette in drive, etc.), the `Protect` routine returns a value of 0 and displays an error message.

The `CLI` command `LIST` displays the protection status of each file. The normal file attributes are "`rwed`" (read, write, execute, delete). This means that the file is unprotected. If you prevent it from being deleted, for instance, the result would be "`rwe-`", and you could no longer delete the file or overwrite it.

```
PROTECT "SYS:LIBS/graphics.bmap","delete"
```

The entry "`rwe-`" appears in the `CLI LIST` output.

If you want to unprotect a program again, just reprotect it while omitting the undesired protection:

```
PROTECT "SYS:LIBS/graphics.bmap","
```

removes all protection from the program.

5.4 Renaming files

Here's a short but very practical program that changes the name of any file or directory. AmigaBASIC doesn't have a command of this kind. Your only alternative is to load the program and save it under another name.

This program uses two pointers and requires a filename ended by a nullbyte.

```
'#######################¶
'#                      #¶
'# Program:Rename       #¶
'# Author: tob          #¶
'# Date:    4.8.87      #¶
'# Version:1.0          #¶
'#                      #¶
'#######################¶
¶
DECLARE FUNCTION Rename% LIBRARY¶
LIBRARY "dos.library"¶
¶
demo: '*Demonstration¶
      Rename "prg1", "program1"¶
      ¶
      LIBRARY CLOSE¶
      END¶
      ¶
SUB Rename (file$, anew$) STATIC¶
    file0$ = file$ + CHR$(0)¶
    anew0$  = anew$ + CHR$(0)¶
    suc%    = Rename%(SADD(file0$),SADD(anew0$))    ¶
    IF suc% <> -1 THEN¶
        PRINT "Rename unsuccessful."¶
        END IF¶
END SUB¶
```

Variables

file$	name of existing file
anew$	new filename
file0$	like file$, but terminated by 0
anew0$	like anew$, but terminated by 0
suc&	DOS function error flag; 0=error

Program description

The function is similar in function to the DOS rename command. Both the current and new program names must be terminated by zero bytes. The addresses of the two names are passed to DOS for renaming. If an error occurs, an error message appears on the screen and the program sets the error flag.

5.5 Directory access

Wouldn't it be nice if you could read the directory from within a BASIC program? The FILES command helps very little, because it prints all of the filenames on the screen and does nothing else. This GetDir routine reads all of the important data from the current directory and stores it in arrays.

```
'#######################¶
'#                      #¶
'# Program:GetDir       #¶
'# Author: tob          #¶
'# Date:   4.8.87       #¶
'# Version:1.0          #¶
'#                      #¶
'#######################¶
¶
DECLARE FUNCTION Examine% LIBRARY¶
DECLARE FUNCTION ExNext% LIBRARY¶
DECLARE FUNCTION Lock& LIBRARY¶
DECLARE FUNCTION AllocMem& LIBRARY¶
DECLARE FUNCTION IoErr% LIBRARY¶
¶
LIBRARY "dos.library"¶
LIBRARY "exec.library"¶
¶
var:    '* Variable / array set-up¶
        x% = 100¶
        DIM SHARED dir.name$(x%) ¶
        DIM SHARED dir.prot$(x%) ¶
        DIM SHARED dir.type$(x%) ¶
        DIM SHARED dir.size&(x%) ¶
        DIM SHARED dir.blocks&(x%) ¶
        DIM SHARED dir.comm$(x%) ¶
¶
demo:   '*Demonstration¶
        PRINT "Searching..."¶
        GetDir "df0:",x%¶
        FOR loop% = 0 TO x%¶
          CLS¶
          PRINT "Entry number:";loop%+1¶
          COLOR 0,1¶
          PRINT dir.name$(loop%) ¶
          COLOR 1,0¶
          PRINT "Protection:  ";dir.prot$(loop%) ¶
          PRINT "Type       : ";dir.type$(loop%) ¶
          PRINT "Size       : ";dir.size&(loop%) ¶
          PRINT "Blocks     : ";dir.blocks&(loop%) ¶
          PRINT "Commentary:  ";dir.comm$(loop%) ¶
          PRINT STRING$(60,"-") ¶
          WHILE INKEY$="":WEND¶
        NEXT loop%¶
                 ¶
        LIBRARY CLOSE¶
        END¶
        ¶
SUB GetDir (dir$, max%) STATIC¶
        a.read% = -2¶
        mode$(0) = "delete-,"¶
        mode$(1) = "execute-,"¶
        mode$(2) = "write-,"¶
        mode$(3) = "read-,"¶
```

```
dir0$     = dir$ + CHR$(0)¶
buffer&   = 252¶
add&      = Lock&(SADD(dir0$), a.read%)¶
IF add&  = 0 THEN¶
  PRINT"Directory doesn't exist."¶
  EXIT SUB¶
END IF¶
¶
opt&      = 2^16¶
info&     = AllocMem&(buffer&, opt&)¶
IF info& = 0 THEN ERROR 7¶
¶
suc%  = Examine%(add&,info&)      ¶
IF suc% = 0 THEN¶
    PRINT "Can't find the subdirectories."¶
    EXIT SUB¶
END IF¶
¶
WHILE e% <> 232¶
  dir.name& = info& + 8¶
  FOR loop% = 0 TO 29¶
    check% = PEEK(dir.name+loop%)¶
    IF check%<>0 THEN¶
      check$ = check$ + CHR$(check%)¶
    ELSE¶
      loop% = 29¶
    END IF¶
  NEXT loop%¶
  ¶
  dir.name$(counter%) = check$¶
  check$                    = ""¶
  prot&                     = PEEKL(info& + 116)¶
  ¶
  IF prot&<>0 THEN¶
    FOR loop% = 3 TO 0 STEP -1¶
      IF (prot& AND 2^loop%) <>0 THEN¶
        prot$ = prot$ + mode$(loop%)¶
      END IF¶
    NEXT loop%¶
    add$ = LEFT$(prot$,LEN(prot$)-1)+"protected."¶
    dir.prot$(counter%) = add$¶
    prot$ = ""¶
  END IF¶
  ¶
  type& = PEEKL(info& + 120)¶
  IF type& < 0 THEN¶
    dir.type$(counter%) = "FILE"¶
  ELSEIF counter% = 0 THEN¶
    dir.type$(counter%) = "CURR.DIR"¶
  ELSE¶
    dir.type$(counter%) = "DIR"¶
  END IF¶
  ¶
  dir.size&(counter%) = PEEKL (info& + 124)¶
  dir.blocks&(counter%) = PEEKL (info& + 128)¶
  ¶
  FOR loop% = 0 TO 79¶
    check% = PEEK(info& + 144 + loop%)¶
    IF check%<>0 THEN¶
      check$ = check$ + CHR$(check%)¶
    ELSE¶
      loop% = 79¶
    END IF¶
  NEXT loop%¶
  ¶
  dir.comm$(counter%) = check$¶
  check$ = ""¶
  suc% = ExNext%(add&,info&)¶
  IF suc% = 0 THEN¶
    e% = IoErr%¶
```

```
            IF e%<>232 THEN¶
              PRINT"Error in directory."¶
              EXIT SUB¶
            END IF¶
          ELSE¶
            counter% = counter% + 1¶
            IF counter% > max% THEN¶
              e% = 232¶
            ELSE¶
              e% = 0¶
            END IF¶
          END IF¶
        WEND¶
        ¶
        CALL FreeMem(info&,buffer&)¶
        CALL Unlock(add&)¶
        max% = counter%¶
      END SUB¶
        ¶
```

Variables

dir.name$()	file/directory name
dir.prot$()	file protection status
dir.type$()	type:DIR or FILE
dir.size&()	program size in bytes
dir.blocks&()	program size in diskette blocks
dir.comm$()	comment string
dir$	name of directory to be read
max%	maximum number of desired entries
a.read%	ACCESS_READ
mode$()	protection mode
dir0$	null-terminated dir$
buffer&	size of necessary buffer
add&	BPTR pointer to lock structure of directory being read
opt&	memory option, MEM_CLEAR = clear memory
info&	starting address of buffer& byte sized buffer
suc&	DOS function error flag;0=error
e%	I/OErr() flag; 232 = NO
check%	ASCII code of character read
check$	string read
prot&	protection bits
type&	type bits
counter&	counter for found entries

Program description

GetDir reads the name, protection status, type, size and commentary of every file on the directory. The maximum number of entries depends on the size of x%. This example sets x% to 100, supplying room for 100 entries. If you have a directory containing more than 100 entries, simply increase the number assigned to x%. Remember that this takes up memory.

The SUB program searches for the directory named in dir$. If the named directory doesn't exist, the program displays an error message and exits the SUB program. The program allocates a 252-byte buffer when it finds the directory. Examine() loads the information of the first directory entry into the buffer. The WHILE/WEND loop that follows filters the information from this block of memory and places the values into the corresponding arrays. ExNext() looks for the next entry and performs the above processes. All entries are read until a NO_MORE_ENTRIES error (code 232) occurs. This ends the WHILE/WEND loop, closes the buffer and unlocks the Lock structure.

The last line of this SUB, max%=counter%, is extremely important. This example lets GetDir store up to 100 entries, but there are few directories that contain that many entries. Therefore, it's important for the program to know when it reaches the last entry on the diskette. One solution is to declare a variable as SHARED, give it the number of entries found and pass this information on to the main program. This program has a simpler and more elegant solution: All parameter variables in the SUB...STATIC lines are automatically declared as SHARED. The number of entries automatically goes to max%. The main program call can then look like this:

```
max% = 100
(...)
GetDir "SYS:", max%
FOR loop% = 1 to max%
(...)
NEXT loop%
```

After the GetDir call, max% receives the correct number of found entries.

The info block in info& has the following format:

+000	LONG	Disk lock
+004	LONG	Buffer contents type (greater then 0: Dir)
+008		Entry name (only 30 of the 118 bytes are usable)
+116	LONG	Protection bits (definitions of least significant bytes):

	Bit	Meaning
	0	Delete
	1	Execute
	2	Write
	3	Read

+120	LONG	Entry type (greater than 0=Dir)
+124	LONG	Bytes in file
+128	LONG	Blocks in file
+132	LONG	Days since January 1, 1978
+136	LONG	Minutes since midnight
+140	LONG	Ticks since the last minute
+144	CHAR	Comment, previously only 80 bytes usable

161

5.6   GetTree

AmigaDOS works with a variety of subdirectories. The main directory on the Workbench diskette named Workbench contains subdirectories like fonts, in which the system fonts are stored. There are other subdirectories inside fonts like sapphire, which houses the various sapphire fonts, ruby which contains the ruby fonts, etc. This *tree* can have even more subdirectories inside subdirectories.

Subdirectories increase the readability of a directory. But have you ever looked at such a directory with the FILES command? The files of the current directory appear on the screen, but subdirectories are only listed by name, not listed in detail. You can access each subdirectory by using CHDIR to change directories, but this can be inconvenient.

The following program looks for all the files on a diskette, ignoring the directories. This bypasses the whole tree structure. First the printout displays the files in the main directory, then the files in all of the subdirectories of the main directory, then all the subdirectories in these subdirectories, and so on. The program sends the output directly to a printer, since there is more information than can fit on the screen.

To keep the list readable, the program also prints the name of the directory currently being printed. Also, the program size in bytes and blocks, as well the entry type (FILE or DIRECTORY), list on the printout. The entries are printed in alphabetical order.

```
'#######################¶
'#                       #¶
'# Program:GetTree       #¶
'# Author: tob           #¶
'# Date:    4.8.87       #¶
'# Version:1.0           #¶
'#                       #¶
'#######################¶
¶
DECLARE FUNCTION Examine% LIBRARY¶
DECLARE FUNCTION ExNext% LIBRARY¶
DECLARE FUNCTION Lock& LIBRARY¶
DECLARE FUNCTION AllocMem& LIBRARY¶
DECLARE FUNCTION IoErr% LIBRARY¶
¶
LIBRARY "dos.library"¶
LIBRARY "exec.library"¶
¶
var:    '* Variable / array set-up¶
        x% = 100¶
        y% = 100¶
        DIM SHARED dir.name$(x%)¶
        DIM SHARED dir.prot$(x%)¶
        DIM SHARED dir.type$(x%)¶
        DIM SHARED dir.size&(x%)¶
        DIM SHARED dir.blocks&(x%)¶
        DIM SHARED dir.comm$(x%)¶
        DIM a$(y%)¶
```

```
        DIM a&(y%)¶
        filler$ = "."¶
        count%  = 1¶
        fil$    = "_"¶
        ¶
demo: '* Application¶
       GOSUB PrintTree¶
        ¶
       LIBRARY CLOSE¶
       END¶
        ¶
PrintTree: '* This uses GetDir...¶
       GOSUB Specifier¶
       GOSUB Header¶
       GOSUB Level¶
        ¶
Entry:    FOR loop% = previous TO count% -1¶
            IF a&(loop%) = Level% THEN¶
              search$ = a$(loop%)¶
              z% = x%¶
              GetDir search$, x%¶
              max% = x%¶
              x% = z%¶
              sort¶
              LOCATE 1,1¶
              PRINT "Print ";a$(loop%);¶
              PRINT STRING$(60,fil$)¶
              ¶
              IF loop% = 0 THEN¶
                a$(0) = dir.name$(0) + ":"¶
              END IF¶
              ¶
              z$ = a$(loop%)¶
              directory$ = LEFT$(z$, LEN(z$) - 1)¶
              ¶
              LPRINT¶
              LPRINT "Directory: ....... 1";directory$¶
              ¶
              FOR show% = 1 TO max%¶
                info$ = dir.name$(show%)¶
                ¶
                diff% = 32 - LEN(dir.name$(show%))¶
                IF diff%>0 THEN¶
                  info$ = info$ + STRING$(diff%,filler$)¶

                END IF¶
                ¶
                IF dir.type$(show%) <>"DIR" THEN¶
                  info$ = info$ + dir.type$(show%)¶
                  info$ = info$ + "." + dir.prot$(show%)¶

                    FOR fill% = LEN(dir.prot$(show%)) TO
3¶
                      info$ = info$ + filler$¶
                    NEXT fill%¶
                    LPRINT "- "; info$;¶
                    LPRINT USING "#######";
dir.size&(show%);¶
                    LPRINT "Bytes, ";¶
                    LPRINT USING "###";
dir.blocks&(show%);¶
                    LPRINT " blocks."¶
                ELSE¶
                    fl = 1¶
                    LPRINT "- " + info$ + "DIRECTORY"¶
                    a$(count%) = a$(loop%) +
dir.name$(show%) + "/"¶
                    a&(count%) = Level% + 1¶
                    count% = count% + 1¶
```

```
                          END IF¶
                      NEXT show%¶
                      END IF¶
                  NEXT loop%¶
                  previous% = loop%¶
                  ¶
                  IF fl = 1 THEN¶
                      fl = 0¶
                      Level% = Level% + 1¶
                      GOSUB Level¶
                      GOTO Entry¶
                  END IF¶
                  GOSUB EndTree¶
                  RETURN¶
              ¶
Specifier:¶
              LINE INPUT "Which disk drive (0-3)?"; dr$¶
              dr%   = VAL(RIGHT$(dr$,1))¶
              dr$   = RIGHT$(STR$(dr%),1)¶
              a$(0) = "df"+ dr$ +":"¶
              RETURN¶
              ¶
Header:      '*Print header¶
              LPRINT "* DOS DIRECTORY *"¶
              LPRINT¶
              LPRINT "(C) 1988 by Abacus for Amiga Tricks
and Tips"¶
              LPRINT¶
              LPRINT ¶
              RETURN¶
              ¶
Level:       '* Current level of disk hierarchy¶
              LPRINT STRING$(70,"_")¶
              LPRINT¶
              LPRINT "Level";Level%¶
              RETURN¶
¶
EndTree:     '* End printout¶
              LPRINT STRING$(70,"_")¶
              LPRINT¶
              LOCATE 1,1¶
              PRINT "OK." + STRING$(60, fil$)¶
              RETURN¶
          SUB sort STATIC¶
            SHARED max%, fil$¶
            LOCATE 1,1¶
            PRINT "Sorting ";dir.name$(0);STRING$(60,fil$)¶

            ¶
            FOR mode% = 0 TO 1¶
              FOR sort1% = 1 TO max%¶
                FOR sort2% = sort1% + 1 TO max% - 1¶
                  IF mode% = 1 THEN¶
                    bb$ = dir.type$(sort1%)¶
                    aa$ = dir.type$(sort2%)¶
                  ELSE¶
                    aa$ = dir.name$(sort1%)¶
                    bb$ = dir.name$(sort2%)¶
                  END IF¶
                  ¶
                  IF UCASE$(aa$)>UCASE$(bb$) THEN¶
                    SWAP dir.name$(sort1%),
dir.name$(sort2%)¶
                    SWAP dir.prot$(sort1%),
dir.prot$(sort2%)¶
                    SWAP dir.type$(sort1%),
dir.type$(sort2%)¶
```

```
                    SWAP dir.size&(sort1%),
dir.size&(sort2%)¶
                    SWAP dir.blocks&(sort1%),
dir.blocks&(sort2%)¶
          END IF¶
        NEXT sort2%¶
      NEXT sort1%¶
    NEXT mode%¶
    LOCATE 1,1¶
    PRINT "Ready. ";STRING$(70,fil$)¶
  END SUB¶
  ¶
  SUB GetDir (dir$,max%) STATIC¶
    a.read%  = -2¶
    mode$(0) = "delete-,"¶
    mode$(1) = "execute-,"¶
    mode$(2) = "write-,"¶
    mode$(3) = "read-,"¶
    dir0$    = dir$ + CHR$(0)¶
    buffer&  = 252¶
    add&     = Lock&(SADD(dir0$), a.read%)¶
    counter% = 0¶
    e%       = 0¶
    IF add&  = 0 THEN¶
      PRINT"Directory doesn't exist."¶
      EXIT SUB¶
    END IF¶
¶
  opt&     = 2^16¶
  info&    = AllocMem&(buffer&, opt&)¶
  IF info& = 0 THEN ERROR 7¶
¶
  suc%  = Examine%(add&,info&)     ¶
  IF suc% = 0 THEN¶
    PRINT "Can't find the subdirectories."¶
    EXIT SUB¶
  END IF¶
¶
  WHILE e% <> 232¶
    dir.name& = info& + 8¶
    FOR loop% = 0 TO 29¶
      check% = PEEK(dir.name&+loop%)¶
      IF check%<>0 THEN¶
        check$ = check$ + CHR$(check%)¶
      ELSE¶
        loop% = 29¶
      END IF¶
    NEXT loop%¶
    ¶
    dir.name$(counter%) = check$¶
    check$              = ""¶
    prot&              = PEEKL(info& + 116)¶
    ¶
    IF prot&<>0 THEN¶
      FOR loop% = 3 TO 0 STEP -1¶
        IF (prot& AND 2^loop%) <>0 THEN¶
          prot$ = prot$ + mode$(loop%)¶
        END IF¶
      NEXT loop%¶
      add$ = LEFT$(prot$,LEN(prot$)-1)+"protected."¶
      dir.prot$(counter%) = add$¶
      prot$ = ""¶
    END IF         ¶
    ¶
    type& = PEEKL(info& + 120)¶
    IF type& < 0 THEN¶
      dir.type$(counter%) = "FILE"¶
    ELSEIF counter% = 0 THEN¶
      dir.type$(counter%) = "CURR.DIR"¶
```

```
        ELSE¶
          dir.type$(counter%) = "DIR"¶
        END IF¶
        ¶
        dir.size&(counter%) = PEEKL (info& + 124)¶
        dir.blocks&(counter%) = PEEKL (info& + 128)¶
        ¶
        FOR loop% = 0 TO 79¶
          check% = PEEK(info& + 144 + loop%)¶
          IF check%<>0 THEN¶
            check$ = check$ + CHR$(check%)¶
          ELSE¶
            loop% = 79¶
          END IF¶
        NEXT loop%¶
        ¶
        dir.comm$(counter%) = check$¶
        check$ = ""¶
        ¶
        suc% = ExNext%(add&,info&)¶
        IF suc% = 0 THEN¶
          e% = IoErr%¶
          IF e%<>232 THEN¶
            PRINT"Error in directory."¶
            EXIT SUB¶
          END IF¶
        ELSE¶
          counter% = counter% + 1¶
          IF counter% > max% THEN¶
            e% = 232¶
          ELSE¶
            e% = 0¶
          END IF¶
        END IF¶
      WEND¶
      ¶
      CALL FreeMem(info&,buffer&)¶
      CALL Unlock(add&)¶
      max% = counter%¶
    END SUB¶
      ¶
```

Variables

y%:	maximum number of subdirectories
filler$	fill character
fil$	second fill character
count%	directory counter
dr$	disk drive number
dr%	count number
previous%	previous loop value
level%	hierarchy level
search$	name of directory under research
directory$	directory name
show%	display loop variable
info$	directory information
mode%	0=DIR/FILE, 1=alphabetical sort
sort1%	bubble sort loop 1
sort2%	bubble sort loop 2

Program
description

All new entries in a$(x) are examined in the loop loop%. At first this entry is just dfx:. The GetDir subprogram reads the corresponding directory and initializes the appropriate DirXXX() arrays. These are then sorted by Sort. If loop% = 0 (first entry), then the directory name is printed. a$(loop%) contains the name of the current directory with a zero byte added to the end of the name. This zero byte is removed when the name is printed. The show% loop then displays all the entries in the current directory. previous% is set to the end of the previous data block in a$() so that it points to new data for the next pass.

If fl = 1, meaning that there is at least one directory on the next level, the next directory is printed.

Sort sorts the entire set of data contained in the current directory. This occurs through a bubble sort procedure. The directory actually sorts twice. The first sort criterion is in alphabetical order (modus%=0). Then from the alphabetized list, the data records sort by type. The end result is data sorted by filename, filetype and directory.

5.7   Reading DOS files

Have you ever read a data record using the BASIC OPEN/INPUT#1
/CLOSE commands? This works fine in most cases, but not always. If
a text contains zeros, AmigaBASIC treats zeros as CHR$(0) and
removes them from the text display.

You may not see this as a problem, but data records often contain zeros.
For example, when a program stores number information in string
form. Or, when you want to look at the .bmap files mentioned in
Chapter 3.

DOS commands are an alternative to BASIC commands. The following
program offers the necessary SUB components. It has four commands:
OpenFile, CloseFile, ReadFile and SeekFile. OpenFile
is the equivalent of OPEN, and opens the file for DOS read access.
CloseFile closes a file like BASIC's CLOSE. ReadFile reads a
string of any length from the open data record (this string can contain
null bytes). SeekFile can move the internal "pointer" around the
data. This pointer signals the place within the open file where the next
ReadFile command should begin.

To help you adapt this routine to real-life applications, this program
includes the SUB routine ExBMAP. It only works in conjunction with
the DOS routines (SeekFile is unused in the sample program
below). This SUB helps you view the .bmap files from Chapter 3.
These files contain the names and parameters of several hundred
machine language routines kept in ROM by the Amiga. The SUB in
this program looks at the files in the libs directory of the Workbench
diskette. If your .bmap files are in another directory or on another
diskette, then you must change the appropriate line in the SUB.

The program reads the .bmap file dos.bmap. It displays the command
names, offsets and parameters in this file. You can easily make sure
that your .bmap files are complete, and identify the newest versions
and/or errors. A further application is reading unknown .bmap files, if
only to see when machine language routines are in the file.

```
'#######################¶
'#                      #¶
'# Program:bmap decoder #¶
'# Author: tob          #¶
'# Date:   4.8.87        #¶
'# Version:1.0           #¶
'#                      #¶
'#######################¶
¶
DECLARE FUNCTION xRead& LIBRARY¶
DECLARE FUNCTION xOpen& LIBRARY¶
DECLARE FUNCTION Seek& LIBRARY¶
'xClose()¶
```

```
¶
LIBRARY "dos.library"¶
¶
ExBMAP "dos.bmap"¶
¶
SUB ExBMAP (lib$) STATIC¶
    SHARED anerror, handle&, store$, xEOF¶
    file$ = "LIBS"+lib$¶
    '*Change LIBS to whatever directory you need¶
        ¶
    '* Open file¶
    OpenFile file$¶
    IF anerror = 1 THEN¶
      ErrorMessage¶
    END IF¶
        ¶
    '* Read file¶
    CLS¶
    WIDTH "scrn:", 150¶
    COLOR 0,3¶
    PRINT "Contents of library file ";file$¶
    PRINT¶
    ReadFile handle&, 1&¶
    IF anerror = 1 THEN¶
      ErrorMessage¶
    END IF¶
    WHILE xEOF<>1¶
      code% = PEEK(SADD(store$))¶
      IF (flag = 3 AND code% = 0) THEN¶
        flag = 4¶
      END IF¶
      ¶
      IF flag = 0 THEN¶
        IF code% > 0 THEN¶
          command$ = command$ + CHR$(code%)¶
        END IF¶
      ELSEIF flag = 1 THEN¶
        hi% = code%¶
        flag = 2¶
      ELSEIF flag = 2 THEN¶
        lo% = code%¶
        value& = hi%*256 + lo%¶
        offset% = 2^16 - value&¶
        flag = 3¶
      ELSEIF flag = 3 THEN¶
        IF code% < 9 THEN¶
          attr$ = attr$ + "d" + RIGHT$(STR$(code%-1),1)¶

        ELSE¶
          attr$ = attr$ + "a" + RIGHT$(STR$(code%-9),1)¶

        END IF¶
        attr$ = attr$ + ", "¶
      ELSEIF flag = 4 THEN¶
        flag = 0¶
        out$ = command$ + "  ("¶
        IF attr$ = "" THEN attr$ = SPACE$(2)¶
        out$ = out$ + LEFT$(attr$,LEN(attr$)-2) + ")"¶
        ¶
        COLOR 2,1¶
        PRINT "Offset: ";¶
        PRINT USING "####";offset%;¶
        PRINT " ... ";¶
        COLOR 1,2¶
        PRINT " "; out$;STRING$(60, " ")¶
        out$     = ""¶
        command$ = ""¶
        attr$    = ""¶
        offset%  = 0¶
      END IF¶
```

```
                    IF (command$ <> "" AND code% = 0) THEN¶
                       flag = 1¶
                    END IF¶
                    ¶
                    ReadFile handle&, 1&¶
                    IF anerror = 1 THEN¶
                       ErrorMessage¶
                    END IF¶
                 WEND¶
                 CloseFile handle&¶
                 COLOR 3,0¶
                 PRINT "A-OK."¶
                 COLOR 1¶
              END SUB¶
              ¶
              SUB ErrorMessage STATIC¶
                 SHARED handle&¶
                 BEEP¶
                 PRINT "Sorry, an error occurred."¶
                 CloseFile handle&¶
              END SUB¶
              ¶
              SUB OpenFile (dat$) STATIC¶
                 SHARED anerror, handle&¶
                 handle& = xOpen&(SADD(dat$),1005)¶
                 IF handle& = 0 THEN¶
                    anerror = 1¶
                    EXIT SUB¶
                 ELSE¶
                    anerror = 0¶
                 END IF¶
              END SUB¶
              ¶
              SUB CloseFile (hand&) STATIC¶
                 IF hand&<>0 THEN¶
                    CALL xClose(hand&)¶
                 ELSE¶
                    BEEP¶
                 END IF¶
              END SUB¶
              ¶
              SUB ReadFile (hand&, num&) STATIC¶
                 SHARED anerror, store$, xEOF¶
                 IF hand& <> 0 THEN¶
                    store$ = SPACE$(num&+10)¶
                    red&    = xRead&(hand&, SADD(store$),num&)¶
                    IF gel& < num& THEN¶
                       xEOF = 1¶
                    ELSE¶
                       xEOF = 0¶
                    END IF¶
                    anerror = 0¶
                 ELSE¶
                    anerror = 1¶
                 END IF¶
                 ¶
                 'Seekfile hand&,1¶
              END SUB¶
              ¶
              SUB SeekFile(hand&,offset%) STATIC¶
                 old% = Seek&(hand&, offset%, 0)¶
              END SUB¶
              ¶
```

Variables   lib$ name of the desired .bmap file
                 handle&   File handle of the xOpen command
                 store$ memory string for Read

xEOF	End-Of-File: 1=end of data block
file$	full name of file to be opened
anerror	1=DOS I/O error
code%	read character
command$	machine command read
hi%, lo%	high and lowbyte of offset
attr$	input parameter for current command
out$	output string
hand&	local handle& variable
red&	number of bytes actually read

Program description

The OpenFile SUB opens the desired file for input. You enter the name of the file; the routine returns a file handle. This handle goes into the variable handle& and must be used by later SUBs. The value in handle& corresponds to the file number used in the BASIC OPEN command. This helps DOS to remember which file to handle.

The ReadFile SUB reads any number of characters from a file opened by OpenFile. You enter the file handle returned from OpenFile, as well as the number of bytes you want read. Both these entries go into a & variable. For example:

```
OpenFile "Example"
ReadFile handle&, 100&
```

This example reads 100 bytes from the file named "Example." The SUB stores the read bytes into store$. When the SUB reaches the end of the file, xEOF=1. Otherwise, xEOF=0.

SeekFile moves the internal data pointer to any offset from the current pointer position. You enter the file handle and the positive or negative offset.

```
loop:
ReadFile handle&, 100&
SeekFile handl&, -100
```

The above example reads the same 100 bytes again.

CloseFile closes a file opened by OpenFile (this is absolutely necessary). The command requires the file handle as input.

Now for the sample program, the ExBMAP SUB. It waits for the name of a .bmap file (any file with the .bmap suffix). The program searches for the file in the Workbench directory libs:. If the file doesn't exist, an error message appears on the screen. Otherwise, the routine reads the file. A character loads into memory from ReadFile and goes into code%. If flag is equal to 0, then the program reads the command name. If code% is equal to 0, however, that means that the command names are done. This increments flag by 1. Now the program reads the high byte of the offset and increments flag by 2. The low byte is then read, the value computed and subtracted from 2^{16} of the library offset of this routine. The result goes into `offset%`. `flag` becomes equal to 3. The input parameters are set. If `code%` > 9, then they handle address registers `a0` to `a4`. If `code%` < 10, then they are at the data registers `d0` to `d9`. As soon as `code%` is equal to 0, `flag` is equal to 4. The entire set of information appears on the screen as a string. Finally the variables clear for the next round. The program reads another character. When it reaches the end of the file (`xEOF` = 1), the program exits the `WHILE`/`WEND` loop and closes the file.

5.8   CLI from AmigaBASIC

The Command Line Interface (CLI) can also be used directly from
AmigaBASIC programs. The AmigaBASIC disk commands can be
enhanced by a complete set of disk-oriented commands. The following
program uses the DOS library and gives you a new BASIC command,
CLI, which can be used to execute any of the CLI commands. The
format is:

        CLI "command string"

This example sends the fonts subdirectory of the disk in drive 0 to
the printer:

        CLI "list df0:fonts keys to prt:"

Here's the program listing:

```
'##############################¶
'# Program: CLI from BASIC    #¶
'# Date:     7/26/87          #¶
'# Author:   tob              #¶
'# Version: 2.0               #¶
'##############################¶
¶
PRINT "Loading libraries..."¶
DECLARE FUNCTION xOpen& LIBRARY¶
DECLARE FUNCTION Execute% LIBRARY¶
LIBRARY "dos.library"¶
¶
main:       '*CLI gets called here¶
            CLI "LIST SYS: QUICK"¶
            ¶
finish:     '*End demo¶
            LIBRARY CLOSE¶
            END¶
            ¶
SUB CLI (command$) STATIC¶
    SHARED error.code%¶
    work$ = command$ + CHR$(0)¶
    count%=0¶
    ¶
    '* start output¶
    out.filename$ = "RAM:cli out"¶
    out$ = out.filename$ + CHR$(0)¶
    ¶
    out.handle& = xOpen&(SADD(out$),1006)¶
    IF out.handle&=0 THEN¶
      error.code% = 1¶
      BEEP¶
      EXIT SUB¶
END IF¶
    ¶
```

```
               '*CLI command execution¶
               follow% = Execute%(SADD(work$),0,out.handle&)¶
               IF follow% = false THEN¶
               error.code% = 2¶
               BEEP¶
               EXIT SUB¶
           END IF¶
           ¶
               '* End output and compute parameters¶
               CALL xClose(out.handle&)¶
               text.height%    = PEEKW(WINDOW(8)+58)¶
               window.height% = PEEKW(WINDOW(7)+10)-11¶
               lines%          = INT(window.height%/text.height%)-3¶

           ¶
               '* Send result to the RAM disk¶
               OPEN out.filename$ FOR INPUT AS 1¶
                  WHILE (EOF(1)=0)¶
                     INPUT#1, reader$¶
                     PRINT reader$¶
                     count%=count%+1¶
                     IF count%>lines% THEN¶
                        count%=0¶
                        PRINT"<<<Press any key to continue>>>";¶
                        WHILE INKEY$="":WEND¶
                        PRINT¶
                     END IF¶
                  WEND¶
                  PRINT "## End output ##"¶
               CLOSE 1¶
               KILL out.filename$¶
           END SUB¶
```

Variables

command$	CLI command sequence
error.code%	DOS error
work$	command string terminated by null
count%	counter
out.filename$	output device name
out$	output device name terminated by null
out.handle&	file handle for output device
follow%	execute command result; 0=false=error
text.height%	height in pixels of present font
window.height	window height in pixels
lines%	number of text lines in current window

Program description

The heart of this program is the DOS function Execute. This routine calls the necessary CLI routines. Before that can happen, a proper output device must be opened. This can be a window, the printer or a disk file. Since this CLI display in the **BASIC** window is unable to access DOS, you can specify the RAM disk as an output medium. As soon as Execute stores its information, you can transfer the data from the RAM disk to the main window and edit data from there.

Execute waits for three entries: A pointer to the command string terminated by a null; an input device (0 in this case); and the above-mentioned output device (the file handle of the xOpen call). If the command executes correctly, follow% is greater than or less than 0. When this is equal to 0, a DOS error occurs.

After the Execute function runs, the result goes into the RAM disk. The type of result depends upon the type of command used. For example, if you start Preferences like this, no information goes to the RAM disk:

```
CLI "SYS:Preferences"
```

This call waits until the user is ready to reconfigure the computer. The next call activates the multitasking system:

```
CLI "run SYS:preferences"
```

This continues with your BASIC program immediately after Prefer-ences opens.

```
CLI "list df0:"
```

The above command stores data on the RAM disk.

The file in the RAM disk closes through the xClose command, then loads its data character by character into memory with the help of the BASIC commands OPEN and CLOSE. A certain number of lines appear on the screen before it scrolls up. The SUB waits for a keypress from the user before it continues with the output. At the end, the RAM disk is erased with KILL.

Note:

You can use almost all CLI commands from the BASIC CLI com-mand. There are just two things to remember: First, you can't change the current directory with cd, since AmigaBASIC still has control over directories with CHDIR. Second, you can't use the asterisk (*), since this CLI doesn't use the CLI window.

6
AmigaBASIC
internals

6.   AmigaBASIC internals

AmigaBASIC has a very powerful command set. The manual that comes with it, however, contains many unclear descriptions of commands. Those of you who may have owned another computer before buying an Amiga probably had a number of *utility* programs. Utilities help programmers to program better. Some utilities help users change programs, create new program code or extract old program code. Others allow you to load any program at another starting address.

Since memory manipulation is so complex on the Amiga, there are no memory handling programs in this chapter. However, there are a number of other utilities here to let you change program code. The authors have devised a diskette configuration so that you can load a program into a utility, change the program and save the program back in its edited form. This configuration uses internal drive df0:, the RAM disk ram:, and any external drives (optional). More on diskette configuration later.

Before continuing with the utilities, you must know about the filetypes supported by AmigaBASIC. Section 6.2 gives detailed information about Amiga file structues. This information will help you later on with adapting these utilities to your own uses.

6.1   File analyzer

This program lets you display the programs in the following chapters.
It acts as a simple file monitor, independent of the built-in CLI editor
and the AmigaBASIC editor. The program is menu controlled. The left
border of the screen displays the offset address from the beginning of the
file. The screen's center shows 16 bytes in hexadecimal notation. The
right border of the screen lists the same data in ASCII form. When you
want to expand the program, remember to adjust the menu activation
and de-activation as needed.

```
GOTO start¶
' ####################################¶
' #  F I L E - A N A L Y Z E R  AMIGA  #¶
' #----------------------------------#¶
' #      (W) 1987 by Stefan Maelger    #¶
' ####################################¶
'¶
' "dos.bmap" and "exec.bmap" must¶
'   exist on the Disk or in LIBS:¶
' ------------------------------------------¶
' Declare ROM functions and routines¶
'¶
start:¶
  DECLARE FUNCTION xOpen&      LIBRARY¶
  DECLARE FUNCTION xRead%      LIBRARY¶
  DECLARE FUNCTION AllocMem&   LIBRARY¶
  DECLARE FUNCTION Examine&    LIBRARY¶
  DECLARE FUNCTION Seek%       LIBRARY¶
  DECLARE FUNCTION Lock&       LIBRARY¶
' ------------------------------------------¶
' Open Libraries¶
'¶
  LIBRARY "exec.library"¶
  LIBRARY "dos.library"¶
  ¶
' ------------------------------------------¶
' Initialize screen and window¶
'¶
  SCREEN 2,640,200,1,2¶
  WINDOW 2," F I L E - A N A L Y Z E R",,0,2¶
  ¶
  MENU 1,0,1,"File"¶
  MENU 1,1,1,"Open"¶
  MENU 1,2,0,"Close"¶
  MENU 2,0,0,"Block"¶
  MENU 2,1,1,"Next"¶
  MENU 2,2,0,"Back"¶
  ¶
  ¶
' ------------------------------------------¶
' Setup InfoBlock and Buffer¶
'¶
  Infobytes&   =   252¶
  Bufferbytes&=  400¶
  PublicRAM&  =65537&¶
  ChipRAM&    =65538&¶
  ¶
```

```
        Info&   =AllocMem&(Infobytes&   ,ChipRAM&  )¶
        Buffer&=AllocMem&(Bufferbytes&,PublicRAM&)¶
        IF Info&=0 OR Buffer&=0 THEN ERROR 7¶
      ¶
        ON MENU GOSUB menus¶
        MENU ON¶
      ¶
        WHILE NOT finished¶
        WEND¶
      ¶
        CALL FreeMem(Buffer&,Bufferbytes&)¶
        CALL FreeMem(Info&   ,Infobytes&  )¶
        LIBRARY CLOSE ¶
        END¶
      ' ----------------------------------------¶
      ' Menu-Selection result¶
      '¶
      menus:¶
        number=MENU(1)+2*MENU(0)-2¶
        ON number GOTO fopen,fclose,bnext,bback¶
      ¶
      fopen:¶
        MENU OFF¶
        CLS¶
        LINE INPUT "FILENAME: ";Filename$¶
        File$=Filename$+CHR$(0)¶
        DosLock&=Lock&(SADD(File$),-2)¶
        IF DosLock&=0 THEN¶
          PRINT :PRINT "File not found!"¶
          MENU ON¶
          RETURN¶
        END IF¶
      ¶
        Dummy&=Examine&(DosLock&,Info&)¶
      ¶
        IF PEEKL(Info&+4)>0 THEN¶
          PRINT :PRINT "Can't display Directories!"¶
          CALL UnLock(DosLock&)¶
          MENU ON:RETURN¶
        END IF¶
        Length&=PEEKL(Info&+124)¶
        CALL UnLock(DosLock&)¶
        Handle&=xOpen&(SADD(File$),1005)¶
        IF Handle&=0 THEN¶
          PRINT :PRINT "Can't open file!"¶
          MENU ON¶
          RETURN¶
        END IF¶
        inBuffer%=xRead%(Handle&,Buffer&,400)¶
        Block%=1 ¶
        IF Length&>400 THEN MENU 2,0,1¶
        MENU 1,1,0¶
        MENU 1,2,1¶
        CLS ¶
        PRINT "File: ";Filename$;TAB(38);" Length: ";Length&;¶

        PRINT " Byte"¶
        Display Buffer&,inBuffer%,Block%¶
        MENU ON¶
        RETURN¶
      ¶
```

```
                fclose:¶
                  MENU OFF¶
                  CALL xClose(Handle&)¶
                  CLS ¶
                  MENU 1,1,1¶
                  MENU 1,2,0¶
                  MENU 2,0,0¶
                  MENU 2,1,1¶
                  MENU 2,2,0¶
                  MENU ON¶
                  RETURN¶
                ¶
                bnext:¶
                  MENU OFF¶
                  inBuffer%=xRead%(Handle&,Buffer&,400)¶
                  Block%=Block%+1¶
                  MENU 2,2,1¶
                  IF Length&<=Block%*400 THEN MENU 2,1,0¶
                  Display Buffer&,inBuffer%,Block%¶
                  MENU ON¶
                  RETURN¶
                ¶
                bback:¶
                  MENU OFF¶
                  begin%=Seek%(Handle&,-400-inBuffer%,0)¶
                  inBuffer%=xRead%(Handle&,Buffer&,400)¶
                  Block%=Block%-1 ¶
                  MENU 2,1,1¶
                  IF Block%<2 THEN MENU 2,2,0¶
                  Display Buffer&,inBuffer%,Block%¶
                  MENU ON¶
                  RETURN¶
                ¶
                ' ----------------------------------------¶
                ' SUBroutine¶
                '¶
                ¶
                SUB Display(Buffer&,Bytes%,Block%) STATIC¶
                  Counter%=0¶
                  Address&=(Block%-1)*336¶
                  FOR y=0 TO 20   ¶
                    LOCATE y+3,1:COLOR 0,1¶
                    PRINT RIGHT$("00000"+HEX$(Address&),6);":";¶
                    Address&=Address&+16¶
                    FOR x=0 TO 15¶
                      LOCATE y+3,x*3+9¶
                      COLOR 1,0¶
                      Counter%=Counter%+1¶
                      w%=PEEK(Buffer&+x+y*16)¶
                      hexa$=RIGHT$("0"+HEX$(w%),2)¶
                      IF (w%>31 AND w%<128)OR w%>159 THEN¶
                        ASCII$=CHR$(w%)¶
                      ELSE¶
                        ASCII$="."¶
                      END IF¶
                      IF Counter%>Bytes% THEN hexa$="  ":ASCII$=" "¶
                      PRINT hexa$; ¶
                      LOCATE y+3,x+57¶
                      COLOR 0,1¶
                      PRINT ASCII$;¶
                    NEXT x,y¶
                  COLOR 1,0¶
                END SUB¶
```

Variables

InfoBytes&	size of file info structure
Bufferbytes&	buffer size for file
PublicRAM&	range for allocate + clear
ChipRAM&	DMA range for allocate + range clear
Info&	address of file info block
Buffer&	file buffer address
finished	dummy variable
number	number of menu item
Filename$	filename
File$	filename ended with CHR$(0)
DosLock	internal file number
Dummy&	dummy variable
Length&	file length in bytes
Handle&	internal file number
inBuffer%	number of bytes presently read into buffer
Block%	number of 400-byte block read
begin%	old start-of-file offset
Counter%	number of displayed bytes
Address&	read pointer
w%	value PEEKed from buffer
hexa$	two-character display string for middle
ASCII$	single-character string for ASCII array

6.2   AmigaBASIC file structure

AmigaBASIC's SAVE command lets users save programs in three different ways:

> SAVE "Test",a stores the program Test as an ASCII file.
> SAVE "Test",b stores the program in binary form.
> SAVE "Test",p stores the program in protected form.

Before you save a program, you should know what you want done with this file later on. That is, the purpose of a file, and the situations in which it is used later.

ASCII files

ASCII files are necessary when you want to combine files using MERGE or CHAIN. When you want to store a program as an ASCII file, you can reload it later and save it out again as an ASCII, binary (normal) or protected file.

The disadvantage of ASCII files is the amount of memory they consume, especially when many variable names are used (more on this later). This disadvantage also applies to the entire concept of modular programming.

Binary files

Binary files are shorter; the computer converts commands and variables into *tokens*. A binary file can be saved out later in ASCII, binary or protected form.

Protected files

Protected files cannot be corrected or changed in any way. Once you save a file in protected form, you can't change it. Unlike the other file forms, you can't resave a protected file in ASCII or binary form. Before saving a file as a protected program, make sure you have a backup copy or two of the file in ASCII or binary form.

6.2.1   Determining filetype

Now you may want to manipulate AmigaBASIC programs, whether they are on diskette or in buffer memory. As soon as you know the structure of an AmigaBASIC file, there should be no problem with this.

There is one glitch: Say you wrote a program that generates a new
AmigaBASIC program from a program already on diskette. This program waits for the user to tell it which program he wants modified (let's
assume that this program is on the diskette currently in the drive). The
programmer must know whether this file is an AmigaBASIC file.

6.2.1.1   Checking for a BASIC file

This program examines a file and tells the user whether or not the file
is an AmigaBASIC program.

```
GOTO start¶
¶
REM ####################################¶
REM #  B  A  S  I  C  -  C  H  E  C  K  #¶
REM #----------------------------------#¶
REM #       (W) 1987 by Stefan Maelger  #¶
REM ####################################¶
¶
REM SUB-Routine to check whether a File¶
REM is a AmigaBASIC-Program¶
¶
start:¶
¶
    DECLARE FUNCTION xOpen& LIBRARY¶
    DECLARE FUNCTION xRead% LIBRARY¶
    DECLARE FUNCTION Seek%  LIBRARY¶
¶
    LIBRARY "dos.library"¶
¶
main:¶
¶
    CLS¶
    LOCATE 2,2¶
    PRINT "Name of AmigaBASIC-Program:"¶
    LOCATE 4,1¶
    PRINT ">";:LINE INPUT Filename$¶
    BASICcheck Filename$,Flag%¶
    LOCATE 6,2¶
    IF Flag% THEN ¶
        PRINT "It is an AmigaBASIC-Program!"¶
    ELSE¶
        PRINT "No, it's not an AmigaBASIC-Program..."¶
    END IF¶
    LIBRARY CLOSE¶
    END¶
¶
SUB BASICcheck (Filename$,ok%) STATIC¶
¶
    File$ = Filename$+".info"+CHR$(0)¶
    Default.Tool$ = SPACE$(12)¶
```

```
        OpenOldFile% = 1005¶
        OffsetEOF% = 1¶
        Offset% = -12¶
¶
OpenFile:¶
¶
        File.handle& = xOpen&(SADD(File$),OpenOldFile%)¶
        IF File.handle& = 0 THEN¶
            CLS¶
            LOCATE 2,2¶
            PRINT "I can't find ";Filename$;"!"¶
            BEEP¶
            EXIT SUB¶
        ELSE¶

OldPosition%=Seek%(File.handle&,Offset%,OffsetEOF%)¶

GotThem%=xRead%(File.handle&,SADD(Default.Tool$),12)¶
            IF GotThem%<12 THEN¶
                CLS¶
                LOCATE 2,2¶
                PRINT "READ-ERROR"¶
                BEEP¶
                EXIT SUB¶
            ELSE¶
                IF INSTR(Default.Tool$,":AmigaBASIC")>0 THEN¶
                    ok%=-1¶
                ELSE¶
                    ok%=0¶
                END IF¶
            END IF¶
            CALL xClose(File.handle&)¶
        END IF¶
END SUB¶
```

Variables

Filename$	name of the potential AmigaBASIC program
Flag%	=-1: the file is an AmigaBASIC program
ok%	SUB variable indicator from flag%
File$	name of the info file from Filename$+CHR$(0)
Default.Tool$	12-byte string, taken from the last 12 bytes of file$
OpenOldFile%	parameter used when file opens (1006=new file open)
OffsetEOF%	sets cursor to end of file during file read routine (-1= beginning, 0=present position)
File.handle&	file handle address (0=file not open)
OldPosition%	old file cursor offset
GotThem%	number of bytes read so far

Program
description

If you've tried out the Info item from the Workbench pulldown menu, you've seen the Default Tool string gadget in the Info window. Default Tool is the main program that loads when you double-click a program's icon. For example, if you double-click an AmigaBASIC program's icon, AmigaBASIC loads first, then the program loads and runs. So, the Default Tool gadget of an Amiga-BASIC program contains the entry :AmigaBASIC. Every Amiga-BASIC program (and most programs) have a companion file called an *info* file. This file has the same name as the program with an added file extension of .info. This info file holds the bitmap of the program's icon, as well as the Default Tool designation.

To find out whether or not a file is an AmigaBASIC program, this program opens the matching info file, moves the cursor to a location 12 bytes from the end of the file and reads the Default Tool gadget. Why 12 bytes? The entry only has 11 bytes, but AmigaDOS only accepts names ended by CHR$(0).

Note:

Some programs that allow icon editing and creation may not work quite right. These program errors can result in a misplaced Default Tool. You can get around this error by raising the number of bytes you want read.

6.2.1.2   Checking the program header

Now you know how to identify a file as an AmigaBASIC program. You still can't change the program yet; you have to determine the program type before any changes can be made. The AmigaBASIC interpreter must know the program type.

Header
bytes

The first byte of an AmigaBASIC program conveys the program type. This byte is called the *header byte*. Programs stored in binary (normal) form and protected form attach this header byte to the beginning of the file. ASCII files contain no header bytes, since they don't need header bytes (see Section 6.2.2 below for details on ASCII file structure).

The header byte assignments are as follows:

$F5	binary program
$F4	protected program
no header byte	ASCII file

The program below performs this function. This program requires the dos.library routines xRead and xWrite. Remember to have this library file available on the diskette currently in the drive.

```
GOTO start¶
¶
' ######################################¶
' # H E A D E R - C H E C K #¶
' #-----------------------------------#¶
' #      (W) 1987 by Stefan Maelger   #¶
' ######################################¶
'¶
' SUB-Routine to determine the File-Type¶
' of an AmigaBASIC-Program from the¶
' File-Headers.¶
' -----------------------------------------¶
'  ¶
start:¶
¶
   DECLARE FUNCTION xOpen& LIBRARY¶
   DECLARE FUNCTION xRead% LIBRARY¶
   ¶
   LIBRARY "dos.library"¶
   ¶
main:¶
   ¶
   ProgramType$(0)="n ASCII-File"¶
   ProgramType$(1)=" Binary-File"¶
   ProgramType$(2)=" Protected-Binary-File"¶
   ¶
   LINE INPUT "Filename: >";Filename$¶
   ¶
   HeaderCheck Filename$,Result%¶
   ¶
   LOCATE 10,1¶
   ¶
   PRINT "The Program ";CHR$(34);¶
   PRINT Filename$;CHR$(34);¶
   PRINT " is a";ProgramType$(Result%)¶
   ¶
   LOCATE 15,1¶
   ¶
   LIBRARY CLOSE¶
   END¶
   ¶
 SUB HeaderCheck(Filename$,Result%) STATIC¶
    ¶
    File$=Filename$+CHR$(0)¶
    OpenOldFile%=1005¶
    handle&=xOpen&(SADD(File$),OpenOldFile%)¶
    IF handle&=0 THEN ERROR 53¶
    s$="1"¶
    Byte&=1¶
    Count&=xRead%(handle&,SADD(s$),Byte&)¶
    CALL xClose(handle&)¶
    Result%=0¶
    d%=ASC(s$)¶
    IF d%=&HF5 THEN¶
       Result%=1¶
    ELSEIF d%=&HF4 THEN¶
```

```
        Result%=2¶
    END IF¶
      ¶
END SUB¶
```

Variables

ProgramType$	program type
Filename$	name of the AmigaBASIC program
Result%	0=ASCII; 1=binary; 2=protected
File$	Filename$+CHR$(0)
OpenOldFile%	parameter used for open file
handle&	file handle address
s$	string from which first byte is read
Byte&	number of bytes to be read
Read&	number of bytes read so far
d%	ASCII value from s$

6.2.2   ASCII files

ASCII file structure is really quite simple. Load AmigaBASIC and enter the following program code:

```
a=1¶
PRINT a¶
```

Save this program using the following syntax:

```
SAVE "Test",A¶
```

Now quit AmigaBASIC and load up the file analyzer program from Section 6.1 (or use some other file monitor if you have one available). When the file analyzer finishes loading, select the Open item from the menu and enter the name of the program you just saved.

The program code appears on the right hand side of the screen:

```
a=1.PRINT a..
```

And the hex dump of the program appears on the left hand side of the screen:

```
61 3D 31 0A 50 52 49 4E 54 20 61 0A 0A
```

If you convert these hex numbers to decimal notation, they look like this:

```
97 61 49 10 80 82 73 78 84 32 97 10 10
```

Look in Appendix A of your AmigaBASIC manual for a list of ASCII character codes. You'll see that these numbers match the text. Character code 10 executes a linefeed (next line).

If you want to read a program saved as an ASCII file, use the following program in AmigaBASIC:

```
LINE INPUT File$¶
OPEN File$ FOR INPUT AS 1¶
 WHILE NOT EOF(1) ¶
  PRINT INPUT$(1,1);
 WEND¶
CLOSE 1¶
```

Insert your Workbench diskette.

•   Make sure the CLI is on in Preferences and start up the CLI.

•   Enter the following:

    ed Diskname:Test

Diskname is the name of the diskette on which you saved the Test program. You can edit ASCII programs using Ed (the editor) from the Workbench diskette. The main disadvantage to Ed is that you cannot test programs using it.

If you thought of simply creating a new program using OPEN name FOR OUTPUT, you had a good idea. The problem with that, though, comes up when you try loading the new program into the directory. The filename .info has no :AmigaBASIC listed as its Default Tool. Just do the following to create a new info file:

    SAVE "Dummy":KILL File$+".info"¶
    NAME "Dummy.info" AS File$+".info"¶
    KILL "Dummy"¶

See Section 6.3 for practical applications using ASCII files.

6.2.3   Binary files

Binary file structure is extremely important since this is the usual file format directly accessible from the AmigaBASIC interpreter. All other filetypes must be converted to binary format before AmigaBASIC can execute them.

Binary programs have a header byte containing $F5.

The first program line begins at the second byte of the program. This would be a good time to examine the structure of an AmigaBASIC line.

Line header

The first byte of a line is the line header. This byte can have one of two values: 0 or 128 ($80 hexadecimal). If the line begins with 0, the line is handled as if it has no line number. If the line begins with 128, then it has a line number. Labels do not apply to this header (more on this later).

Line offset

The second byte of a line is the offset to the next line. It would be pretty complicated to try figuring out pointers to the next line every time an AmigaBASIC program loads and runs at different memory locations. Instead, AmigaBASIC counts the total length of the current line. The interpreter then figures out the address at which the line begins, and takes the number of occupied bytes from it. If the interpreter must jump a number of lines forward (e.g., during a jump command), it just adds the line length of the current line to the starting address.

Line length is represented in only one byte. This is why a program line can be no longer than 255 bytes.

Indenting program lines can make your program code more easily readable for debugging or when trying to read a program for its flow of execution. A program might look something like this:

```
multiple.FOR.NEXT.loops:                          0
    FOR FirstLoop=1 TO 100                         2
        FOR secondLoop=1 TO 10                     4
            FOR thirdLoop=1 TO 50                  6
                LPRINT FNstepon (x,y,z)            8
        NEXT thirdLoop, secondLoop, FirstLoop      2
```

The numbers at the right of the lines above don't belong to the program itself. These are the numbers taken up by the third byte of the matching program line. Take a look at these with the file monitor. Only LIST and editing commands make use of this byte. It gives the spacing of the first command from the left margin. This answers the question as to whether the program length or execution speed are affected by indentation. You see, the single change is in the value of the third byte.

Line numbers

Now look at the difference between the structures of a line containing a line number and a line without a line number. Up to now, you've seen how a line without line numbers is handled. Here's a review:

Byte	Value	Definition
1	00	Line without line number follows
2	xx	Line length in bytes (with head and end)
3	xx	Spacing from left margin to first command (for LISTing programs only)

Lines with line numbers have two additional bytes, making the line header a total of five bytes long. Bytes four and five give the line number in high byte/low byte format. For example, if the line number is 10000, the fourth and fifth byte return $27 and $10 respectively (39 and 16 decimal: 39*256+16=line number). The structure looks like this:

Byte number	Value	Definition
1	128	Line with line number follows
2	xx	Line length in bytes (with head and end)
3	xx	Spacing from left margin to first command (for LISTing programs only)
4	xx	Line number (high byte)
5	xx	Line number (low byte)

Both line structures are similar. The bytes following are the *tokens* (commands coded into two-byte numbers).

BASIC lines end with the value 0 (an extra byte). To summarize, a program line consists of

1)   a program header with or without line numbers

2)   tokens (commands, labels,.variables and values)

3)   end byte of 0

Blank lines   Now that you know about line storage, you may already know how blank spaces are stored. The blanks discussed here are those spaces between one line and the next.

Here's the problem: The first byte must contain a zero, so no line number follows. The third byte (indentation) is also zero most of the time). The fourth byte starts the token list. If this line is blank, the end-of-line code (another zero) follows. The line ends and the total line length (four bytes) goes to the second byte of the line.

A blank line looks something like this:

       $00 – $04 – $xx – $00

It's obvious here that every blank line takes up four bytes of memory and slows down the computer's execution time, since the interpreter checks these blank lines for commands. You should remove blank lines from your programs, especially programs that are time-critical. You know the old saying–little things add up. See Section 6.3 for a program that removes blank lines.

The last line   The last line of a program begins with a null byte. There is no line number offset. The next byte is the line length byte, which is also set to null, then the end-of-line code (again, a zero).

Other bytes could follow, say when a program has been edited. These bytes can have some strange values.

Variable tables

Variable names can be up to 40 characters long in AmigaBASIC. The problem comes up every time access occurs on a variable stored under its full name. In order to use long-named variables without slowing the computer down, the programmer must do the following in this BASIC dialect:

When a variable occurs, the interpreter reads a special token. This token always has the value $01. Following this token is a number in high byte/low byte format. The interpreter simply numbers each variable and continues program execution based upon variable numbers. These variables must be stored under their full names so that LIST lists these variables under their full names. The end of the program contains a variable table to accomplish this. An entry in this table appears in the following format:

1st byte	Length of the variable name in bytes
successive bytes	Variable names in ASCII code.

For example, if you use the variables a%, String$ and Address& in your program, the variable table would look something like this:

Hexadecimal	ASCII	
01	61	.a
06	5A 74 72 69 6E 67	.String
07	41 64 64 72 65 73 73	.Address

The last byte of your program would then be $65. It doesn't matter what type the variable is to the table—these follow the variable number set by the token $01. If you look at the above example, the a% variable lies in the program as follows:

Byte number	Value	Definition
1	1	Variable number follows
2	0	High byte of variable number
3	0	Low byte of variable number
4	37	ASCII code of % character

The above table shows you that the first variable is assigned the number zero.

Unfortunately, the variables in AmigaBASIC aren't as simple as all that. The order of the variables in the variable table is the order in which you first typed them in. To see this bug in action, do the following:

• Load AmigaBASIC.

• Enter the following:

```
The.big.error%=0
Blahblahblah%=The.error%
```

```
Hello%=0
```

•   Change `Blahblahblah%` to read:

```
Blahblahblah%=The.big.error%
```

•   Save the program in binary form, and look at it with the file monitor.

The program itself no longer contains the `error%` variable. However, the variable table still has this variable. If you write a long program and mistype some variable names, or change a few names, you're still stuck with the original errors/variable names in the variable table, whether you use them or not. Your program could end up several kilobytes longer than you need, and execution time suffers as well.

See Section 6.3.6 for a solution to this problem.

Another bug in AmigaBASIC is the fact that all SUB programs, their calls and all operating system routines called by LIBRARY and/or DECLARE FUNCTION are set up as *variables*—in the table and the program text. AmigaBASIC can only recognize these names in complete syntax checking as functions or SUB extensions. This makes no difference to the BASIC interpreter, which goes through a complete check of the program before starting it. This means that some delay can occur between a program loading and eventually starting.

Label handling

Labels are similar to variables. The developers of AmigaBASIC had some problems dealing with long label names. The solution is as follows: Labels are treated as special variables—different from other variables in that they are used for program branching.

This means that labels are sorted out in the variable table like a normal variable. Now the BASIC interpreter must be able to recognize a label, since no memory is set aside for labels. A special token ($02) marks labels in program code. When the interpreter encounters a $02, the number immediately following is the high byte/low byte number of a label. For example:

Byte number	Value	Definition
1	2	Label number follows
2	xx	High byte of label number
3	xx	Low byte of label number

If the interpreter finds $02 $00 $09 in the program, it knows that there is a label here whose name is at the tenth place in the variable table (this table begins its numbering at 0).

Label branching

You can jump to any label you want, especially useless ones like REMarks. This section talks about GOTO and labels, but the same applies to GOSUB.

Example: `GOTO division`

Let's assume that `division` stands at the third place in the variable table. The interpreter finds the following in the program:

Byte number	Value	Definition
1	151	Token for GOTO (see Appendices)
2	32	Space
3	3	Token=label that should be branched to
4	0	Always 0
5	0	High byte of number in variable table
6	2	Low byte of number

You've just learned a new token—$03. The interpreter looks for a $02-$00-$02 and continues program execution at that point.

Line number branching

Line number branches are very different from label branches. The reason is that line numbers aren't stored in the variable table. A new token is required:

Example: `GOTO 10000`

Byte number	Value	Definition
1	151	Token for GOTO (see Appendices)
2	32	Space
3	14	Token=branch to following line number
4	0	Always 0
5	39	High byte of line number (39*256)
6	16	Low byte of line number (+16=10000)

The $0E token means that in all lines containing header bytes of $80, bytes 4 and 5 must be compared with bytes 5 and 6 to find the branch line.

Values in Amiga-BASIC

AmigaBASIC has another big difference from other versions of BASIC: AmigaBASIC uses its own methods of handling values in its program codes. For example, take a simple variable assignment like the one listed below:

`Amiga=1`

The item of interest here is the way the "1" is stored in the program. Unlike the methods used in other BASIC dialects, in which numbers are converted to their ASCII equivalents, which takes time during program execution, AmigaBASIC stores numbers and values in the necessary format. For every format (e.g., floating-point or octal), a new token must exist. Let's go through this process step by step.

The process used to differentiate the format selection is a stupid one; it's not dependent upon the needs of the variable. Look at the above example. It goes without saying that the number 1 would be handled as an integer. The next important fact is that the number is a single-digit number. When it comes down to the leading character of the number (positive or negative), the following occurs:

Positive integers from 0 to 9 go into the program without tokens. The ASCII code is unused. Direct storage in memory is impossible, since the numbers can be interpreted as other values (e.g., "0" means end-of-line and "1" means "Variable number"). The values are coded as follows:

Hex	Dec	Value (decimal)
$11	17	0
$12	18	1
$13	19	2
...	...	...
$19	25	8
$1A	26	9

When the interpreter finds a byte between 17 and 26, it replaces the value 17 with the proper value.

Now take a look at positive integer values between 10 and 255. One byte is enough for storing these numbers. Again, a token is required so that the interpreter cannot mistake the number for a command token or other token. The format is:

Byte number	Value	Definition
1	15	A positive integer from 10 to 255 follows
2	xx	Value between 10 and 255

Integer values can also be larger than 255, and positive or negative. These numbers use this format:

Byte number	Value	Definition
1	28	A 2-byte integer with leading character follows
2	xx	High byte (bit 7=leading character bit)
3	xx	Low byte

Integers larger than 32767 are represented in long-integer format:

Byte number	Value	Definition
1	30	A 4-byte integer with leading character follows
2-5	xx	4-byte integer (bit 7 in byte 2=leading character bit)

If the value should be handled as a floating-point number, use the following format:

Byte number	Value	Definition
1	29	A 4-byte floating-point number follows
2-5	xx	4-byte floating-point (7-place accuracy)

Double-length floating-point numbers:

Byte number	Value	Definition
1	31	An 8-byte floating-point number follows
2-9	xx	8-byte floating-point (16-place accuracy)

Notation

The Amiga has ways to recognize and fix incorrect numerical notation. Enter the following into a program from AmigaBASIC:

```
a=&hff
```

When you exit the line, the Amiga corrects the error:

```
a=&HFF
```

Tokens help the Amiga recognize the number system used:

Byte number	Value	Definition
1	12	Hexadecimal number follows
2	xx	High byte
3	xx	Low byte

Then there are the larger octal numbers like &O123456. These must be converted into 2-byte format:

Byte number	Value	Definition
1	11	Octal number follows
2 + 3	xx	Octal number (accuracy to 6 places)

Assigning values to strings has one major change from the other variables: Strings are stored in ASCII. To save memory, no new memory is set aside for a direct value assignment. The pointer is set in the program to the starting address of the string.

For example, type this in AmigaBASIC and run it:

```
a$="--------------------------"
b$="These lines I am a'changing."
FOR i=1 TO LEN(b$)
  POKE SADD(a$)+i-1,ASC(MID$(b$,i,1))
NEXT
LIST
```

SADD may be an unfamiliar command to you. It returns the starting address of the string contained in a variable (in this case a$).

After you run this program, compare the listing above with the program you entered and ran. It looks like this:

```
a$="These lines I am a'changing."
b$="These lines I am a'changing."
```

```
FOR i=1 TO LEN(b$)
   POKE SADD(a$)+i-1,ASC(MID$(b$,i,1))
NEXT
LIST
```

You can see from this little example lots of potential for self-modifying programs. For example, you could put the name of a window in a$. The user could enter a new name while the program runs. The program then POKEs the name into the system and saves the altered program to diskette.

Command tokens

Command tokens (characters having ASCII codes higher than 127) have their own peculiarities that you should know about. These tokens are stored by AmigaBASIC as single- or double-character codes. They represent direct commands, but require less memory than if the Amiga stored commands by their full names.

$8E (ELSE) never happens in program code by itself. The interpreter can only determine the end of a command when it either finds code $00 (end-of-line) or code $3A (colon). If the interpreter finds IF and THEN without an ELSE, then IF/THEN are handled by the interpreter as one command. If ELSE follows, you can see that the BASIC interpreter adds a colon before the $8E (you can't see this colon when you call LIST). If you put your own colons in preceding the ELSEs in your programs, the file monitor shows two colons. The colon originally added by the interpreter itself is invisible to LIST.

REMarks cause a similar problem—the interpreter adds a colon. This is strange, since it happens even when REM is the only command in the line. A line can look like this:

    '*1.*

Its structure can look like this:

00 0E 00	3A	AF E8	20	2A	20	31	2E	20	2A	00
Header	:	'		*		1	.		*	End

Another strange thing happens when you create a program and use the token $BE for the WHILE command. Under certain circumstances, the Amiga stops the program and returns ERROR 22 (Missing operand). If you write a program in AmigaBASIC, once in a while the interpreter places an $EC after the visible single-byte token $BE.

Important:
There is one token that you can't list and you almost never use. You know that you can only call SUB routines directly through THEN or ELSE with the CALL command. You can use BASIC commands as well as SUB programs. The SUB program has one purpose alone: It allows the programming of command extensions in BASIC. Those who know this never use the CALL command, aside from calling operating system routines. Instead they use this token. Unlike CALL, this token goes after the pointers to the variable table. The token is the double token $F8-$D1.

In closing, a few words about the DATA command. DATA statements are placed in ASCII text, like the data following a REMark. This data can be read into variables, and can be of any type:

```
DATA &hffe2,123,&06666
```

SUB
programs
Why were the SUB programs implemented in AmigaBASIC? The first reason is that they allow modular programming. Also, SUB programs allow the retention of variable names, even when programs are combined through CHAIN and MERGE. Any of these variables can be shared with other routines by stating the names with STATIC.

It's a good move to edit each and every SUB program separately, store them as ASCII files, and combine the SUBs with the BASIC program currently in memory using MERGE in direct mode or program mode (the syntax check takes up a lot of time). The call convention (e.g., which operating system routines must be declared as functions, etc.) should be declared and archived with a file manager. The second point of interest was that unlike earlier computers with incomplete command sets, SUB programs allow extension of the command set:

```
PRINTAT 10,20,"Sample text"

SUB PRINTAT (x,y,Text$) STATIC
   LOCATE y,x
   PRINT Text$
END SUB
```

The third point is the pressure on the programmer to learn Pascal or another language. Why learn more complex languages, when BASIC can do it just as well and just as fast? Unlike Pascal, SUB programs cannot call themselves. However, a command can be called multiple times, with the help of a label at the beginning of a routine made up of SUB programs.

Programs handle SUB routines like variables. Only in this way does the Amiga recognize these routines.

Important details

What would the make-believe manipulation program do when it encounters the code sequence $20-$F8-$8F-$20? Turn to the token list in the Appendix. The code stands for the $F8 double token END, placed between two spaces. The program hasn't ended, though. What about this $F8-$BE? That's the double code for SUB. You see, a token by itself can cause trouble. First the connection in which the token is compared to other tokens sets the type of execution. This also goes for PRINT# and ?#—the token numbers are the same.

Other tokens

No time has been spent discussing tokens below 128. These tokens are used, though. There are occasions when you try saving an edited program in direct mode when the Amiga displays an error requester instead. Apparently the Amiga gets stuck in the error checking routine, and keeps registering an error. Clicking on the OK gadget eventually gets you past the error, but you may have to click it a few times over.

A simple program check can change commands around. An occasional gap in the token list can control the program. For example, $8, which acts as the branch offset of the IF/THEN construction that may not be in the same place in another program. In order to make life with manipulation programs as simple as possible, try to follow these ground rules:

1)   Manipulation programs or programs for reading data from other programs which require binary file format should:

  •   allow storage of the modified file as an ASCII file.

  •   allow you to save the file back in binary file format after loading.

2)   ASCII files require no special treatment, as long as the program control codes aren't saved as well.

6.3   Utility programs

The following section presents programs that let you change Amiga-BASIC program code.

6.3.1   DATA generator

This program demonstrates how you can create a program from an AmigaBASIC program saved in ASCII format.

A good program should allow you to type it in direct from a magazine. But what if this program has sprites, bobs, machine language or something similar? Then a DATA generator is necessary. This program makes DATA statements out of any program. The ASCII file created can be appended to a program using MERGE.

To keep the DATA list short, the statements are displayed in hexadecimal notation. You may recognize the reader routine from the AmigaBASIC manual program for converting hex to decimal numbers. The reverse routine can be found anywhere, although it's not standard to AmigaBASIC. Just type:

```
stuff: DATA ff,ec,0,1,f
RESTORE stuff:FOR i=1 TO 5:READ a$:x(i)=VAL("&H"+a$):NEXT
```

Now for the listing:

```
GOTO Start¶
' ####################################¶
' # D A T A - G E N E R A T O R  AMIGA #¶
' #------------------------------------#¶
' #     (W) 1987 by Stefan Maelger     #¶
' ####################################¶
'¶
' "dos.bmap" and "exec.bmap" must be on¶
' Disk or in LIBS: !¶
' ------------------------------------¶
' Declare System Routines and Functions¶
'¶
Start: ¶
   DECLARE FUNCTION xOpen&      LIBRARY¶
   DECLARE FUNCTION xRead%      LIBRARY¶
   DECLARE FUNCTION AllocMem&   LIBRARY¶
   DECLARE FUNCTION Examine&    LIBRARY¶
   DECLARE FUNCTION Lock&       LIBRARY¶
   ' ------------------------------------¶
```

```
' Open Libraries¶
'  ¶
  LIBRARY "exec.library"¶
  LIBRARY "dos.library"¶
' ----------------------------------------¶
' Input¶
'¶
sourcefile:¶
  CLS¶
  LINE INPUT "Name of Source-File: ";source$¶
  PRINT¶
  PRINT "Insert Diskette and Press <RETURN>"¶
  WHILE A$<>CHR$(13)¶
    A$=INKEY$¶
  WEND¶
  LOCATE 3,1:PRINT "Checking File...              "¶
  CHDIR "df0:"¶
  CheckFile source$,Bytes&¶
¶
¶
  IF Bytes&=0 THEN¶
    LOCATE 3,1:PRINT "File not found...":BEEP¶
    A=TIMER+3 :WHILE A>TIMER:WEND¶
    GOTO sourcefile¶
  ELSEIF Bytes&=-1 THEN¶
    LOCATE 3,1:PRINT "I can't find the Directory..."¶
    BEEP :A=TIMER+3:WHILE A>TIMER:WEND¶
    GOTO sourcefile¶
  END IF¶
  LOCATE 3,1:PRINT "File Found. Length=";Bytes&;" Byte"¶
' ----------------------------------------¶
' Setup Buffer¶
'¶
  PublicRAM&=65537&¶
  Buffer&=AllocMem&(Bytes&,PublicRAM&)¶
  IF Buffer&=0 THEN¶
    LOCATE 5,1:PRINT "Not enough memory."¶
    LOCATE 7,1¶
    PRINT "Program can re-started with RUN."¶
    BEEP :END¶
  END IF¶
' ----------------------------------------¶
' Load File in Buffer¶
'¶
  source$=source$+CHR$(0)¶
  Opened&=xOpen&(SADD(source$),1005)¶
  IF Opened&=0 THEN¶
    LOCATE 5,1:PRINT "I can not open the File!"¶
    BEEP :A=TIMER+3:WHILE A>TIMER:WEND¶
    GOTO sourcefile¶
  END IF¶
  sofar%=xRead%(Opened&,Buffer&,Bytes&)¶
  CALL xClose(Opened&)¶
' ----------------------------------------¶
' Input Target-File¶
'¶
```

```
targetfile: ¶
  LOCATE 9,1:PRINT "Name of BASIC-ASCII-File"¶
¶
¶
  FOR i=11 TO 17 STEP 2¶
    LOCATE i,1:PRINT SPACE$(80)¶
  NEXT¶
  LOCATE 11,1:LINE INPUT "to be produced: ";target$¶
  LOCATE 13,1:PRINT "Insert Target-Disk and Press
<RETURN>"¶
  A$="" :WHILE A$<>CHR$(13):A$=INKEY$:WEND¶
  CHDIR "df0:"¶
  LOCATE 15,1:PRINT "Checking Disk..."¶
  CheckFile target$,exist&¶
  IF exist&=-1 THEN¶
    LOCATE 15,1:PRINT "This is the Name of a Directory!"¶
    BEEP :A=TIMER+3:WHILE A>TIMER:WEND¶
    GOTO targetfile¶
  ELSEIF exist&<>0 THEN¶
    LOCATE 15,1:PRINT "A File with that name already"¶
    LOCATE 17,1:PRINT "exists! Replace File? (Y/N)"¶
pause:      ¶
    A$=INKEY$ :IF A$<>"" THEN A$=UCASE$(A$)¶
    IF A$="Y" GOTO continue¶
    IF A$<>"N" GOTO pause¶
    GOTO targetfile¶
  END IF¶
continue:¶
' -------------------------------------------¶
' Produce DATA-ASCII-File¶
'¶
  LOCATE 19,1:PRINT "Producing ASCII-File."¶
  LOCATE 21,1:PRINT "Please be Patient..."¶
  OPEN target$ FOR OUTPUT AS 1¶
    Number&=0¶
    PRINT#1,"RESTORE datas";CHR$(10);¶
    PRINT#1,"datastring$=";CHR$(34);CHR$(34);CHR$(10);¶
    PRINT#1,"FOR i=1 TO ";STR$(Bytes&);CHR$(10);¶
    PRINT#1,"READ a$";CHR$(10);¶
    PRINT#1,"a$=";CHR$(34);"&H";CHR$(34);"+a$";CHR$(10);¶
    PRINT#1,"datastring$=datastring$+CHR$(VAL(a$))";¶
     PRINT#1,CHR$(10);¶
    PRINT#1,"NEXT";CHR$(10);¶
    PRINT#1,"datas:";CHR$(10);¶
¶
¶
Loop:¶
    PRINT#1,"DATA ";¶
    BCount=0¶
Value:      ¶
    PRINT#1,HEX$(PEEK(Buffer&+Number&));¶
    BCount=BCount+1 :Number&=Number&+1¶
    IF Number&<Bytes& THEN¶
      IF BCount<20 THEN ¶
        PRINT#1,",";¶
        GOTO Value¶
```

```
        ELSE¶
           PRINT#1,CHR$(10);¶
           GOTO Loop¶
         END IF¶
       END IF¶
       PRINT#1,CHR$(10);CHR$(10);¶
     CLOSE 1¶
 ' ----------------------------------------¶
 ' Alter .info-file¶
 '¶
   SAVE "DATA-GENINFO"¶
   tmp$=target$+".info"¶
   KILL tmp$¶
   NAME "DATA-GENINFO.info" AS target$+".info"¶
   KILL "DATA-GENINFO"¶
   CLS¶
   PRINT "finished."¶
   CALL FreeMem(Buffer&,Bytes&)¶
   END¶
 ' ----------------------------------------¶
 ' SUBROUTINE¶
 '¶
 SUB CheckFile(Filename$,Length&) STATIC¶
   ChipRAM&=65538&¶
   InfoBytes&=252¶
   Info&=AllocMem&(InfoBytes&,ChipRAM&)¶
   IF Info&=0 THEN ERROR 7¶
   File$=Filename$+CHR$(0)¶
           ¶
 ¶
   DosLock&=Lock&(SADD(File$),-2)¶
   IF DosLock&=0 THEN¶
     Length&=0¶
   ELSE¶
     Dummy&=Examine&(DosLock&,Info&)¶
     Length&=PEEKL(Info&+4)¶
     IF Length&>0 THEN ¶
       Length&=-1¶
     ELSE¶
       Length&=PEEKL(Info&+124)¶
     END IF¶
   END IF¶
   CALL UnLock(DosLock&)¶
   CALL FreeMem(Info&,InfoBytes&)¶
 END SUB¶
```

Variables

A	string, help variable
AllocMem	EXEC routine; reserves memory
Buffer	address of reserved memory
Bytes	length of file being edited
CheckFile	SUB routine; tests for file availability: if yes, then it checks for directory; if not, it checks for length
ChipRAM	option for AllocMem; 2^16 (65536)=clear range, 2^1(2)=chip RAM range
DosLock	file handle for Checkfile routine

`Dummy`	unused variable
`Examine`	DOS routine; looks for file
`File`	filename with concluding 0 for DOS
`Filename`	name of file being edited
`FreeMem`	EXEC routine; frees memory range
`Info`	address of file info structure
`InfoBytes`	length of file info structure
`Length`	file length
`Lock`	DOS routine; blocks access from other programs and provides handle
`Opened`	address of file handle for source file
`PublicRAM`	option for AllocMem; 2^16 (65536)=clear range, 2^1(2)=public range
`UnLock`	DOS routine; releases Lock
`Number&`	counter for DATA values written
`sofar&`	number of bytes read so far
`i`	loop variable
`source`	source file
`target`	target file in ASCII format for DATA
`exist&`	flag:does file exist?
`Tmp`	help variable - temporary file
`xClose`	DOS routine; closes file
`xOpen`	DOS routine; opens file
`xRead`	DOS routine; reads file
`BCount`	byte counter for a line of DATA

6.3.2   Cross-reference list

This program demonstrates a method of reading values from Amiga-BASIC programs stored in binary format. Before doing this, the program you wish to read must have its onboard program control codes removed, as well as any program "garbage" that can occur between the program body and the variable table. Do the following to clean up the program code:

- Load the file you want to check

- SAVE "Filename",A

- Quit AmigaBASIC

- Reload AmigaBASIC

- LOAD "Filename"

- SAVE "Filename",B

Once you do this, you can now send a cross-reference list of this program to a printer using the program below. It displays labels as well as line numbers in the output. Places where branches are set (e.g., GOTO place) are marked by "<- -". If a branch goes to a section of a program not set by a branch marker (e.g., the beginning of a program), a pseudo label appears in parentheses (e.g., "(Program start)"). A "- ->" marks the destination of the branch. Bear in mind that operating system calls and SUB routines are viewed by the AmigaBASIC interpreter as variables. Aside from that, this program is a great method of documenting your programs.

```
' ####################################¶
' # C r o s s R e f e r e n c e  Amiga #¶
' #-----------------------------------#¶
' #      (W) 1987 by Stefan Maelger    #¶
' ####################################¶
'¶
' This program creates a Cross-Reference¶
' of a program on your Printer.¶
' It allows every BINARY format¶
' AmigaBASIC-Program to be documented.¶
' ---------------------------------------¶
' How the AmigaBASIC programmer handled¶
' SUB-Routines and System calls is still¶
' not well known.¶
' ---------------------------------------¶
' ¶
'----Reserve Memory, load PrinterDriver, ----¶
'----Open Library and Variables----¶
 CLEAR,45000&¶
 LPRINT¶
 DECLARE FUNCTION xOpen& LIBRARY¶
 DECLARE FUNCTION xRead% LIBRARY¶
 DECLARE FUNCTION Seek% LIBRARY¶
 LIBRARY "dos.library"¶
 DIM Cross$(5000),names$(1000)¶
¶
 LOCATE 2,2¶
 PRINT CHR$(187);" Cross Reference Amiga ";CHR$(171)¶
 LOCATE 5,2¶
 PRINT "Name of the binary AmigaBASIC-Program:"¶
 LOCATE 7,2¶
 LINE INPUT Filename$¶
 CHDIR "df0:"¶
¶
 BASICcheck Filename$,Result%¶
¶
 LOCATE 10,2¶
 IF Result%=-1 THEN¶
  PRINT "I can not find any Info-File."¶
 ELSEIF Result%=0 THEN¶
  PRINT "Read-Error!"¶
 ELSEIF Result%=1 THEN¶
  PRINT "This is Not an AmigaBASIC-Program."¶
 END IF¶
```

```
IF Result%<>2 THEN¶
 BEEP¶
 WHILE INKEY$=""¶
 WEND¶
 RUN¶
END IF¶
PRINT CHR$(34);Filename$;".info";CHR$(34)¶
PRINT ¶
PRINT " made with this Program as AmigaBASIC-File."¶
¶
OpenFile Filename$,handle&¶
¶
LOCATE 14,2¶
IF handle&=0 THEN¶
 PRINT "AAAaargh! I can't find ";CHR$(34);¶
 PRINT Filename$;CHR$(34);"!!!"¶
 BEEP¶
 WHILE INKEY$="":WEND:RUN¶
ELSE¶
 PRINT "File opened."¶
END IF¶
LOCATE 16,2¶
¶
HeaderCheck handle&,Header$¶
¶
IF ASC(Header$)<>&HF5 THEN¶
 PRINT "Sorry, I can only Cross-Reference binary-Files"¶
 BEEP¶
 WHILE INKEY$="":WEND:RUN¶
ELSE¶
 PRINT "File has binary Format"¶
 PRINT :PRINT "Please be patient. ";¶
 PRINT "I'll report on my status..."¶
END IF¶
pointer%=-1¶
¶
main:¶
¶
GetLine handle&,Current$¶
¶
IF LEN(Current$)<4 THEN¶
 PRINT ¶
 PRINT " Reached the end of Binary-Codes"¶
 PRINT :PRINT " getting Variable Table."¶
 GOTO Vartab¶
END IF¶
IF ASC(Current$)=128 THEN¶
 pointer%=pointer%+1¶
 Cross$(pointer%)=CHR$(128)+MID$(Current$,4,2)¶
 Current$=MID$(Current$,6)¶
ELSE¶
 Current$=MID$(Current$,4)¶
END IF¶
¶
GetToken:¶
¶
```

```
  Token%=ASC(Current$+CHR$(0))¶
  IF Token%=0 GOTO main¶
¶
'----Command Token?----   ¶
 IF Token%>127 THEN¶
  IF Token%=175 OR Token%=141 GOTO main¶
  IF Token%=190 OR Token%>247 THEN¶
   Current$=MID$(Current$,3)¶
  ELSE¶
   Current$=MID$(Current$,2)¶
  END IF¶
  GOTO GetToken¶
 END IF¶
¶
'----String?----   ¶
 IF Token%=34 THEN¶
  Byte%=INSTR(2,Current$,CHR$(34))¶
  IF Byte%=0 GOTO main¶
  Current$=MID$(Current$,Byte%+1)¶
  GOTO GetToken¶
 END IF¶
¶
'---- 2-Byte-Value Sequence?----   ¶
 IF Token%=1 OR Token%=11 OR Token%=12 OR Token%=28 THEN¶
  Current$=MID$(Current$,4)¶
  GOTO GetToken¶
 END IF¶
¶
'---- 1-Byte-Value Sequence?----   ¶
 IF Token%=15 THEN Current$=MID$(Current$,3):GOTO
GetToken¶
¶
'---- 4-Byte-Value Sequence?----   ¶
 IF Token%=29 OR Token%=30 THEN¶
  Current$=MID$(Current$,6)¶
  GOTO GetToken¶
 END IF¶
¶
'---- 8-Byte-Value Sequence?----   ¶
 IF Token%=31 THEN Current$=MID$(Current$,10):GOTO
GetToken¶
¶
'---- Is it a Label?----   ¶
 IF Token%=2 THEN¶
  pointer%=pointer%+1¶
  Cross$(pointer%)=LEFT$(Current$,3)¶
  Current$=MID$(Current$,4)¶
  GOTO GetToken¶
 END IF¶
¶
'---- Is it a Branch Statement?----   ¶
 IF Token%=3 OR Token%=14 THEN¶
  pointer%=pointer%+1¶
  Cross$(pointer%)=CHR$(Token%)+MID$(Current$,3,2)¶
  Current$=MID$(Current$,5)¶
  GOTO GetToken¶
```

```
      END IF¶
      Current$=MID$(Current$,2)¶
      GOTO GetToken¶
    ¶
    Vartab:¶
    ¶
      p2%=-1¶
    ¶
    notforever:¶
    ¶
      GetLength handle&,bytes%¶
    ¶
      IF bytes%=0 GOTO GoOn¶
    ¶
      GetName handle&,Current$,bytes%¶
    ¶
      p2%=p2%+1¶
      names$(p2%)=Current$¶
      GOTO notforever¶
    ¶
    GoOn:¶
    ¶
      IF pointer%=-1 THEN¶
        PRINT ¶
        PRINT "I have no Label or Line Number"¶
        PRINT ¶
        PRINT "that I can discover!"¶
        BEEP¶
        WHILE INKEY$="":WEND:RUN¶
      ELSEIF p2%=-1 THEN¶
        PRINT ¶
        PRINT "Hmm - no Variable Table"¶
        BEEP¶
        WHILE INKEY$="":WEND:RUN¶
      ELSE ¶
        PRINT :PRINT " Getting Data."¶
      END IF¶
    ¶
      LPRINT ">>> CrossReference Amiga <<<"¶
      LPRINT "----------------------------"¶
      LPRINT "Program: ";Filename$¶
      LPRINT¶
      FOR i=0 TO pointer%¶
        ascii%=ASC(Cross$(i))¶
        IF ascii%=2 THEN¶
          LPRINT names$(CVI(MID$(Cross$(i),2)));":"¶
          FOR j=0 TO pointer%¶
            IF ASC(Cross$(j))=3 THEN¶
              IF CVI(MID$(Cross$(j),2))=CVI(MID$(Cross$(i),2))
    THEN¶
                k=j¶
                WHILE k>-1¶
                  k=k-1¶
                  IF k>-1 THEN¶
                    IF ASC(Cross$(k))=2 THEN¶
                      LPRINT "  <-- ";¶
```

```
        LPRINT names$(CVI(MID$(Cross$(k),2)))¶
        k=-2¶
      ELSEIF ASC(Cross$(k))=128 THEN¶
        LPRINT "  <-- ";CVI(MID$(Cross$(k),2))¶
        k=-2¶
      END IF¶
     END IF¶
    WEND  ¶
    IF k=-1 THEN LPRINT "  <--(Program-Start)"¶
   END IF¶
  END IF¶
 NEXT j¶
ELSEIF ascii%=3 THEN¶
 LPRINT "  --> ";names$(CVI(MID$(Cross$(i),2)))¶
ELSEIF ascii%=14 THEN¶
 LPRINT "  --> ";CVI(MID$(Cross$(i),2))¶
ELSEIF ascii%=128 THEN¶
 LPRINT CVI(MID$(Cross$(i),2))¶
 FOR j=0 TO pointer%¶
  IF ASC(Cross$(j))=14 THEN¶
   IF CVI(MID$(Cross$(j),2))=CVI(MID$(Cross$(i),2))
THEN¶
     k=j¶
     WHILE k>-1¶
      k=k-1¶
      IF k>-1 THEN¶
       IF ASC(Cross$(k))=2 THEN¶
        LPRINT "  <-- ";¶
        LPRINT names$(CVI(MID$(Cross$(k),2)))¶
        k=-2¶
       ELSEIF ASC(Cross$(k))=128 THEN¶
        LPRINT "  <-- ";CVI(MID$(Cross$(k),2))¶
        k=-2¶
       END IF¶
      END IF¶
     WEND  ¶
     IF k=-1 THEN LPRINT "  <--(Programm-Start)"¶
    END IF¶
   END IF¶
  NEXT j¶
 END IF¶
NEXT i¶
PRINT :PRINT "Finished."¶
BEEP¶
WHILE INKEY$="":WEND:RUN¶
    ¶
SUB GetName(handle&,Current$,bytes%) STATIC¶
  Current$=SPACE$(bytes%)¶
  Length%=xRead%(handle&,SADD(Current$),bytes%)¶
END SUB¶
¶
SUB GetLength(handle&,bytes%) STATIC¶
  Current$=CHR$(0)¶
readit:  ¶
  Length%=xRead%(handle&,SADD(Current$),1)¶
  IF Length%=0 THEN¶
```

```
        CALL xClose(handle&)¶
        bytes%=0¶
        EXIT SUB¶
      END IF¶
      bytes%=ASC(Current$)¶
      IF bytes%=0 THEN readit¶
      IF bytes%>60 THEN readit¶
      ¶
   END SUB¶
        ¶
   SUB GetLine(handle&,Current$) STATIC¶
     Current$=STRING$(3,0)¶
     Length%=xRead%(handle&,SADD(Current$),3)¶
     OldPos%=Seek%(handle&,-3,0)¶
     LoL%=ASC(MID$(Current$,2,1))¶
     IF LoL%=0 THEN¶
        EXIT SUB¶
     ELSE¶
        Current$=STRING$(LoL%,0)¶
        Length%=xRead%(handle&,SADD(Current$),LoL%)¶
     END IF¶
   END SUB¶
      ¶
   SUB HeaderCheck(handle&,Header$) STATIC¶
     Header$="1"¶
     OldPos%=Seek%(handle&,0,-1)¶
     gotit%=xRead%(handle&,SADD(Header$),1)¶
   END SUB¶
          ¶
   SUB OpenFile(Filename$,handle&) STATIC¶
     file$=Filename$+CHR$(0)¶
     handle&=xOpen&(SADD(file$),1005)¶
   END SUB¶
       ¶
   SUB BASICcheck(Filename$,Result%) STATIC¶
     file$=Filename$+".info"+CHR$(0)¶
     Default.Tool$=SPACE$(20)¶
     handle&=xOpen&(SADD(file$),1005)¶
     IF handle&=0 THEN¶
       Result%=-1¶
     ELSE¶
       OldPos%=Seek%(handle&,-20,1)¶
       gotit%=xRead%(handle&,SADD(Default.Tool$),20)¶
       IF gotit%<20 THEN¶
         Result%=0¶
       ELSE¶
         IF INSTR(Default.Tool$,"AmigaBASIC")>0 THEN¶
           Result%=2¶
         ELSE¶
           Result%=1¶
         END IF¶
       END IF¶
       CALL xClose(handle&)¶
     END IF¶
   END SUB¶
```

Variables
BASICcheck	SUB routine; test for Default Tools
Byte	pointer to byte in string
Bytes	length of file being edited
Cross	string array; buffer for branch markers and jumps
Current	string; BASIC line read
Default.Tool	string; reads Default Tool
Filename	string; name of file to be edited
GetLength	SUB routine; reads label length
GetLine	SUB routine; reads line
GetName	SUB routine; reads label name
Header	string; file header byte
HeaderCheck	SUB routine; checks for header type
Length	file length
LoL	line length
OldPos	old pointer position in file
OpenFile	SUB routine; opens file
Result	flag; result of search
Seek	DOS routine; moves read/write pointer in file
Token	address of file handle for source file
ascii	code value in Cross$
File	string; filename ended with 0 for DOS routines
gotit	bytes read so far
handle	file handle address
i	loop variable
j	loop variable
k	loop variable
names	string array; branch marker names
p2	help variable
pointer	help variable
xClose	DOS routine; closes file
xOpen	DOS routine; opens file
xRead	DOS routine; reads file

6.3.3   Blank line killer

Now that you know how to make blank lines, you should know how to get rid of them. The following program removes these lines for you. Before using this program, any control codes and garbage must be removed (see the preceding section for instructions on doing this).

Note: When you type in this program, you could create small errors that can ruin the programs being modified. Use *copies* of the program you want to modify only, and test the main program with these copies to make sure that it runs properly. This program alters the file and saves it out again. The current window closes to save memory. If there are small errors in the line killer program, such as an endless loop, you won't be able to recover the program. If the program seems as if it's taking a while at first, don't panic—the time factor depends on the file being modified.

```
' #####################################¶
' #      Blank Line-Killer   Amiga        #¶
' #-------------------------------------#¶
' #     (W) 1987 by Stefan Maelger      #¶
' #####################################¶
'¶
' "dos.bmap" and "exec.bmap" must be on¶
' Disk or in LIBS:¶
' -------------------------------------¶
'¶
  DECLARE FUNCTION AllocMem&  LIBRARY¶
  DECLARE FUNCTION Lock&      LIBRARY¶
  DECLARE FUNCTION Examine&   LIBRARY¶
  DECLARE FUNCTION xOpen&     LIBRARY¶
  DECLARE FUNCTION xRead&     LIBRARY¶
  DECLARE FUNCTION xWrite&    LIBRARY¶
  LIBRARY "exec.library"¶
  LIBRARY "dos.library"¶
  WINDOW CLOSE WINDOW(0)¶
  WINDOW 1,"Blank Line-Killer",(0,0)-(250,50),16¶
Allocation.1:¶
  COLOR 3,1:CLS¶
  info&=AllocMem&(252&,65538&)¶
  IF info&=0 THEN¶
    ALLOCERR ¶
    GOTO Allocation.1¶
  END IF ¶
Source:  ¶
  REQUEST "SOURCE"¶
  SELECT box%¶
  IF box% THEN CALL FreeMem(info&,252):SYSTEM¶
  CHDIR "df0:"¶
GetFilename:  ¶
  LINPUT Filename$¶
  GETINFO Filename$,info&,Length&¶
  IF Length&<1 THEN¶
    IF Length&=-1 THEN¶
      DIRERR¶
    ELSEIF Length&=0 THEN¶
      FILEERR¶
    END IF¶
    GOTO GetFilename¶
  END IF¶
Allocation.2:¶
  COLOR 3,1:CLS  ¶
  buffer&=AllocMem&(Length&,65537&)¶
```

```
      IF buffer&=0 THEN¶
        ALLOCERR¶
        GOTO Allocation.2¶
      END IF¶
      LOADFILE Filename$,buffer&,Length&¶
      IF Filename$="" THEN¶
        CALL FreeMem(buffer&,Length&)¶
        LOADERR¶
        GOTO GetFilename¶
      END IF¶
      IF PEEK(buffer&)<>&HF5 THEN¶
        CALL FreeMem(buffer&,Length&)¶
        FORMERR¶
        GOTO GetFilename¶
      END IF¶
      NEWFILE Filename$,handle&¶
      IF handle&=0 THEN¶
        CALL FreeMem(buffer&,Length&)¶
        CALL FreeMem(info&,252&)¶
        OPENERR¶
        SYSTEM¶
      END IF¶
      Bytes&=1¶
      DWRITE handle&,buffer&,Bytes&¶
      IF Bytes&=0 THEN¶
        CALL xClose(handle&)¶
        CALL FreeMem(buffer&,Length&)¶
        CALL FreeMem(info&,252&)¶
        WRITEERR¶
        SYSTEM¶
      END IF¶
      pointer&=buffer&+1¶
GetLength:¶
    Bytes&=PEEK(pointer&+1)¶
    IF Bytes&=4 THEN¶
      pointer&=pointer&+4¶
      GOTO GetLength¶
    ELSEIF Bytes&>4 THEN¶
      DWRITE handle&,pointer&,Bytes&¶
      IF Bytes&=0 THEN¶
        CALL xClose(handle&)¶
        CALL FreeMem(buffer&,Length&)¶
        CALL FreeMem(info&,252&)¶
        WRITEERR¶
        SYSTEM¶
      END IF¶
      pointer&=pointer&+Bytes&¶
      GOTO GetLength¶
    ELSE¶
      Bytes&=Length&-(pointer&-buffer&+1)¶
      DWRITE handle&,pointer&,Bytes&¶
      IF Bytes&=0 THEN¶
        CALL xClose(handle&)¶
        CALL FreeMem(buffer&,Length&)¶
        CALL FreeMem(info&,252&)¶
        WRITEERR¶
```

```
            SYSTEM¶
          END IF¶
      END IF¶
      CALL xClose(handle&)¶
      CALL FreeMem(buffer&,Length&)¶
      CALL FreeMem(info&,252&)¶
      LIBRARY CLOSE¶
      COLOR 3,1:CLS:LOCATE 2,2:PRINT "Ready."¶
      WHILE INKEY$="":WEND¶
      SYSTEM¶
  SUB WRITEERR STATIC¶
      COLOR 1,3:CLS:LOCATE 2,2:PRINT "ERROR:  Write-error."¶
      ShowCont¶
  END SUB  ¶
  SUB DWRITE(handle&,adr&,Length&) STATIC¶
      written&=xWrite&(handle&,adr&,Length&)¶
      IF written&<>Length& THEN Length&=0¶
  END SUB¶
  SUB OPENERR STATIC¶
      COLOR 1,3:CLS:LOCATE 2,2:PRINT "ERROR:  Can't open
  File."¶
      ShowCont¶
  END SUB  ¶
  SUB NEWFILE(Filename$,handle&) STATIC¶
      File$=Filename$+CHR$(0)¶
      handle&=xOpen&(SADD(File$),1005)¶
  END SUB  ¶
  SUB FORMERR STATIC¶
      COLOR 1,3:CLS:LOCATE 2,2:PRINT "ERROR:  Not a binary
  File."¶
      ShowCont¶
  END SUB  ¶
  SUB LOADERR STATIC¶
      COLOR 1,3:CLS:LOCATE 2,2:PRINT "ERROR:  Load-error."¶
      ShowCont¶
  END SUB¶
  SUB LOADFILE(Filename$,buffer&,Length&) STATIC¶
      File$=Filename$+CHR$(0)
  :handle&=xOpen&(SADD(File$),1005)¶
      IF handle&=0 THEN¶
         Filename$=""¶
      ELSE ¶
         inBuffer&=xRead&(handle&,buffer&,Length&)¶
         CALL xClose(handle&)¶
         IF inBuffer&<>Length& THEN Filename$=""¶
      END IF¶
  END SUB¶
  SUB FILEERR STATIC¶
      COLOR 1,3:CLS:LOCATE 2,2:PRINT "ERROR:  File not
  found."¶
      ShowCont¶
  END SUB  ¶
  SUB DIRERR STATIC¶
      COLOR 1,3:CLS:LOCATE 2,2¶
      PRINT "ERROR:  File is a Directory."¶
      ShowCont¶
```

```
END SUB¶
SUB GETINFO(Filename$,info&,Length&) STATIC¶
  File$=Filename$+CHR$(0) :DosLock&=Lock&(SADD(File$),-
2)¶
  IF DosLock&=0 THEN              ¶
    Length&=0¶
  ELSE¶
    Dummy&=Examine&(DosLock&,info&)¶
    IF PEEKL(info&+4)>0 THEN¶
      Length&=-1¶
    ELSE¶
      Length&=PEEKL(info&+124)¶
    END IF¶
  END IF¶
  CALL UnLock(DosLock&)¶
END SUB¶
SUB LINPUT(Filename$) STATIC¶
  COLOR 3,1:CLS:WINDOW 2,"Filename:",(0,0)-(250,10),0¶
  WINDOW OUTPUT 1:LOCATE 5,2¶
  PRINT "Name of a binary saved File";¶
  LINE INPUT Filename$:WINDOW CLOSE 2¶
END SUB¶
SUB SELECT(box%) STATIC¶
Check:  ¶
  WHILE MOUSE(0)=0:WEND:x=MOUSE(1):y=MOUSE(2)¶
  IF y>27 AND y<43 THEN¶
     IF x>9 AND x<38 THEN box%=0:EXIT SUB¶
     IF x>177 AND x<238 THEN box%=-1:EXIT SUB¶
  END IF¶
  GOTO Check¶
END SUB¶
SUB ALLOCERR STATIC¶
COLOR 1,3:CLS:LOCATE 2,2:PRINT "ERROR:  Allocation
denied."¶
  ShowCont¶
END SUB¶
SUB ShowCont STATIC¶
  LOCATE 4,2:PRINT "Press SPACE to continue,"¶
  LOCATE 5,7:PRINT "ESCAPE to exit.";¶
  WHILE a$<>CHR$(32) AND a$<>CHR$(27)¶
    a$=INKEY$¶
  WEND¶
  IF a$=CHR$(27) THEN SYSTEM¶
END SUB¶
SUB REQUEST(disk$) STATIC¶
  COLOR 3,1:CLS¶
  LOCATE 2,2:PRINT "INSERT ";disk$;" DISK INTO DRIVE"¶
  LOCATE 3,14:PRINT "DF0:":LOCATE 5,3:PRINT "OK";¶
  LOCATE 5,24:PRINT "CANCEL";:LINE(10,28)-(37,42),3,b¶
  LINE(178,28)-(237,42),3,b¶
END SUB¶
```

Variables		
	ALLOCERR	SUB routine; memory reservation error
	AllocMem	EXEC routine; reserves memory
	Bytes	length of file being edited
	DIERR	SUB routine; error—no file

DWRITE	SUB routine; write to file
DosLock	file handle of Lock
Dummy	unused variable
Examine	DOS routine; looks for file
FILEERR	SUB routine; error
FORMERR	SUB routine; error
File	filename with concluding 0 for DOS
Filename	name of file being edited
FreeMem	EXEC routine; frees memory range
GETINFO	SUB routine; file check
LINPUT	SUB routine; input
LOADERR	SUB routine; error
LOADFILE	SUB routine; load program
Length	file length
Lock	DOS routine; blocks access from other programs and provides handle
NEWFILE	SUB routine; create new file
OPENERR	SUB routine; error
REQUEST	SUB routine; draw primitive requester
SELECT	SUB routine; select through mouse click
ShowCont	SUB routine; show options
UnLock	DOS routine; releases Lock
WRITEERR	SUB routine; error
a	help variable
adr	address
b	help variable
box	help variable
buffer	address of reserved memory
disk	diskette
handle	address of file handle
inBuffer	bytes read
info	address of file info structure
pointer	help variable
written	bytes written
x	help variable
xClose	DOS routine; closes file
xOpen	DOS routine; opens file
xRead	DOS routine; reads file
xWrite	DOS routine; writes to file
y	help variable

6.3.4   REM killer

This program has a lot of the same code as the line killer in Section
6.3.3. Load that program, change the necessary text and save the new
program under a different name from the name you assigned in Section
6.3.3.

```
' ######################################¶
' #   K i l l - R e m a r k    Amiga    #¶
' #------------------------------------#¶
' #      (W) 1987 by Stefan Maelger     #¶
' ######################################¶
'¶
' "dos.bmap" and "exec.bmap" must be on¶
' Disk or in LIB:¶
' ------------------------------------¶
'¶
  DECLARE FUNCTION AllocMem& LIBRARY¶
  DECLARE FUNCTION Lock&     LIBRARY¶
  DECLARE FUNCTION Examine&  LIBRARY¶
  DECLARE FUNCTION xOpen&    LIBRARY¶
  DECLARE FUNCTION xRead&    LIBRARY¶
  LIBRARY "exec.library"¶
  LIBRARY "dos.library"¶
  WINDOW CLOSE WINDOW(0)¶
  WINDOW 1,"Kill-Remark",(0,0)-(250,50),16¶
Allocation.1:¶
  COLOR 3,1:CLS¶
  info&=AllocMem&(252&,65538&)¶
  IF info&=0 THEN¶
    ALLOCERR ¶
    GOTO Allocation.1¶
  END IF ¶
Source:   ¶
  REQUEST "SOURCE"¶
  SELECT box%¶
  IF box% THEN CALL FreeMem(info&,252):SYSTEM¶
  CHDIR "df0:"¶
GetFilename:   ¶
  LINPUT filename$¶
  GETINFO filename$,info&,Length&¶
  IF Length&<1 THEN¶
    IF Length&=-1 THEN¶
      DIRERR¶
    ELSEIF Length&=0 THEN¶
      FILEERR¶
    END IF¶
    GOTO GetFilename¶
  END IF¶
Allocation.2:¶
  COLOR 3,1:CLS  ¶
  buffer&=AllocMem&(Length&,65537&)¶
  IF buffer&=0 THEN¶
    ALLOCERR¶
    GOTO Allocation.2¶
  END IF¶
  LOADFILE filename$,buffer&,Length&¶
  IF filename$="" THEN¶
    CALL FreeMem(buffer&,Length&) ¶
    LOADERR¶
    GOTO GetFilename¶
  END IF¶
  IF PEEK(buffer&)<>&HF5 THEN¶
```

```
              CALL FreeMem(buffer&,Length&)¶
              FORMERR¶
              GOTO GetFilename¶
          END IF¶
          NEWFILE filename$¶
          Bytes&=1¶
          DWRITE buffer&,Bytes&¶
          pointer&=buffer&+1¶
     GetLength:¶
        Bytes&=PEEK(pointer&+1)¶
        IF Bytes&=4 THEN¶
          pointer&=pointer&+4¶
          GOTO GetLength¶
        ELSEIF Bytes&>4 THEN¶
          IF PEEK(pointer&)=128 THEN offs&=6 ELSE offs&=4¶
          IF PEEK(pointer&+offs&)<>175 THEN¶
            DWRITE pointer&,Bytes&¶
          END IF   ¶
          pointer&=pointer&+Bytes&¶
          GOTO GetLength¶
        ELSE¶
          IF ((pointer&-buffer&+1)MOD 2)=1 THEN¶
            pointer&=pointer&-1¶
          END IF¶
          Bytes&=Length&-(pointer&-buffer&+1)+1¶
          DWRITE pointer&,Bytes&¶
        END IF¶
        CLOSE 1¶
        OPEN filename$+"-RL.info" FOR OUTPUT AS 1¶
        OPEN filename$+".info" FOR INPUT AS 2¶
        PRINT#1,INPUT$(LOF(2),2);¶
        CLOSE 2,1¶
        KILL filename$+"-RL.info.info"¶
        ¶
        CALL FreeMem(buffer&,Length&)¶
        CALL FreeMem(info&,252&)¶
        LIBRARY CLOSE¶
        COLOR 3,1:CLS:LOCATE 2,2:PRINT "Ready."¶
        WHILE INKEY$="":WEND¶
        SYSTEM¶
     SUB WRITEERR STATIC¶
        COLOR 1,3:CLS:LOCATE 2,2:PRINT "ERROR:  Write-error."¶
        ShowCont¶
     END SUB   ¶
     SUB DWRITE(adr&,Length&) STATIC¶
        FOR i&=1 TO Length&¶
          PRINT#1,CHR$(PEEK(adr&-1+i&));¶
        NEXT¶
     END SUB¶
     SUB OPENERR STATIC¶
        COLOR 1,3:CLS:LOCATE 2,2:PRINT "ERROR:  Can't open
     File."¶
        ShowCont¶
     END SUB   ¶
     SUB NEWFILE(filename$) STATIC¶
        File$=filename$+"-RL"¶
```

```
    OPEN File$ FOR OUTPUT AS 1  ¶
END SUB  ¶
SUB FORMERR STATIC¶
COLOR 1,3:CLS:LOCATE 2,2:PRINT "ERROR:   Not a binary
File."¶
  ShowCont¶
END SUB  ¶
SUB LOADERR STATIC¶
  COLOR 1,3:CLS:LOCATE 2,2:PRINT "ERROR:   Load-error."¶
  ShowCont¶
END SUB¶
SUB LOADFILE(filename$,buffer&,Length&) STATIC¶
  File$=filename$+CHR$(0)
:handle&=xOpen&(SADD(File$),1005)¶
  IF handle&=0 THEN¶
    filename$=""¶
  ELSE  ¶
    inBuffer&=xRead&(handle&,buffer&,Length&)¶
    CALL xClose(handle&)¶
    IF inBuffer&<>Length& THEN filename$=""¶
  END IF¶
END SUB¶
SUB FILEERR STATIC¶
  COLOR 1,3:CLS:LOCATE 2,2:PRINT "ERROR:   File not
found."¶
  ShowCont¶
END SUB  ¶
SUB DIRERR STATIC¶
  COLOR 1,3:CLS:LOCATE 2,2¶
  PRINT "ERROR:  File is a Directory."¶
  ShowCont¶
END SUB¶
SUB GETINFO(filename$,info&,Length&) STATIC¶
  File$=filename$+CHR$(0)  :DosLock&=Lock&(SADD(File$),-
2)¶
  IF DosLock&=0 THEN                ¶
    Length&=0¶
  ELSE¶
    Dummy&=Examine&(DosLock&,info&)¶
    IF PEEKL(info&+4)>0 THEN  ¶
      Length&=-1  ¶
    ELSE  ¶
      Length&=PEEKL(info&+124)¶
    END IF¶
  END IF¶
  CALL UnLock(DosLock&)¶
END SUB¶
SUB LINPUT(filename$) STATIC¶
  COLOR 3,1:CLS:WINDOW 2,"Filename:",(0,0)-(250,10),0¶
  WINDOW OUTPUT 1:LOCATE 5,2¶
  PRINT "Name of a binary saved File";¶
  LINE INPUT filename$:WINDOW CLOSE 2¶
END SUB¶
SUB SELECT(box%) STATIC¶
Check:  ¶
  WHILE MOUSE(0)=0:WEND:x=MOUSE(1):y=MOUSE(2)¶
```

```
           IF y>27 AND y<43 THEN¶
             IF x>9 AND x<38 THEN box%=0:EXIT SUB¶
             IF x>177 AND x<238 THEN box%=-1:EXIT SUB¶
           END IF¶
           GOTO Check¶
        END SUB¶
        SUB ALLOCERR STATIC¶
          COLOR 1,3:CLS:LOCATE 2,2:PRINT "ERROR:  Allocation
        denied."¶
          ShowCont¶
        END SUB¶
        SUB ShowCont STATIC¶
          LOCATE 4,2:PRINT "Press SPACE to continue,"¶
          LOCATE 5,7:PRINT "ESCAPE to exit.";¶
          WHILE a$<>CHR$(32) AND a$<>CHR$(27)¶
            a$=INKEY$¶
          WEND¶
          IF a$=CHR$(27) THEN SYSTEM¶
        END SUB¶
        SUB REQUEST(disk$) STATIC¶
          COLOR 3,1:CLS¶
          LOCATE 2,2:PRINT "INSERT ";disk$;" DISK INTO DRIVE"¶
          LOCATE 3,14:PRINT "DF0:":LOCATE 5,3:PRINT "OK";¶
          LOCATE 5,24:PRINT "CANCEL";:LINE(10,28)-(37,42),3,b¶
          LINE(178,28)-(237,42),3,b¶
        END SUB¶
```

Variables	ALLOCERR	SUB routine; memory reservation error
	AllocMem	EXEC routine; reserves memory
	Bytes	length of file being edited
	DIERR	SUB routine; error—no file
	DWRITE	SUB routine; write to file
	DosLock	file handle of Lock
	Dummy	unused variable
	Examine	DOS routine; looks for file
	FILEERR	SUB routine; error
	FORMERR	SUB routine; error
	File	filename with concluding 0 for DOS
	FreeMem	EXEC routine; frees memory range
	GETINFO	SUB routine; file check
	LINPUT	SUB routine; input
	LOADERR	SUB routine; error
	LOAD LE	SUB routine; load program
	Length	file length
	Lock	DOS routine; blocks access from other programs and provides handle
	NEWFILE	SUB routine; create new file
	OPENERR	SUB routine; error
	REQUEST	SUB routine; draw primitive requester
	SELECT	SUB routine; select through mouse click
	ShowCont	SUB routine; show options
	UnLock	DOS routine; releases Lock
	WRITEERR	SUB routine; error
	a	help variable

```
adr           address
b             help variable
box           help variable
buffer        address of reserved memory
disk          diskette
filename      name of file
handle        address of file handle
i             help variable
inBuffer      bytes read
info          address of file info structure
offs          offset
pointer       help variable
written       bytes written
x             help variable
xClose        DOS routine; closes file
xOpen         DOS routine; opens file
xRead         DOS routine; reads file
y             help variable
```

6.3.5   Listing variables

You may look at a listing for an older BASIC program, and wonder how you can solve any of its problems. Part of human nature lies in doing no more work than necessary. You want to avoid detailed documentation, and at the same time, keep from being buried in a stack of program printouts.

Thanks to modular programming, you can store a collection of short routines on diskette, and merge them into programs as needed. Documenting these short routines is indispensable. Also, many magazines from which you get program listings usually supply detailed documentation.

The program here gives variable lists and label names. These items are vital to documenting program code. For example, you could check out the variable lists of two files before MERGEing one to the other. This avoids any major rewrites on both programs for changing variables to match/conflict. Bear in mind that the variable list program can view SUB programs and operating system routines as variables, even if the variable types are different. This kind of thing can occur in other aspects of BASIC with DEFINT xxx (e.g., DEFINT a-c). For example, if you use a variable named Anton$, this variable appears in the list under Anton. If you want the program to ignore uppercase and lowercase during sorting, remove the four UCASE$() statements after the display label.

Note: The loading and saving conventions used in the two preceding programs apply to this section as well.

```
' #####################################¶
' #  V a r i a b l e - L i s t  Amiga  #¶
' #-----------------------------------#¶
' #       (W) 1987 by Stefan Maelger   #¶
' #####################################¶
'¶
' "dos.bmap" and "exec.bmap" must be on¶
' Disk of in LIB:¶
' -----------------------------------¶
'¶
  CLEAR,50000&¶
  DECLARE FUNCTION AllocMem& LIBRARY¶
  DECLARE FUNCTION Lock&     LIBRARY¶
  DECLARE FUNCTION Examine&  LIBRARY¶
  DECLARE FUNCTION xOpen&    LIBRARY¶
  DECLARE FUNCTION xRead&    LIBRARY¶
  LIBRARY "exec.library"¶
  LIBRARY "dos.library"¶
  WINDOW CLOSE WINDOW(0)¶
  DIM varname$(2000),var%(2000),er$(5)¶
  FOR i=0 TO 5:READ er$(i):NEXT¶
¶
DATA "File contains no binary."¶
DATA "Read-Error.","File open error."¶
DATA "File is a directory.","File not found."¶
DATA "Allocation denied."¶
¶
nextTry:¶
  REQUEST "Place Disk into Drive df0.",1,"OK","",flag%¶
  WINPUT filename$¶
  CHECKFILE filename$,buffer&¶
  IF buffer&<0 THEN¶
    e%=6+buffer&¶
    REQUEST er$(e%),2,"CANCEL","QUIT",flag%¶
    IF flag%=2 THEN LIBRARY CLOSE:SYSTEM¶
    GOTO nextTry¶
  END IF¶
  pointer&=buffer&+1¶
¶
ReadLine:¶
  SETPOINTER pointer&,flag%¶
  IF flag%=1 GOTO ReadNames¶
¶
ReadToken:¶
  CHECKTOKEN pointer&,number%¶
  IF number%<0 GOTO ReadLine¶
  var%(number%)=1:GOTO ReadToken¶
¶
ReadNames:¶
  current%=0¶
¶
searching:¶
  IF PEEK(pointer&)=0 OR PEEK(pointer&)>&H60 THEN¶
    pointer&=pointer&+1:GOTO searching¶
  END IF¶
¶
```

```
getlength:¶
  length%=PEEK(pointer&)¶
  IF length%=0 GOTO display¶
  FOR i%=1 TO length%¶
    pointer&=pointer&+1¶

varname$(current%)=varname$(current%)+CHR$(PEEK(pointer&)
)¶
  NEXT¶
  current%=current%+1¶
  pointer&=pointer&+1:GOTO getlength¶
¶
display:¶
  flag%=1:first%=0:last%=current%-2¶
  WHILE flag%=1¶
    flag%=0¶
    FOR i%=first% TO last%¶
      IF UCASE$(varname$(i%))>UCASE$(varname$(i%+1))
THEN¶
        SWAP varname$(i%),varname$(i%+1)¶
        SWAP var%(i%),var%(i%+1)¶
        flag%=1¶
      END IF¶
    NEXT¶
    start%=start%+1:flag%=0¶
    FOR i%=last% TO first% STEP -1¶
      IF UCASE$(varname$(i%))<UCASE$(varname$(i%-1))
THEN¶
        SWAP varname$(i%),varname$(i%-1)¶
        SWAP var%(i%),var%(i%-1)¶
        flag%=1¶
      END IF¶
    NEXT¶
    last%=last%-1¶
  WEND¶
¶
Display2:   ¶
  BEEP¶
  REQUEST "List to Screen?",2,"YES","NO",sflag%¶
  REQUEST "List to Printer?",2,"YES","NO",pflag%¶
  REQUEST "Save as ASCII-File?",2,"YES","NO",fflag%¶
  IF sflag%=2 AND pflag%=2 AND fflag%=2 GOTO ausgabe2¶
  IF sflag%=1 THEN WINDOW 2,"Variables:",(0,0)-
(240,180),31¶
  IF fflag%=1 THEN¶
    OPEN filename$+".V" FOR OUTPUT AS 1¶
    PRINT#1,CHR$(10);"Variable-List:";¶
    PRINT#1,CHR$(10);"--------------";CHR$(10);CHR$(10);¶
  END IF¶
  IF pflag%=1 THEN¶
    LPRINT "Variable-List from:"¶
    LPRINT filename$:LPRINT¶
  END IF¶
  FOR i%=0 TO current%-1¶
    IF var%(i%)=1 THEN¶
      IF sflag%=1 THEN PRINT varname$(i%)¶
```

224

```
         IF pflag%=1 THEN LPRINT varname$(i%)¶
         IF fflag%=1 THEN PRINT#1,varname$(i%);CHR$(10);¶
      END IF¶
   NEXT¶
   IF fflag%=1 THEN CLOSE 1¶
   REQUEST "Ready.",1,"OK","",flag%¶
   LIBRARY CLOSE¶
   SYSTEM¶
   ¶
SUB CHECKTOKEN(a&,n%) STATIC¶
PeekToken:¶
   t%=PEEK(a&):a&=a&+1¶
   IF t%=0 THEN strflag%=0:n%=-1:EXIT SUB¶
   IF strflag%=1 AND t%<>34 GOTO PeekToken¶
   IF t%>127 THEN¶
      IF t%>247 THEN a&=a&+1¶
      GOTO PeekToken¶
   ELSEIF t%=1 THEN¶
      n%=CVI(CHR$(PEEK(a&))+CHR$(PEEK(a&+1))):a&=a&+2:EXIT
SUB¶
   ELSEIF t%=2 OR t%=11 OR t%=12 OR t%=28 THEN¶
      a&=a&+2:GOTO PeekToken¶
   ELSEIF t%=15 THEN¶
      a&=a&+1:GOTO PeekToken¶
   ELSEIF t%=29 OR t%=30 THEN¶
      a&=a&+4:GOTO PeekToken¶
   ELSEIF t%=31 THEN¶
      a&=a&+8:GOTO PeekToken¶
   ELSEIF t%=3 OR t%=14 THEN¶
      a&=a&+3:GOTO PeekToken¶
   ELSEIF t%=34 THEN¶
      IF strflag%=1 THEN strflag%=0 ELSE strflag%=1¶
      GOTO PeekToken¶
   ELSE¶
      GOTO PeekToken¶
   END IF¶
END SUB¶
         ¶
SUB SETPOINTER(a&,f%) STATIC¶
   IF PEEK(a&+1)=0 THEN f%=1 ELSE f%=0¶
   IF PEEK(a&)=0 THEN a&=a&+3 ELSE a&=a&+5¶
END SUB¶
   ¶
SUB CHECKFILE(a$,f&) STATIC¶
   i&=AllocMem&(252&,65538&)¶
   IF i&=0 THEN ¶
      f&=-1:EXIT SUB¶
   ELSE¶
      b$=a$+CHR$(0):l&=Lock&(SADD(b$),-2)¶
      IF l&=0 THEN¶
         f&=-2:EXIT SUB¶
      ELSE¶
         s&=Examine&(l&,i&)¶
         IF PEEKL(i&+4)>0 THEN¶
            f&=-3:CALL UnLock(l&):EXIT SUB¶
         ELSE¶
```

```
          f&=PEEKL(i&+124):CALL UnLock(l&)¶
          CALL FreeMem(i&,252&):v&=f&+3¶
          c&=AllocMem&(v&,65537&)¶
          IF c&=0 THEN¶
            f&=-1:EXIT SUB¶
          ELSE¶
            h&=xOpen&(SADD(b$),1005)¶
            IF h&=0 THEN¶
              f&=-4:EXIT SUB¶
            ELSE¶
              r&=xRead&(h&,c&,f&):CALL xClose(h&)¶
              IF r&<>f& THEN¶
                f&=-5:EXIT SUB¶
              ELSE¶
                f&=c&¶
                IF PEEK(f&)<>&HF5 THEN f&=-6:EXIT SUB¶
              END IF¶
            END IF      ¶
          END IF¶
        END IF¶
      END IF¶
    END IF¶
END SUB¶
¶
SUB WINPUT (a$) STATIC¶
  WINDOW 1,"Input: Filename",(0,0)-(240,8),0¶
  LINE INPUT a$¶
  WINDOW CLOSE 1¶
END SUB¶
¶
SUB REQUEST(a$,m%,b$,c$,b%) STATIC¶
  WINDOW 1,"System Request",(0,0)-(240,40),22¶
  COLOR 0,1:CLS:LOCATE 2,(30-LEN(a$))\2:PRINT a$;:COLOR
1,0¶
  IF m%=1 THEN¶
    l%=LEN(b$)/2:LOCATE 4,15-l%:PRINT " ";b$;" ";¶
  ELSEIF m%=2 THEN¶
    LOCATE 4,2:PRINT " ";b$;" ";:LOCATE 4,27-LEN(c$)¶
    PRINT " ";c$;" ";¶
  END IF¶
mouse1:¶
  WHILE MOUSE(0)<>0:WEND¶
  WHILE MOUSE(0)=0:WEND¶
  x%=(MOUSE(1)+8)\8:y%=(MOUSE(2)+8)\8:b%=0¶
  IF y%=4 THEN¶
    IF m%=1 THEN¶
      IF x%>14-l% AND x%<17+l% THEN b%=1¶
    ELSEIF m%=2 THEN¶
      IF x%>1 AND x%<LEN(b$)+4 THEN b%=1¶
      IF x%>26-LEN(c$) AND x%<30 THEN b%=2¶
    END IF¶
  END IF¶
  IF b%>0 THEN¶
    WINDOW CLOSE 1¶
    EXIT SUB¶
  END IF¶
```

```
  GOTO mouse1¶
END SUB¶
```

This program created many of the variable lists in this book.

6.3.6   Removing "extra" variables

Maybe you've wondered why a binary format BASIC program becomes longer when you load, shorten and resave it, instead of shorter. Or you've noticed when your BASIC program stops with an error, the orange error box surrounds a couple of blank lines. You find that there's garbage in the program that you can only see with the file monitor. Why does the big program you've been working on run slower and slower every time you edit it? And how can you manipulate internal errors in a binary program?

There is a solution to these problems. As you repeatedly save programs from the AmigaBASIC interpreter, the interpreter adds bits of extraneous data to the file (garbage). Like a garbage can, the program can only hold so much of this garbage. This also goes for the entire memory range assigned to the variable table. When you save a program, the interpreter saves it without checking which variables still belong to the program and which don't. The final problem is that important pointers remain uninitialized—especially if these pointers stay unset before saving or reloading a program.

There is, as always, a loophole. When you save a program in ASCII format, what you get in the file is what you see on the screen: Plain text separated by linefeeds (CHR$(10)).

• Save your program once with the extension ,A.

• Quit AmigaBASIC (if you just type new, the garbage still stays on the screen, and the pointers stay unchanged).

• Restart AmigaBASIC's interpreter.

• Load the program.

• Save the program with the extension of ,B (binary format—very important).

Remember the following rules when trying this resaving:

1)   This process works best when you save incomplete programs as ASCII files in the first place. Save the program out in binary form when you wish to try running the program and/or debugging it.

2) When a program runs into a problem you may not be able to see, the logical solution is to save the file in ASCII format; you might recover the program.

3) The worst thing you can do is save a program in binary format after a test run that resulted in an error message. This causes the most garbage sent from the interpreter.

4) If your program doesn't run after all, it may be due to programmer error or memory error, or an error in AmigaBASIC itself.

6.3.7   Self-modifying programs

There are methods that allow changing program code as a program runs. The two programs listed below can bring this about.

The first method of program modifying is direct access through POKE. The prinicple is simple: You assign a set of characters to a string variable at any point in the program. It is important that you make no changes to the string itself, such as A$=A$+CHR$(0). You can point the variable pointer direct to the string in your program.

This first example lets you change strings within a program. This routine opens the window named in the string. Selecting the CHANGE item from the menu lets you insert a new window title, after which the new program loads and starts.

```
REM *******************************************¶
REM *     S e l f   M o d i f y i n g    I     *¶
REM *-----------------------------------------*¶
REM *    (W) 1987 by Stefan Maelger, Hamburg    *¶
REM *******************************************¶
¶
REM * The new Title String will be changed here:¶
¶
Title$="Self Modifying I"¶
¶
SCREEN 1,320,200,2,1¶
WINDOW 2,Title$,,16,1¶
MENU 1,0,1,"CHANGE"¶
MENU 1,1,1,"TITLE"¶
¶
ON MENU GOSUB checkmenu¶
MENU ON¶
¶
WHILE Maelger=0¶
SLEEP¶
WEND¶
¶
MENU RESET¶
```

```
WINDOW CLOSE 2¶
SCREEN CLOSE 1¶
END¶
¶
checkmenu:¶
IF MENU(1)=1 AND MENU(0)=1 GOTO newtitle¶
RETURN¶
¶
newtitle:¶
PRINT "Please enter new Title"¶
PRINT LEN(Title$);"Characters Long."¶
LINE INPUT newt$¶
neu$=LEFT$(newt$+SPACE$(LEN(Title$)),LEN(Title$))¶
¶
REM * Here is where the String is changed:¶
¶
FOR i=1 TO LEN(newt$)¶
   POKE SADD(Title$)+i-1,ASC(MID$(newt$,i,1))¶
NEXT¶
¶
REM * Start Program again (with the new Title)¶
¶
PRINT "Program with new title being saved."¶
SAVE "Programname"¶
PRINT "New Program is saved."¶
PRINT "Re-Load or start this"¶
PRINT "program over again."¶
t=TIMER+15:WHILE t>TIMER:WEND¶
Maelger=1¶
RETURN¶
```

You can see how simple it is. Replace "Programname" with your own program name.

This method lets you change commands in a binary format program. However, it also allows changes to files saved in protected format.

Now we come to the second method—the ASCII file method. Here, too, you can completely change a program. The clincher to this method is the ease in changing entire program sections.

Using POKE to change parameters in a binary format program can have serious consequences: It isn't that easy to change commands. The ASCII file route makes this replacement much simpler.

How it works

Here's the principle behind it. First the program section must be found for replacement. User input works with a syntax check to find the area that needs changing. The running program deletes the program lines you want changed (DELETE from-to). The program then saves to diskette as an ASCII file. While the change waits under its own name, the RAM disk supplies the most speed. Now the saved ASCII program opens for appending (OPEN x$ FOR APPEND AS y), and the DATA generator creates the new program segment.

In order to get this program into memory, all you need to enter is RUN filename$ or LOAD filename$. The program starts all over again, so that you can create the new program section as an ASCII file in the RAM disk, then join the programs with CHAIN MERGE. You can also restart the altered program with a starting label, and merge a series of program segments (e.g., CHAIN stuff,lines,ALL).

```
REM ****************************************¶
REM *     S e l f M o d i f y i n g  II    *¶
REM *--------------------------------------*¶
REM *   (W) 1987 by Stefan Maelger, Hamburg *¶
REM ****************************************¶
¶
REM * Get the Screens Resolution¶
¶
GOSUB VariableLabel¶
¶
SCREEN 1,SWidth%,Height%,Depth%,Mode%¶
WINDOW 2,"Hello!",,0,1¶
¶
PRINT "Width in Pixels:";SWidth%¶
PRINT "Height in Pixels:";Height%¶
PRINT "Depth in Planes:";Depth%¶
¶
PRINT¶
PRINT "Please enter the"¶
PRINT "New Width:";¶
INPUT NewWidth%¶
IF NewWidth%<20 OR NewWidth%>640 THEN¶
  NewWidth%=SWidth%¶
END IF¶
INPUT "New Height:";NewHeight%¶
IF NewHeight%<10 OR NewHeight%>512 THEN¶
  NewHeight%=Height%¶
END IF¶
INPUT "New Depth:";NewDepth%¶
IF NewDepth%<1 OR NewDepth%>5 THEN¶
  NewDepth%=Depth%¶
END IF¶
PRINT¶
Mode%=1¶
IF NewWidth%>320 THEN Mode%=2¶
IF NewHeight%>256 THEN Mode%=Mode%+2¶
IF Mode%=4 AND NewDepth%>2 THEN¶
  NewDepth%=2¶
ELSEIF Mode%>1 AND NewDepth%>4 THEN¶
  NewDepth%=4¶
END IF¶
OPEN "Programname.t" FOR OUTPUT AS 1¶
PRINT#1,"VariableLabel:";CHR$(10);¶
PRINT#1,"SWidth%=";STR$(NewWidth%);CHR$(10);¶
PRINT#1,"Height%=";STR$(NewHeight%);CHR$(10);¶
PRINT#1,"Depth%=";STR$(NewDepth%);CHR$(10);¶
PRINT#1,"Mode%=";STR$(Mode%);CHR$(10);¶
PRINT#1,"RETURN";CHR$(10);¶
PRINT#1,"VariableLabelEnd:";CHR$(10);¶
```

```
CLOSE 1¶
¶
DELETE VariableLabel-VariableLabelEnd¶
SAVE "Programname",A¶
OPEN "Programname.t" FOR INPUT AS 1¶
OPEN "Programname" FOR APPEND AS 2¶
PRINT#2,INPUT$(LOF(1),1);¶
CLOSE 2¶
CLOSE 1¶
KILL "Programname.t"¶
WINDOW CLOSE 2¶
SCREEN CLOSE 1¶
LOAD "Programname",R¶
END¶
¶
¶
VariableLabel:¶
SWidth%= 320¶
Height%= 200¶
Depth%= 2¶
Mode%= 1¶
RETURN¶
VariableLabelEnd:¶
```

Amazing, isn't it? This procedure is particularly good for any kind of graphic program. For example, you could enter user-defined functions in a function plot, palette values in a drawing program, etc.

7
The Workbench

7.   The Workbench

The Amiga's user interface leaves nothing to the imagination. All important operations are realized through icons. These icons make text input almost unnecessary, thus removing the barriers so often caused by language.

There are some Workbench functions that few users even know about. These users can form easy solutions to tough problems. This chapter shows how effectively these functions can be used, with a minimum of time and effort.

7.1   Using the Workbench

The Workbench is the one part of the Amiga that the user sees most often. With that in mind, here are some helpful hints for making your Workbench maintenance and use easier and more efficient.

7.1.1   Keyboard tricks

Do you know what a *string gadget* is? Essentially, it's a miniature input window. String gadgets are used by the Amiga whenever it needs some form of keyboard input (e.g., for renaming a diskette). Instead of pressing the <DEL> key to delete the old name, press and hold the <right Amiga> key and press the <X> key. Presto, the string gadget clears.

In most cases, <right Amiga><Q> acts as an Undo function, restoring the last item changed.

When you want to move the cursor to the first character of the input line, press <SHIFT><Cursor left>. Pressing <SHIFT><Cursor right> to get to the end of the input line.

Now we come to the icons. Suppose you want to select more than one icon. Hold down the <SHIFT> key and click on every icon you want selected. Whatever you do to/with the last icon applies to all the icons selected in this one pass. For example, if you want to throw the multi-selected icons into the Trashcan, just drag the last icon to the Trashcan (you can release the <SHIFT> key).

When CLI output flashes by on the screen (e.g., directory listings), you can stop the listing by pressing the <RETURN> key. Continue the listing by pressing the <Backspace> key.

If you want to go to the beginning of a screen, or just open a fresh window, press <CTRL><L> to clear the screen.

Now and again a prompt may not appear. <CTRL><O> and <RETURN> returns the prompt to the screen.

<CRTL><D> interrupts the startup sequence, while <CRTL><C> interrupts any currently executing command.

Easter eggs

Many programmers and hardware developers place "signatures" on their creations. These signatures are sometimes called *Easter eggs*, because they are hidden in the system for the user to find. This adds a personal touch to the software or hardware design.

The Amiga has a few of these Easter eggs built-in. You can see them on the screen if you have a little patience and very flexible hands.

•   Boot the Workbench diskette.

•   After the Workbench screen appears, press and hold both <ALT> keys AND both <SHIFT> keys.

•   With your free fingers, press function keys <F1> to <F10> and watch the title bar.

Each function key lists the people responsible for different aspects of Amiga design.

7.1.2   The Trashcan

Not everything you make when computing is worthwhile. The developers of the operating system created the Trashcan for disposing of garbage. It's easy to use:

•   Select the icon you want to get rid of.

•   Drag it to the Trashcan.

•   Click on the Trashcan icon.

•   Select the Empty Trash item from the Disk pulldown menu.

There's an even simpler way to do it. The above process works well, on the condition that you remember to empty the trash. However, if you don't the diskette keeps the data placed in the Trashcan in disk memory. Since diskettes only have a capacity of about 880K, this can take up a great deal of disk memory.

Now for the simpler method:

•   Click once on the file icon you want disposed of.

•   Select the Discard item from the Workbench pulldown menu.

•   Click on the ok to discard gadget in the system requester.

7.1.3   Extended selection

Have you ever wondered about how to organize icons in every window. If you put your Extras diskette in the drive and open the BASICdemos drawer, you'll see 25 icons. Most of these icons have such long names that the Clean Up item doesn't put most of them in neat order.

You could conceivably select and move each icon, then execute the Snapshot item from the Special pulldown menu each time you get an icon into position. This takes time, though.

There's a simpler way out. Every icon you click stays active while you hold down one of the <SHIFT> keys. Most of the functions you can perform on single icons work with multiple icons (assuming that these functions match the icons). For example, you can't use Discard on a disk icon.

*   Move each icon into the desired position.

*   Press and hold the <SHIFT> key.

*   Click on all the icons you want organized.

*   Release the <SHIFT> key.

*   Select the Snapshot item from the Special pulldown menu.

If you wish to copy several programs, this *extended selection* helps you to do this copying quickly and easily. You can drag a set of icons across the screen, and onto the windows in other diskettes. The only disadvantage is that diskette exchanges must be made for every program.

If you wish to avoid this constant diskette switching, here's a quick method of getting around this:

*   Copy the Empty drawer of the Workbench diskette onto the formatted source diskette.

*   Move all icons you want copied into this drawer using extended selection.

*   Drag the drawer to the target diskette icon.

7.1.4   Reading and setting Preferences

The name Preferences speaks for itself: This program lets you adjust the Amiga to your individual needs. It allows selection of almost any printer type, any number of screen colors and more. The Preferences icon normally appears in the Workbench window.

What can the intermediate programmer start to do with these Preferences? A lot! Preferences stores its data and parameters in a long data block. This data block has the following structure:

+ Offset	Type	Definition
0	B	Font height
1	B	Printer port: 0=parallel, 1=serial
2	W	Baudrate: 0=110, 1=300, 2=1200, 3=2400, 4=4800, 5=9600, 6=19200, 7=MIDI
4	L	keyboard repeat—seconds
8	L	keyboard repeat—microseconds
12	L	keyboard delay—seconds
16	L	keyboard delay—microseconds
20	W	Sprite pointer definition array, approx. 72 bytes
100	B	X-offset of pointer hot spot
101	B	Y-offset of pointer hot spot
102	W	RGB information for color register 17
104	W	RGB information for color register 18
106	W	RGB information for color register 19
108	W	Pointer ticks (sensitivity)
110	W	RGB information for color register 0
112	W	RGB information for color register 1
114	W	RGB information for color register 2
116	W	RGB information for color register 17
118	B	X-offset of view
119	B	Y-offset of view
120	W	X-offset of view (initialization)
122	W	Y-offset of view
124	W	CLI on/off (0/1)
126	W	Printer type (see following sample program for definitions)
128	B	Bytefield with printer filenames
158	W	Typestyle: 0=Pica, $400=Elist, $800=Fine
160	W	Print quality: 0=draft, $100=NLQ
162	W	Line spacing: 0=6 LPI, $200=8 LPI
164	W	Left border
166	W	Right border
168	W	Print type: 0=positive, 1=negative
170	W	Print direction: 0=horizontal, 1=vertical
172	W	Gray scales: 0=B/W, 1=gray scales, 2=color

174	W	Contrast
176	W	Paper size: 0=US letter, $10=US legal, $20= narrow carriage, $30=wide carriage, $40= custom
178	W	Paper length
180	W	Paper type: 0=endless, $80=single sheet

The following program offers three SUB programs which load this data record, send the modifications back to Preferences and exit.

```
'###########################¶
'# Program:    Preferences   #¶
'# Author:     tob           #¶
'# Date:       8/12/87        #¶
'# Version:    2.0            #¶
'#                            #¶
'###########################¶
¶
DECLARE FUNCTION AllocMem& LIBRARY¶
¶
LIBRARY "exec.library"¶
LIBRARY "intuition.library"¶
¶
demo:    '*Read and change preferences¶
         '*Change screen colors¶
         GetP prefs&, 220¶
         ¶
         POKEW prefs& + 110, 1*15 + 256*15¶
         POKEW prefs& + 112, 1¶
         POKEW prefs& + 114, 16*15¶
    ¶
         SetP prefs&¶
         ¶
         '* Sample printer settings¶
         DIM pr$(12)¶
         pr$(0) = "Custom"¶
         pr$(1) = "Alpha P 101"¶
         pr$(2) = "Brother 15XL"¶
         pr$(3) = "CBM MPS 1000"¶
         pr$(4) = "DIAB 630"¶
         pr$(5) = "DIAB ADV D25"¶
         pr$(6) = "DIAB C 150"¶
         pr$(7) = "Epson"¶
         pr$(8) = "Epson JX 80"¶
         pr$(9) = "Okimate 20"¶
         pr$(10) = "Qume LP 20"¶
         pr$(11) = "HP Laserjet"¶
         pr$(12) = "HP Lasertjet +"¶
         PRINT"Please select a printer type:"¶
         PRINT¶
         ¶
         FOR loop% = 0 TO 12¶
           PRINT pr$(loop%)¶
         NEXT loop%¶
         ¶
         PRINT¶
         LINE INPUT"Your selection...";in$¶
         ¶
         FOR loop% = 0 TO 12¶
           IF UCASE$(in$) = UCASE$(pr$(loop%)) THEN¶
             pr% = loop%¶
             loop% = 12¶
             flag% = 1¶
           END IF¶
         NEXT loop%¶
```

```
        ¶
        IF flag% = 1 THEN¶
            flag% = 0¶
            CLS¶
            POKEW prefs& + 126, pr%¶
            SetP prefs&¶
            LINE INPUT "Would you like to run a printer
test? (y/n)";yn$¶
            IF yn$ = "y" THEN¶
                LPRINT"testTESTtestTESTtestTESTtestTEST"¶
                LPRINT"TESTtestTESTtestTESTtestTESTtest"¶
            END IF   ¶
        ELSE    ¶
            CLS  ¶
            PRINT"Your printer type not listed."¶
        END IF¶
        ¶
        Finish pref&¶
        ¶
        LIBRARY CLOSE¶
        END¶
        ¶
SUB GetP (datum&, size%) STATIC¶
    opt&    = 2^16¶
    mem&    = size% + 4¶
    add&    = AllocMem&(mem&,opt&)¶
    IF add& <> 0 THEN¶
      POKEL add&, mem&¶
      datum& = add& + 4¶
      CALL GetPrefs(datum&, size%)¶
    ELSE¶
      datum&=0¶
    END IF¶
END SUB¶
    ¶
SUB SetP (datum&) STATIC¶
    IF datum&<>0 THEN¶
        size& = PEEKL(datum& - 4) - 4¶
        CALL SetPrefs(datum&,size&, -1)¶
    END IF¶
END SUB¶
    ¶
SUB Finish (datum&) STATIC¶
    IF datum& <>0 THEN¶
        mem& = PEEKL(datum& - 4)¶
        add& = datum& - 4¶
        CALL FreeMem(add&,mem&)¶
    END IF¶
END SUB¶
```

Program description

GetP makes a copy of the abovementioned Preferences data block. Enter a variable into which the address of the copy is placed, as well as the desired number of bytes. In normal cases, the entire data record requires 180 bytes. However, if you're just interested in the first entry, you can enter far fewer bytes.

Now you can change the copy as you want it to appear in the program. If all changes are as you want them, then SetP puts the changed copy into Preferences, thus activating the changes.

Finish returns the copy memory to the system.

7.1.4.1   Info

The `Info` item from the `Workbench` pulldown menu allows the user to look at information in programs and data files. But which information can you change? These are questions that the Amiga manual doesn't discuss. Here are some answers.

7.1.4.2   The `Info` screen

This screen appears after selecting any kind of icon and selecting the `Info` item from the `Workbench` pulldown menu. The `Info` screen lists all the vital information about the program. The Workbench diskette should not be removed during the selection of `Info`.

The `Info` screen has several areas. The upper left corner lists common data about the file and/or diskette—name, type and the size in two different measurements. Beneath `Stack` the number of bytes the file uses in memory is listed.

`Type` describes the type of icon for a file or diskette. The normal icon types are Disk, Drawer, Tool, Project and Garbage:

Disk

Disks are the diskette icons which lie outside of directory windows. Double-clicking on a disk opens the disk window (the diskette's main directory).

The only item of interest about this icon type is that, like the other icons, you can change its shape. Computer owners into nostalgia can change the disk icons to look like 5-1/4" diskettes.

Drawers

Drawers are the icons which represent subdirectories. Moving programs into a drawer easily lets you find programs on the same diskette. This operation takes a lot of time, though. Here's a suggestion: Use the RENAME command from AmigaDOS. Enter the first name with the full path specification, then enter the new name with the path under which you want the program placed (don't forget to copy the `.info` file to the new path as well).

Tools

Any executable program is called a tool. Tools can lie in drawers, windows and on the Workbench screen. They have their own icons which execute programs when you double-click on them.

AmigaBASIC, `Preferences` and *BeckerText Amiga* from Abacus are tools.

Projects

Amiga projects are any files that contain data saved from a tool (program).

Notepad texts, word processing files, BASIC programs and .bmap files are projects.

Trashcan

This last type is actually another form of drawer. Normally you can place drawers inside of drawers. The Trashcan drawer can only lie in the main directory. Plus, it can't be moved onto the Workbench screen. Whenever you need a Trashcan icon, look in the main directory.

On the right side of the screen you'll see a box which lists the Status of the file. This refers to the access options offered to the user (see the AmigaDOS manual under LIST). When the write protect is set on the diskette, you can't change the read, write or executable attributes. When you get information from a diskette, this area lists whether the diskette is write-protected or write-enabled. Clicking this Status changes nothing; you must change the write-protect by hand.

The user's Comments appear in the line below Status. Amiga-DOS's FILENOTE lets you write a text of up to 80 characters long. This function is suppressed by diskettes, since a diskette cannot be supplied with a comment.

The Info screen does more than give information about programs or diskettes. They also supply details about projects (text and data files). Default Tool tells the user which tool created the project, or which diskette has the copy. The Workbench knows which project to load when you double-click a tool's icon.

The last line displays Tool Types. This information is given by the main program. The Notepad, for example, states which font is in use, and the window size for input.

7.1.4.3   A closer look at the Info screen

You can change the available information in the Info screen. Write and save a text from the Notepad, and open its Info screen to look at the information.

What you put under Comment has no effect on other parts of the system—it's just commentary.

The Default Tool gadget is much more important. As mentioned earlier, this gadget lists the name of the tool (program) which created the project (file). There's a bug in this, though. For example: You set up two Workbench diskettes named user and cli. The first diskette, user, is a nearly normal Workbench. The second diskette, cli, has been modified so that on startup it copies all the important CLI commands to RAM, and stays in the DOS window. Both diskettes have a Notepad tool. If you write a text on the user diskette, the Default Tool gadget reads:

> Workbench user:Utilities/Notepad

If you want to load a text, the user diskette must be in the drive. But the cli diskette also has a Notepad. All you need to do to read the same text from the cli diskette's Notepad is change the Default Tool text to read as follows:

> sys:Utilities/Notepad

The Tool Types gadget holds all the information needed by the program. You can change this also. Here are the types and meanings:

Name	Example	Definition
FILETYPE	notepad	Notepad text
FONT	topaz.8	Global font
WINDOW	0,0,50,50	Window coordinates
FLAGS	NOGLOBAL	Flag listing

The FILETYPE line identifies the tool that created the project. FONT gives the name of the global font; you can change this, provided the font you change it to exists on the Workbench diskette. WINDOW lists the X- and Y-coordinates of the input window. Other values can go here as desired. The FLAGS gadget may be new to you, since it isn't used in normal saving. This gadget lists some parameters that are normally used in loading:

Parameter	Definition
NOGLOBAL	Disable global font function
GLOBAL	Enable global font function
NOWRAP	Disable word wrap
WRAP	Enable word wrap
NOFONTS	Skip font table generation
FORMFEED	Add formfeed to printer driver
DRAFT	Print in draft quality

Try these procedures out in other programs, such as programs that place data into files. Read the section on icons for information on saving these parameters to diskette and more.

8
Icons

8.   Icons

The Amiga's Workbench user interface uses *icons* to help the user easily identify programs, data file, directories and diskettes. These icons appear as pictures that quickly indicate their purposes to the user. You start programs by double-clicking on their icons, instead of typing in the program name as you would from the CLI.

Clicking icons saves the trouble of typing in disk paths to open directories and subdirectories to the file you want. All you have to do is click on a drawer; click on the drawer inside the drawer that opens; and so on, until you get to the file icon you need.

This chapter gives detailed information on icon design, drawer structure and image structure. Programs are included that let you edit icons and examine the structure of an icon from AmigaBASIC. You'll also find information about icon structure and creating multiple graphics for one icon (before double-clicking and after double-clicking) .

8.1   Icon types

There's a problem with this title: All icon symbols can stand for different objects. You have to be able to differentiate between directories and diskettes, and between programs. So, you wouldn't assign a drawer icon to the Trashcan, any more than you should assign a program icon to a directory. The program still runs, but using "other" icons can cause some confusion later on.

For this reason, this section uses certain icon descriptions in certain contexts. For example, the book consistently calls the icon for a diskette a disk icon, etc.

As you've seen in Chapter 7, the following icon types exist:

Name	Identifier	Object	Number
Diskette icon	WBDISK	standard diskette	1
Drawer icon	WBDRAWER	directory	2
Tool icon	WBTOOL	executable program	3
Project icon	WBPROJECT	program data file	4
Trashcan icon	WBGARBAGE	Trashcan	5
Kickstart icon	WBKICK	Kickstart diskette (Amiga 1000)	5

You can get additional information on the icon types from the Workbench. Check the following sources:

Disk icon information corresponds to drawer icons. The drawer icon stores the pictures of all icons and data which can be opened by double-clicking.

Projects (files) are of the same general design as the tools (programs) used to create them. Double-clicking a project icon opens the tools used to create that file, then the project itself.

The Trashcan is really just another form of drawer. The main difference is that you can't move it from one directory to another, nor can you move it to the Workbench.

8.2   Icon design

Now for the structure, so you can start thinking about designing your
own icons. Icon data goes into a directory. Every file that has an icon
has an extra file with the same name and a file extension of .info.
This info file contains the information that goes into the Workbench.

8.2.1   DiskObject structure

Every icon file begins with a DiskObject structure, which contains
all sorts of information (see the table below):

Identifier	Parameter	Bytes
do_Magic	magic number	2
do_Version	version number	2
do_Gadget	click structure	4
gg_LeftEdge	left click range	2
gg_TopEdge	top click range	2
gg_Width	width of click range	2
gg_Height	height of click range	2
gg_Flags	invert flag	2
gg_Activation	$0003	2
gg_Type	$0001	2
gg_GadgetRender	pointer1 picture data	4
gg_SelectRender	pointer2 picture data	4
gg_IntuiText	"not used?"	4
gg_MutualExclude	"not useable!"	4
gg_SpecialInfo	"not useable!"	4
gg_GadgetID	"for own use!"	2
gg_UserData	"your Pointer!"	4
do_Type	icon type	1
nothing	fillbyte	1
do_DefaultTool	text structure	4
do_ToolTypes	text structure	4
do_CurrentX	current X-position	4
do_CurrentY	current Y-position	4
do_DrawerData	window structure	4
do_ToolWindow	program window	4
do_StackSize	reserved memory	4

For starters, the magic number is equal to $E310. This tells the system
that this is where an icon is read. Next follows the version number,

which at the time of this writing is always $0001. The above table indicates how many bytes each value occupies.

Four unused bytes follow the structure. These are normally reserved for a gadget click structure. Now things get more complicated: The symbol itself is actually divided into two separate areas—the graphic range and the click range. The click range helps determine the range in which you can click on the icon. The X- and Y-offsets of the click position follow, setting the upper left corner of the click range. Next comes the width and height of that range. It's important to remember that text is printed beneath the click range (i.e., under the icon). Be sure that the click range is high enough that the text can be counted as part of the graphic.

Gadgets

Now comes the gadget structure. The next value changes the picture when you activate it. You have three options at your disposal:

1)   The entire rectangular area in which the icon is displayed inverts. Just place a 4 in the Flags register. This is the simplest (but not the most attractive) method.

2)   Only the drawn-in area inverts. This looks and works somewhat better than 1. This mode requires a 5 in the Flags register.

3)   Instead of an inverse version of the icon, another icon appears altogether. Place a 6 in the Flags register.

Next the value constants $0003 and $0001 follow in the DiskObject structure. The first is the activation type, and the second marks a Book gadget. The pointers to icon graphic data follow. If you're switching between two graphics, the second pointer must be initialized.

The next 18 bytes are required by the system for normal gadgets. Its actual purpose appears to make no sense. It works best when you fill this area with zeros. These bytes are important to the next parameter: It distinguishes which icon type is available to the user. You insert the numbers which indicate the abovementioned table. Since this should be given in one byte, and the processor can only address even addresses, these are the same as fillbytes.

Tool types

In order to select the type, the pointer to the Default Tool structure then the pointer to the ToolTypes structure must be set (more on these pointers later).

The system stores the positioning in the DiskObject structure as the current X- and Y-coordinates. However, you also have the option of Workbench coordinates of $80000000, $80000000. These values are called NO_ICON_POSITION. As long as a user-created icon stays unchanged, it is found at the same position. A pointer to the window data follows if necessary, and a pointer to the ToolWindow structure.

To conclude, the stack depth tells the Workbench how much memory to allocate for this program or this data. The value of a data file has higher

priority than a main program. This way you could reserve considerably
more memory for the data records of a file.

8.2.2   Drawer structure

Now that you have the information about the average DiskObject
structure, you can continue on with the individual types.

First comes the Drawer structure, which is almost equal to a diskette.
The big difference is that the directory and the Trashcan use this struc-
ture. It contains all the data needed for opening a new directory window.
The table reads as follows:

Identifier	Parameter	Bytes
wi_LeftEdge	left corner	2
wi_TopEdge	top edge	2
wi_Width	width	2
wi_Height	height	2
wi_DetailPen	drawing color 1	1
wi_BlockPen	drawing color 2	1
wi_IDCMPFlags	gadget flags	4
wi_Flags	window flags	4
wi_FirstGadget	gadget structure	4
wi_CheckMark	checkmark	4
wi_Title	title text	4
wi_Screen	screen pointer	4
wi_BitMap	window bitmap	4
wi_MinWidth	minimum width	2
wi_MinHeight	minimum height	2
wi_MaxWidth	maximum width	2
wi_MaxHeight	maximum height	2
wi_Type	$0001	2
actx-pos	current X-position	2
acty-pos	current Y-position	2

These are handled as an independent window structure, which extends
the coordinates for the current position. This may need some explanation:

The upper left corner coordinates and the window size appear. When the
user moves and closes the window, the diskette doesn't leave the system, so that the directory window isn't opened at the position given by
the current coordinates.

The parameters then follow for color control. The values set the colors
for the lines and blocks used in a window. Normally $FF stands for -1,

251

which takes the color from the screens in use. This makes color control much simpler.

Handling window changes

The next byte contains a pointer and flag used by the system internals. First comes the IDCMP flag, which sets the reaction to any changes to a window. The window flag determines the setup of the directory window. Then five pointers to structures or memory ranges follow, whose changes require knowledge of the operating system.

This way all windows set up in any size within the minimum and maximum limits set by `MinHeight`, `MaxWidth` and `MaxHeight`.

8.2.3   Image structure

Every icon needs an `Image` structure. They contain the graphic data, and are set into the respective file twice when necessary.

Identifier	Parameter	Bytes
im_LeftEdge	left corner	2
im_TopEdge	top edge	2
im_Width	width	2
im_Height	height	2
im_Depth	depth	2
im_ImageData	bitplane pointer	4
im_PlanePick	graphic data	1
im_PlaneOnOff	use	1
im_NextImage	next graphic	4

After information about the sizes and positions of several bitmaps, the image setup contains the graphic itself. The number of bitmaps depend upon the screen's depth. The Workbench has a normal depth of two bitmaps on which the icon is also based.

The image parameters repeat after the icon position is given to the `DiskObject` structure. The position is just an offset of this parameter. No values are left out concerning the width, height and number of bitplanes, just as on the other bitplanes.

The next four bytes are a pointer to the current graphic data. This pointer can change the next couple of parameters somewhat. For example, `PlanePick` depends on the number of bitplanes for its graphic display. And `PlaneOff` controls an unused icon's activity.

The last parameter is a pointer to another `Image` structure. This lets you combine several objects into one unit.

The bytes of the individual bitplanes follow the Image structure. First comes bitplane 1, then bitplane 2, and so on (if more bitplanes are used). The system computes the number of bytes needed for the width by rounding off the number of pixels in to the next highest multiple of 16. The height is calculated by the number of pixels in height, rounded off to the next highest multiple of 8. The Amiga needs these bytes to create any bitplane.

8.2.4   DefaultTool text

Unlike the Image structure, used by every icon, you only need the DefaultTool text for diskettes and data files. Diskettes use the text to state the diskette hierarchy needed to call system programs. For example, every diskette contains the text SYS:System/DiskCopy, used to access the disk copy program (if you remove this text the disk cannot be copied in this manner). Data files use this text to indicate the program used to create these files. If you remove these texts, the main program becomes inaccessible. Here's the parameter setup:

Identifier	Parameter	Bytes
char_num	number of characters	4

This list contains only the truly concrete data (the number of characters). Everything else is flexible. Every text must end with a nullbyte, so that the end is identifiable.

8.2.5   ToolTypes text

The section on the Info function of the Workbench (Section) mentioned that the string gadget under ToolTypes lets you give additional information about the main program. For example, you could set up a text file for handling as an IFF file. The program requires other information that doesn't appear in this area. You can easily add this information, and use the file in other programs as an interchange format file.

Identifier	Parameter	Bytes
string_num	text number	4

Like the DefaultTool text, the size of the ToolTypes gadget is extremely difficult to change. Assuming that this string isn't blank, the beginning of the text has the number of the string. You must increment the number contained here by one, then multiply by four, to compute the string number. You can also find this number when you read the file. If you want the data expressed, you must reverse the procedure.

Next follows a string which begins with the length, and ends with a nullbyte. The number of characters is computed by string_num mentioned above.

8.2.6 Icon analyzer

The following program is a move toward the practical side of icon structure. This BASIC program reads the parameters of the filename, and displays these parameters and their corresponding values. This program would be easier to use if you could print this list to a printer (you may wish to modify it to do so).

```
DIM DiskObject$(26,3),DiskObject(26)¶
DIM DrawerData$(20,3),DrawerData(20)¶
DIM Image$(2,9,3),Image(2,9)¶
DIM DefaultTool$(2,3),DefaultTool(2)¶
¶
¶
DEF FNSize%(Im)=Image(Im,4)*2*INT((Image(Im,3)+15)/16)¶

¶
WIDTH 75¶
¶
INPUT "Filename:";File$¶
¶
OPEN File$+".info" FOR INPUT AS 1¶
  ¶
  summary$=INPUT$(LOF(1),1)¶
  ¶
CLOSE 1¶
¶
summary$=summary$+STRING$(40,0)¶
¶
GOSUB LoadHeader¶
¶
  IF DiskObject(18)=1 THEN¶
     GOSUB LoadDrawer¶
     GOSUB LoadImage¶
     GOSUB LoadDefaultTool¶
     GOSUB LoadToolTypes¶
  END IF¶
 ¶
  IF DiskObject(18)=2 OR DiskObject(18)=5 THEN¶
     GOSUB LoadDrawer¶
     GOSUB LoadImage¶
     GOSUB LoadToolTypes¶
  END IF¶
  ¶
  IF DiskObject(18)=3 THEN¶
     GOSUB LoadImage   ¶
     GOSUB LoadToolTypes¶
  END IF¶
  ¶
  IF DiskObject(18)=4 THEN¶
     GOSUB LoadImage¶
     GOSUB LoadDefaultTool¶
```

```
        GOSUB LoadToolTypes¶
      END IF¶
      ¶
END¶
¶
¶
LoadHeader:¶
  RESTORE DiskObject¶
  po=1 : PRINT¶
  PRINT "Disk Object Structure" : PRINT¶
  FOR i=1 TO 26 ¶
      GetBytes DiskObject$(i,1),DiskObject$(i,2),
DiskObject$(i,3),DiskObject(i)¶
  NEXT i ¶
RETURN¶
¶
LoadDrawer:¶
  RESTORE DrawerData¶
  PRINT¶
  PRINT "Drawer Data Structure" : PRINT¶
  FOR i=1 TO 20¶
      GetBytes DrawerData$(i,1),DrawerData$(i,2),
DrawerData$(i,3),DrawerData(i)¶
  NEXT i¶
RETURN¶
¶
LoadImage:¶
  Im=1¶
  GOSUB GetImage¶
  IF DiskObject(12)<>0 THEN Im=2 : GOSUB GetImage¶
RETURN¶
¶
GetImage:¶
  RESTORE Image¶
  PRINT¶
  PRINT "Image Structure" : PRINT¶
  FOR i=1 TO 9¶
      GetBytes Image$(Im,i,1),Image$(Im,i,2),
Image$(Im,i,3),Image(Im,i)¶
  NEXT i¶
  bytes=FNSize%(Im)¶
  PRINT¶
  PRINT "BitPlanes" : PRINT¶
  WIDTH 60¶
  FOR j=1 TO Image(Im,5)¶
      PRINT¶
      PRINT "Bitplane";j¶
      FOR i=1 TO bytes¶
          a$=HEX$(ASC(MID$(summary$,po,1)))¶
          IF LEN(a$)<2 THEN a$="0"+a$¶
          PRINT a$;¶
          IF i/2=INT(i/2) THEN PRINT " ";¶
          po=po+1¶
      NEXT i¶
      PRINT¶
  NEXT j¶
  WIDTH 75  ¶
RETURN¶
      ¶
LoadDefaultTool:¶
  RESTORE DefaultTool¶
  PRINT¶
  PRINT "Default Tool" : PRINT¶
  GetBytes DefaulTool$(1,1),DefaultTool$(1,2),
DefaultTool$(1,3),DefaultTool(1)¶
  IF DefaultTool(1)>80 THEN
DefaultTool(1)=DefaultTool(1)/16¶
  GetString DefaultTool(1)¶
```

255

```
RETURN¶
  ¶
LoadToolTypes:¶
  RESTORE ToolTypes¶
  PRINT¶
  PRINT "ToolTypes" : PRINT¶
  IF po>LEN(summary$) THEN RETURN¶
  GetBytes ToolTypes$(1,1),ToolTypes$(1,2),
ToolTypes$(1,3),ToolTypes(1)¶
  FOR i=1 TO ToolTypes(1)/4-1¶
      RESTORE DefaultTool¶
      ToolTypes$(2,3)=""¶
      GetBytes ToolTypes$(2,1),ToolTypes$(2,2),
ToolTypes$(2,3),ToolTypes(2)¶
      IF ToolTypes(2)>80 THEN
ToolTypes(2)=ToolTypes(2)/16¶
      GetString ToolTypes(2)¶
  NEXT i    ¶
RETURN¶
  ¶
  ¶
SUB GetString (length) STATIC¶
  ¶
SHARED po,summary$¶
  ¶
  ts=po : a=1¶
  IF length=0 THEN EXIT SUB¶
  ¶
  WHILE a<>0¶
      a=ASC(MID$(summary$,po,1))¶
      a$=HEX$(a)¶
      IF LEN(a$)<2 THEN a$="0"+a$¶
      PRINT a$;" ";¶
      po=po+1¶
  WEND¶
  PRINT¶
  PRINT MID$(summary$,ts,po-ts-1)¶
  ¶
END SUB¶
  ¶
  ¶
SUB Decimal (he$,dec) STATIC¶
  ¶
  dec=0¶
  FOR i=1 TO LEN(he$)  ¶
      a=ASC(MID$(he$,LEN(he$)+1-i,1))-48¶
      IF a>9 THEN a=a-7¶
      dec=dec+16^(i-1)*a¶
  NEXT i¶
  ¶
END SUB¶
  ¶
SUB GetBytes (identifier$,paramater$,value$,dec) STATIC¶
  ¶
  ¶
SHARED po,summary$¶
      READ identifier$,paramater$,bytes¶
      PRINT identifier$;TAB(20);paramater$;TAB(47);¶
      a$=MID$(summary$,po,bytes)¶
      po=po+bytes¶
      IF bytes=1 THEN value=ASC(a$)¶
      IF bytes=2 THEN value=CVI(a$)¶
      IF bytes=4 THEN¶
          FOR j=1 TO 4¶
              a=ASC(MID$(a$,j,1))¶
              h$=HEX$(a)¶
              IF LEN(h$)<2 THEN h$=h$+"0"¶
              value$=value$+h$¶
          NEXT j¶
```

```
            ELSE¶
                value$=HEX$(value)¶
            END IF¶
            PRINT "$";value$;TAB(57);¶
            Decimal value$,dec¶
            PRINT dec    ¶
    ¶
    END SUB¶
    ¶
    ¶
    ¶
    DiskObject:¶
    ¶
    DATA do_Magic,Magic Number,2¶
    DATA do_Version,Version Number,2¶
    DATA do_Gadget,Click Structure,4¶
    DATA gg_LeftEdge,Left Click Range,2¶
    DATA gg_TopEdge,Top Click Range,2¶
    DATA gg_Width,Click Range Width,2¶
    DATA gg_Height,Click Range Height,2¶
    DATA gg_Flags,Invert Flag,2¶
    DATA gg_Activation,$0003,2¶
    DATA gg_Type,$0001,2¶
    DATA gg_GadgetRender,Pointer1 Picture Data,4¶
    DATA gg_SelectRender,Pointer2 Picture Data,4¶
    DATA gg_IntuiText,"not used??",4¶
    DATA gg_MutualExclude,"not usable!",4¶
    DATA gg_SpecialInfo,"not useable!",4¶
    DATA gg_GadgetID,"for own use!",2¶
    DATA gg_UserData,"your Pointer!",4¶
    DATA do_Type,Icon type,1¶
    DATA nothing,Fillbyte,1¶
    DATA do_DefaultTool,Text Structure,4¶
    DATA do_ToolTypes,Text Structure,4¶
    DATA do_CurrentX,Current x-Position,4¶
    DATA do_CurrentY,Current y-Position,4¶
    DATA do_DrawerData,Window Structure,4¶
    DATA do_ToolWindow,Program Window,4¶
    DATA do_StackSize,Reserved Memory,4¶
    ¶
    DrawerData:¶
    ¶
    DATA wi_LeftEdge,Left Edge,2¶
    DATA wi_TopEdge,Top Edge,2¶
    DATA wi_Width,Width,2¶
    DATA wi_Height,Height,2¶
    DATA wi_DetailPen,Drawing Color 1,1¶
    DATA wi_BlockPen,Drawing Color 2,1¶
    DATA wi_IDCMPFlags,Gadget Flags,4¶
    DATA wi_Flags,Window Flags,4¶
    DATA wi_FirstGadget,Gadget Structure,4¶
    DATA wi_CheckMark,CheckMark,4¶
    DATA wi_Title,Title Text,4¶
    DATA wi_Screen,Screen Pointer,4¶
    DATA wi_BitMap,Window BitMap,4¶
    DATA wi_MinWidth,Mininimum Width,2¶
    DATA wi_MinHeight,Minimum Height,2¶
    DATA wi_MaxWidht,Maximum Width,2¶
    DATA wi_MaxHeight,Maximum Height,2¶
    DATA wi_Type,$0001,2¶
    DATA actx-pos,Current x-Position,4¶
    DATA acty-pos,Current y-Position,4¶
    ¶
    Image:¶
    ¶
    DATA im_LeftEdge,Left Edge,2¶
    DATA im_TopEdge,Top Edge,2¶
    DATA im_Width,Width,2¶
    DATA im_Height,Height,2¶
    DATA im_Depth,Depth,2¶
```

257

```
DATA im_ImageData,BitPlane Pointer,4¶
DATA im_PlanePick,Graphic Data,1¶
DATA im_PlaneOnOff,Use,1¶
DATA im_NextImage,Next Graphic,4¶
¶
DefaultTool:¶
¶
DATA char_num,Number of Characters,4¶
¶
ToolTypes:¶
¶
DATA string_num,Text Number,4¶
```

*Program
description*

After creating arrays for all structures, the program prompts for the file-name you want analyzed. Do not enter the .info file extension, since the program provides that extension automatically. Next, all data contained in the file goes into summary$, so that disk access won't be needed later. If the text contains no closing nullbyte (Intuition normally does this), nullbytes are added. The main program jumps to the DiskObject structure reading routine.

Once the routine closes, the program branches to examine the icon type. The available structures are viewed, then the program branches to the required routines for looking into each structure.

The most important subroutine of all, LoadHeader, analyzes the DiskObject structure. This loads the name and the byte lengths of individual parameters from the DATA statements. The DATA lines are searched for the GetBytes subroutine, used by almost every subroutine.

After GetBytes reads the text and data lengths, the text goes into the window. From this text, the program computes the corresponding number to be displayed from the bytes. Then a subroutine executes for converting the hexadecimal values to decimal notation so the user can read the text more easily.

The LoadDrawer subroutine works in the same way as Load-Header. It reads the starting data, but computes the size of the graphic array from Size%; this lets you incorporate this size with your own display routines. Then the routine tests for a possible Double-Image. If there is a Double-Image, both Image structures must be read.

The LoadDefaultTool routine reads the text lenght from Get-Bytes. This number is multiplied by 16 for most test-icons, when this is needed. Next follows the call for the GetString routine, which reads the corresponding number of the string.

The same goes for LoadToolTypes, only the number of the text must be read.

8.3 Making your own icons

Now that you have some information about the structure of icons, you can now learn how to use and create your own icons. It's much easier to take an established icon and change it to your own needs. You can use the icon editor built into the Workbench diskette for this purpose.

8.3.1 Two graphics, one icon

This section tells how you can force the Amiga to display a new graphic for an icon that has been clicked, instead of simply inverting the original icon colors. This is a common method that can be applied to any icon type. Later on, you'll learn other extras, such as changing drawer icons only.

The change must set the pointer to the second Image structure, into which the new data is inserted. This problem is easier to solve than you might think, since the newest edition of the Extras diskette contains a program to do this. You must create two icons with a program like the Icon Editor. The only stipulation is that both icons must be the same size. After you enter the name, both icons are combined into one unit.

With this combined icon, you can create wonderful effects. For example, you can make the Trashcan icon "lid" open up when you click on the Trashcan icon (some versions of the Workbench already have this feature). You can also make a drawer icon "open" when you click on it (again, this already happens on some later Workbench diskettes).

8.3.2 Text in graphics

Another option for enhancing normal icons is placing text above the icon graphic.

As you saw from the DiskObject structure, the graphic range proper is different from the click range. This click range is given in the DiskObject structure at parameters 4-7. The icon's text appears below this click range. If you lower the height of the click range, then you can raise the text proportionally. This means that you can move the text up, and have it somewhere other than underneath the icon.

8.3.3   The icon editor

These changes require a program that allows you to access and change certain bytes, then save these altered bytes to diskette.

The program below is an extension of the analyzer program listed earlier. The entire program is listed below. Load your analyzer program, compare the listing with this listing, and add the new lines. Save the modified program under the name IconEditor.

```
DIM DiskObject$(26,3),DiskObject(26)¶
DIM DrawerData$(20,3),DrawerData(20)¶
DIM Image$(2,9,3),Image(2,9)¶
DIM DefaultTool$(2,3),DefaultTool(2)¶
DIM Address(100,3)¶
¶
ON TIMER(.5) GOSUB KeyTest¶
TIMER ON¶
¶
DEF FNSize%(Im)=Image(Im,4)*2*INT((Image(Im,3)+15)/16)¶


¶
WIDTH 75 : Adr=1 : AdrNum=1¶
¶
INPUT "Pathname:";Path$¶
INPUT "Filename:";File$¶
¶
OPEN Path$+File$+".info" FOR INPUT AS 1¶
¶
   summary$=INPUT$(LOF(1),1)¶
   ¶
CLOSE 1¶
¶
summary$=summary$+STRING$(40,0)¶
¶
LstBytes:¶
number=0 : lst=0¶
GOSUB LoadHeader¶
¶
   IF DiskObject(18)=1 THEN¶
     GOSUB LoadDrawer¶
     GOSUB LoadImage¶
     GOSUB LoadDefaultTool¶
     GOSUB LoadToolTypes¶
   END IF¶
¶
   IF DiskObject(18)=2 OR DiskObject(18)=5 THEN¶
     GOSUB LoadDrawer¶
     GOSUB LoadImage¶
     GOSUB LoadToolTypes¶
   END IF¶
   ¶
   IF DiskObject(18)=3 THEN¶
     GOSUB LoadImage   ¶
     GOSUB LoadToolTypes¶
   END IF¶
   ¶
   IF DiskObject(18)=4 THEN¶
     GOSUB LoadImage¶
     GOSUB LoadDefaultTool¶
     GOSUB LoadToolTypes¶
   END IF¶
```

```
   ¶
PRINT¶
PRINT "End of File!"¶
   ¶
WHILE last=0¶
   SLEEP¶
   IF lst=1 THEN GOTO LstBytes¶
WEND¶
   ¶
END¶
                              ¶
KeyTest:¶
   ¶
 IF INKEY$<>" " THEN RETURN¶
 WINDOW 2,"Input",(0,0)-(631,53),6¶
   ¶
Start:¶
 PRINT "Address:"Adr,Address(AdrNum,3)¶
 INPUT "Command: ",Command$¶
 ComKey$=LEFT$(Command$,1)¶
 ComTxt$=MID$(Command$,2)¶
 ComValue#=VAL(ComTxt$)¶
 IF ComKey$="#" THEN¶
    FOR TestI=1 TO number¶
       IF Address(TestI,1)=ComValue# THEN Adr=ComValue# :
AdrNum=TestI¶
    NEXT TestI¶
    GOTO Start¶
 END IF¶
 IF ComKey$="e" THEN last=1¶
 IF ComKey$="s" THEN¶
    IF LEN(ComTxt$)>0 THEN File$=ComTxt$¶
    OPEN ":mod. Icons/"+File$+".info" FOR OUTPUT AS 1¶
    PRINT#1,summary$¶
    CLOSE 1¶
    KILL ":mod. Icons/"+File$+".info.info"¶
    GOTO Start¶
 END IF¶
 IF ComKey$="a" THEN¶
    bytes$="" : value#=ComValue#¶
    FOR KeyI=Address(AdrNum,2)-1 TO 1 STEP -1¶
       a=INT(value#/256^KeyI)¶
       value#=value#-a*256^KeyI¶
       bytes$=bytes$+CHR$(a)¶
    NEXT KeyI¶
    bytes$=bytes$+CHR$(value#)¶
    MID$(summary$,Adr,Address(AdrNum,2))=bytes$¶
    Address(AdrNum,3)=ComValue#¶
    GOTO Start¶
 END IF¶
 IF ComKey$="l" THEN lst=1¶
   ¶
 WINDOW CLOSE 2¶
   ¶
RETURN¶
   ¶
   ¶
LoadHeader:¶
   RESTORE DiskObject¶
   po=1 : PRINT¶
   PRINT "Disk Object Structure" : PRINT¶
   FOR I=1 TO 26 ¶
       GetBytes DiskObject$(I,1),DiskObject$(I,2),
DiskObject$(I,3),DiskObject(I)¶
   NEXT I ¶
RETURN¶
   ¶
```

```
LoadDrawer:¶
  RESTORE DrawerData¶
  PRINT¶
  PRINT "DrawerData Structure" : PRINT¶
  FOR I=1 TO 20¶
     GetBytes DrawerData$(I,1),DrawerData$(I,2),
DrawerData$(I,3),DrawerData(I)¶
  NEXT I¶
RETURN¶
¶
LoadImage:¶
  Im=1¶
  GOSUB GetImage¶
  IF DiskObject(12)<>0 THEN Im=2 : GOSUB GetImage¶
RETURN¶
¶
GetImage:¶
  RESTORE Image¶
  PRINT¶
  PRINT "Image Structure" : PRINT¶
  FOR I=1 TO 9¶
     GetBytes Image$(Im,I,1),Image$(Im,I,2),
Image$(Im,I,3),Image(Im,I)¶
  NEXT I¶
  bytes=FNSize%(Im)¶
  PRINT¶
  PRINT "BitPlanes" : PRINT¶
  WIDTH 60¶
  FOR j=1 TO Image(Im,5)¶
     PRINT¶
     PRINT "Bitplane";j¶
     FOR I=1 TO bytes¶
        a$=HEX$(ASC(MID$(summary$,po,1)))¶
        IF LEN(a$)<2 THEN a$="0"+a$¶
        PRINT a$;¶
        IF I/2=INT(I/2) THEN PRINT " ";¶
        po=po+1¶
     NEXT I¶
     PRINT¶
  NEXT j¶
  WIDTH 75  ¶
RETURN¶
     ¶
LoadDefaultTool:¶
  RESTORE DefaultTool¶
  PRINT¶
  PRINT "DefaultTool" : PRINT¶
  GetBytes DefaulTool$(1,1),DefaultTool$(1,2),
DefaultTool$(1,3),DefaultTool(1)¶
  IF DefaultTool(1)>80 THEN
DefaultTool(1)=DefaultTool(1)/16¶
     GetString DefaultTool(1)/16¶
RETURN¶
     ¶
LoadToolTypes:¶
  RESTORE ToolTypes¶
  PRINT¶
  PRINT "ToolTypes" : PRINT¶
  IF po>LEN(summary$) THEN RETURN¶
  GetBytes ToolTypes$(1,1),ToolTypes$(1,2),
ToolTypes$(1,3),ToolTypes(1)¶
  FOR I=1 TO ToolTypes(1)/4-1¶
     RESTORE DefaultTool¶
     ToolTypes$(2,3)=""¶
     GetBytes ToolTypes$(2,1),ToolTypes$(2,2),
ToolTypes$(2,3),ToolTypes(2)¶
```

```
        IF ToolTypes(2)>80 THEN
ToolTypes(2)=ToolTypes(2)/16¶
        GetString ToolTypes(2)¶
   NEXT I      ¶
RETURN¶
¶
¶
SUB GetString (length) STATIC¶
¶
SHARED po,summary$¶
¶
 ts=po : a=1¶
 IF length=0 THEN EXIT SUB¶
 ¶
 WHILE a<>0¶
    a=ASC(MID$(summary$,po,1))¶
    a$=HEX$(a)¶
    IF LEN(a$)<2 THEN a$="0"+a$¶
    PRINT a$;" ";¶
    po=po+1¶
 WEND¶
 PRINT¶
 PRINT MID$(summary$,ts,po-ts-1)¶
 ¶
END SUB¶
¶
¶
SUB Decimal (he$,dec) STATIC¶
¶
 dec=0¶
 FOR I=1 TO LEN(he$) ¶
    a=ASC(MID$(he$,LEN(he$)+1-I,1))-48¶
    IF a>9 THEN a=a-7¶
    dec=dec+16^(I-1)*a¶
 NEXT I¶
 ¶
END SUB¶
¶
SUB GetBytes (identifier$,paramater$,value$,dec) STATIC¶

¶
SHARED po,summary$,Address(),number¶
    READ identifier$,paramater$,bytes¶
    PRINT identifier$;TAB(20);paramater$;TAB(47);¶
    a$=MID$(summary$,po,bytes)¶
    IF bytes=1 THEN value=ASC(a$)¶
    IF bytes=2 THEN value=CVI(a$)¶
    IF bytes=4 THEN¶
      value$=""¶
      FOR j=1 TO 4¶
        a=ASC(MID$(a$,j,1))¶
        h$=HEX$(a)¶
        IF LEN(h$)<2 THEN h$=h$+"0"¶
        value$=value$+h$¶
      NEXT j¶
    ELSE¶
        value$=HEX$(value)¶
    END IF¶
    PRINT "$";value$;TAB(57);¶
    Decimal value$,dec¶
    PRINT dec;TAB(71);po¶
    number=number+1¶
    Address(number,1)=po : Address(number,2)=bytes :
Address(number,3)=dec¶
    po=po+bytes¶
    ¶
END SUB¶
¶
¶
```

```
DiskObject:¶
¶
DATA do_Magic,Magic Number,2¶
DATA do_Version,Version Number,2¶
DATA do_Gadget,Click Structure,4¶
DATA gg_LeftEdge,Left Click Range,2¶
DATA gg_TopEdge,Top Click Range,2¶
DATA gg_Width,Click Range Width,2¶
DATA gg_Height,Click Range Height,2¶
DATA gg_Flags,Invert Flag,2¶
DATA gg_Activation,$0003,2¶
DATA gg_Type,$0001,2¶
DATA gg_GadgetRender,Pointer1 Picture Data,4¶
DATA gg_SelectRender,Pointer2 Picture Data,4¶
DATA gg_IntuiText,"not used??",4¶
DATA gg_MutualExclude,"not useable!",4¶
DATA gg_SpecialInfo,"not useable!",4¶
DATA gg_GadgetID,"for own use!",2¶
DATA gg_UserData,"your Pointer!",4¶
DATA do_Type,Icon type,1¶
DATA nothing,Fillbyte,1¶
DATA do_DefaultTool,Text Structure,4¶
DATA do_ToolTypes,Text Structure,4¶
DATA do_CurrentX,Current x-Position,4¶
DATA do_CurrentY,Current y-Position,4¶
DATA do_DrawerData,Window Structure,4¶
DATA do_ToolWindow,Program Window,4¶
DATA do_StackSize,Reserved Memory,4¶
¶
DrawerData:¶
¶
DATA wi_LeftEdge,Left Edge,2¶
DATA wi_TopEdge,Top Edge,2¶
DATA wi_Width,Width,2¶
DATA wi_Height,Height,2¶
DATA wi_DetailPen,Drawing Color 1,1¶
DATA wi_BlockPen,Drawing Color 2,1¶
DATA wi_IDCMPFlags,Gadget Flags,4¶
DATA wi_Flags,Window Flags,4¶
DATA wi_FirstGadget,Gadget Structure,4¶
DATA wi_CheckMark,CheckMark,4¶
DATA wi_Title,Title Text,4¶
DATA wi_Screen,Screen Pointer,4¶
DATA wi_BitMap,Window BitMap,4¶
DATA wi_MinWidth,Mininimum Width,2¶
DATA wi_MinHeight,Minimum Height,2¶
DATA wi_MaxWidht,Maximum Width,2¶
DATA wi_MaxHeight,Maximum Height,2¶
DATA wi_Type,$0001,2¶
DATA actx-pos,Current x-Position,4¶
DATA acty-pos,Current y-Position,4¶
¶
Image:¶
¶
DATA im_LeftEdge,Left Edge,2¶
DATA im_TopEdge,Top Edge,2¶
DATA im_Width,Width,2¶
DATA im_Height,Height,2¶
DATA im_Depth,Depth,2¶
DATA im_ImageData,BitPlane Pointer,4¶
DATA im_PlanePick,Graphic Data,1¶
DATA im_PlaneOnOff,Use,1¶
DATA im_NextImage,Next Graphic,4¶
¶
DefaultTool:¶
¶
DATA char_num,Number of Characters,4¶
¶
ToolTypes:¶
¶
```

```
DATA string_num,Text Number,4¶
```

***Program
description***

Most of this program matches the icon analyzer program in structure and program flow. One change is the byte number following all changeable parameters. In addition, pressing <SPACE> calls a window. This window lets you enter the following simple file management commands:

 # num

Enter the address for num at which you want the change made. From there you can select the position where you want your bytes added.

a num

The current address is assigned the value placed in num. The routine converts the given number to byte format.

s name

This saves the info file bytes in the directory :mod.Icons. You should make this directory before running this program (use makedir mod.Icons in the CLI to create this directory). If you give no name after s, the name used for the previous loading procedure is assigned to s.

l

Once you've made changes, this lets you list the program structure out.

e

This command ends the program. The e command must be given, since the program's display structure is within a delay loop.

When you want to exit the editor, press the <RETURN> key at any prompt without entering any other text.

The authors realize that this editor isn't the most comfortable one in the world to work with. However, a more user-friendly editor would take up much more memory, and the current version of the editor performs all the necessary functions.

8.3.4   Color changes

Any window can open in its own color, including the **Workbench** window. The default Workbench colors are effective enough, but they aren't very interesting. To change these colors, you must change the data and colors before opening the window. Changing window structure is very similar to changing drawer structure.

You can see the Drawing color 1/2 using the icon editor in Section 8.3.3. The Drawing color contains the value $FF or 255. A few details about screen color changes were mentioned earlier. Using the icon editor write a value between 0 and three in the corresponding byte to change the color.

The best thing to do is experiment with these options. Don't be surprised, though, when you try to open one of the stored info files, the Info screen opens for a moment then disappears again. This happens because no subdirectory exists for the window, which is apparently very important to a drawer icon. Enter the CLI and create a directory for every info file using the makedir command.

From there, you can then see all the new window colors. Some color combinations don't work very well. Others cancel out text. Work toward what you can see best in terms of contrast and readability.

9
Error trapping

9   Error trapping

Controlled error handling is an absolute necessity for large programs. These can save the user a lot of trouble from incorrect input. Very few programs are equipped with foolproof error checking. All the user has to do is type in input that the computer can't accept, and the system may crash. Error trapping is another facet of user-friendliness.

However, you must first know how errors are handled in the first place, and where in the program the error occurs. You can't find the latter on your own, but there are a few rules you can follow to help your programs run error-free.

This chapter shows you how you can foolproof your programs from errors. You'll read about routines that check for files on diskette without stopping from an error message, programs that generate requesters, and even a demonstration of easy menu creation.

9.1   Errors—and why

Even when programs shouldn't have errors, they may have some—whether you wrote them, or they were written commercially. These errors can be divided into two generic groups. The first group consists of errors that the programmer may have overlooked. These are the lines that result from leaving out a parenthesis or formula (syntax). This error type happens often when you or the user try modifying a program. The only way to avoid syntax (or any) errors is to completely test a program. But how?

First, write down a list of program sections that must be used. Note the program lines that operate under certain conditions. A number of errors may only occur under certain conditions. When you test the program, you have to test every section by calling them.

There are more error sources to annoy the user and programmer alike. A frequently encountered error is the `Subscript Out of Range` error. This happens when you try to access an array element past the default 10 elements of an array. Make a list of the arrays used, and make sure that you define them all properly. To make control easier, use one particular section for dimensioning arrays at the beginning of the program.

Math errors are another source of problems. Almost any calculation can lead to an error. Any slip of the hand can lead to an `Overflow` error, or a `Division by Zero`. Make sure your computations test for incorrect input, particularly in division, exponentiation, etc.

9.1.1   Disk access errors

Imagine this: You write the perfect data and address base. The user types in the name of the file that uses this program, and all he gets is a `File Not Found` error. Unlike the Workbench, which displays a requester when something is wrong, AmigaBASIC returns an error.

A file under that name may exist, but you may have accidentally created it from another program, and it may have a different format from the program currently in use. The best that can happen is that the data can confuse the program. Most of the time the result is a `Type Mismatch` or similar error.

A much more aggravating error occurs when the file is on the right diskette, but the file you want is in another directory altogether. The result is a File Not Found error.

9.1.2   User input errors

Any database program requires the entry of values. But even values have their limitations! Numbers should be within a certain range, and/or have a certain number of decimal places; texts can only be a certain length or can only contain certain characters. All these conditions aren't considered by the normal INPUT statement. It accepts numeric input as well as text, and the wrong kind of input results in a Redo from Start error message, screen scrolling and repeated input.

The option of selecting only certain characters is unsupported. If the user goes past the assigned text length, the program cuts off these extra characters. This means that important information can be lost.

9.1.3   Menu errors

This is where errors get harder to pinpoint. User menus consist of entire subroutines and functions. The user selects an item and the program reacts. But menus are not infallible.

Under certain circumstances, one or more menu items may be unusable. Selecting a menu item that shouldn't be used could lead to no reaction at all, or even a system failure.

One harmless example could be a Save item on the fictional database program mentioned above. Selecting this item when no data has been entered doesn't crash the computer, but the data diskette now has a blank record that could be very difficult to remove later.

9.2   Trapping errors

It's possible to trap errors, or even bypass them. The keyword in solving these problems mentioned above is *prevention*.

Checking for errors

As already mentioned, you can prevent simple error messages like `Division by Zero` by checking for these errors. This method is much more user-friendly than the program just stopping with an error. Program breaks give the user a new problem—he has to become a programmer and find the bug himself. Either you can set the program up to prompt for the correct data, or at least have the program jump to the beginning. These are crude, but either route is better than a break.

There are other ways to handle errors in BASIC. ON ERROR GOTO sends the system to a given line when an error occurs. The programmer assigns the line or routine. From there, the program can mention the nature of the error, or return to the area just after the incorrect line.

Requester

The system requester is a much friendlier solution to error handling. For example: If the wrong diskette is in the disk drive, a window appears in the upper left hand corner. This window displays the text, "Please insert volume in any drive". From there, you can select the Cancel gadget to exit, or the Retry gadget to go on. The requester is the last chance you get to correct an error, without getting an error message. However, the requester is the only way to get around certain problems, such as exchanging diskettes when you only have one disk drive.

You may not get a chance to test your program under every circumstance, so you may have to create your own errors using subroutines. These errors can test your error checking thoroughly.

9.2.1   User-friendly programming

Now that you've read through the theory, you can go on to practical programming. When an error occurs, nothing angers a user more than a program break. This is because most users aren't professional programmers, and even if they do program, they may not understand most of the material within a program written by someone else. You as a programmer must make things as simple for the user as possible. Programs should offer the user a chance to correct errors with some flexibility. You've already seen an example of user-friendly programming in the system requester mentioned above; it gave you an opportunity to insert the correct diskette.

You can write this kind of flexible programming! You're probably thinking of one way—open a window, write the text, and read for the mouse click. That's one possible solution, but it's also too complicated! Instead, you can let the operating system draw a requester for you. You'll see how this is done, and how you can insert your own information, below.

Before you can program a requester, you must clearly know what you want the requester to do. It can serve the same occasions as those served by the Workbench requesters.

For example, you can set up a requester for a file that the system can't find on diskette. BASIC usually returns an error message. You must first suppress the error message, then call the requester that matches a File not Found error message.

Bypassing errors

Since the File not Found error message usually accompanies opening a file that is neither on the diskette nor in the correct directory, you can't just read status during OPEN. A sequential file gives you another way out, though. You can open the file using the APPEND option. Either the file exists as defined by a pointer, which allows adding to the file, or the file doesn't exist, and a new file opens. The LOF function lets you see if the file existed previously. A file exists if the file is at least one character in length; otherwise, the length is equal to zero. If the length is equal to zero, the program deletes the newly opened file.

Here is a program that demonstrates the above procedures:

```
' Check for existing file¶
' on diskette¶
'¶
'    by Wgb, August '87¶
'¶
¶
¶
FileName$="AmigaBasic2"¶
¶
 Mainprogram:¶
¶
 Again:¶
 ¶
 PRINT "Searching for the file: ";¶
 WRITE FileName$¶
 ¶
 CALL CheckFile (FileName$)¶
 IF exist=-1 THEN¶
   PRINT "Okay, the file exists!"¶
 ELSE¶
   PRINT "File not found...sorry."¶
 END IF¶
 ¶
END¶
¶
' -------------------------------¶
¶
SUB CheckFile (File$) STATIC¶
¶
 SHARED exist¶
```

```
¶
OPEN File$ FOR APPEND AS 255¶
   exist=(LOF(255)>1)¶
CLOSE 255¶
¶
IF exist=0 THEN KILL File$¶
¶
END SUB¶
```

You can use a more elegant (and more complex) method to determine whether a file exists on diskette (see the program below). This other way uses a subroutine that returns a corresponding value: 1 (file exists) or 0 (file not found).

The Lock function must be defined within a program as a function. Then the memory location of the name is given, ending with a null-byte. Next, the routine supplies information about how the file should be accessed. Since the Amiga is a multitasking computer, you can choose one access by itself (Access Mode = Exclusive Write (-1)) or read access by multiple tasks (Access Mode = Shared Access (-2)). The first option provides write and read access for a single user. The second option allows more than one program and/or user to read one file at the same time.

The new routine uses Shared Access, a returned value of -2.

The value returned by the function is equal to zero if no file exists on diskette. The value must go into memory, since it can allow another try at file access.

The access secured through this routine should cancel the list of parameters, since this list takes memory and time. You can use the Un-Lock function for this cancellation. The routine returns the value received by Lock.

```
' Test for existing file on diskette¶
' using  dos.library¶
'¶
' © by Wgb, August '87¶
'¶
¶
DECLARE FUNCTION Lock& LIBRARY¶
¶
LIBRARY "dos.library"¶
¶
FileName$="AmigaBasic2"¶
¶
MainProgram:¶
¶
 Again:¶
 ¶
 PRINT "Searching for the file: ";¶
 WRITE FileName$¶
 ¶
 CALL CheckFile (FileName$)¶
 IF exist=-1 THEN¶
   PRINT "File exists!"¶
   PRINT "File Header begins at Block";blk&;"on this
Disk."¶
```

```
    ELSE¶
     PRINT "File not found!"¶
    END IF¶
    ¶
    LIBRARY CLOSE ¶
    END¶
    ¶
    ' -------------------------------¶
    ¶
    SUB CheckFile (File$) STATIC¶
    ¶
     SHARED exist,blk&¶
    ¶
     File$=File$+CHR$(0)¶
     accessRead%=-2¶
     DosLock&=Lock&(SADD(File$),accessRead%)¶
     IF DosLock&=0 THEN¶
        exist=0¶
     ELSE¶
        exist=-1¶
        blk&=PEEKL(DosLock&*4+4)¶
     END IF¶
    ¶
     CALL UnLock(DosLock&)¶
    ¶
    END SUB¶
```

Now that you have some understanding of how to check for a file on diskette or in a subdirectory, you should learn how you can create a requester in BASIC.

It's possible to write a requester completely in BASIC, as described above. However, it's much easier to use the requester routine provided by the Amiga's operating system. This operating system module is called the `AutoRequest` function. This function takes your text and gadget requests, and does the rest. The program below contains a subroutine that does all this for you. This subroutine returns a value which tells the main program where to branch from that point.

```
' Test for a file on ¶
' diskette¶
'¶
' © by Wgb, June'87¶
'¶
¶
DECLARE FUNCTION AllocRemember& LIBRARY¶
DECLARE FUNCTION AutoRequest& LIBRARY¶
DECLARE FUNCTION Lock& LIBRARY¶
¶
LIBRARY "df1:intuition.library"¶
LIBRARY "df1:dos.library"¶
¶
FileName$="df1:9.Errors/AmigaBasic2"¶
¶
 Mainprogram:¶
¶
 Again:¶
¶
 PRINT "File: ";¶
 WRITE FileName$¶
¶
 CheckFile FileName$¶
 IF exist=-1 THEN¶
    PRINT "File exists!"¶
```

```
     PRINT "File Header begins at Block";blk&;"on this
Disk."¶
 ELSE¶
  Request FileName$¶
  IF res&=1 THEN GOTO Again¶
  PRINT "File not found!"¶
 END IF¶
 ¶
LIBRARY CLOSE ¶
END¶
 ¶
' ------------------------------¶
 ¶
SUB CheckFile (File$) STATIC¶
 ¶
 SHARED exist,blk&¶
 ¶
 TestFile$=File$+CHR$(0)¶
 accessRead%=-2¶
 DosLock&=Lock&(SADD(TestFile$),accessRead%)¶
 IF DosLock&=0 THEN¶
    exist=0¶
 ELSE¶
    exist=-1¶
    blk&=PEEKL(DosLock&*4+4)¶
 END IF¶
 ¶
 CALL UnLock(DosLock&)¶
 ¶
END SUB¶
 ¶
' ------------------------------------¶
 ¶
SUB Request (FileName$) STATIC¶
 ¶
 SHARED add&,st$,res&,offs%¶
 ¶
 Quest$(0)="Please insert volume containing"¶
 Quest$(1)="File "+FileName$¶
 Quest$(2)="Can't find the file!"¶
 yes$="Retry"¶
 no$="Cancel"¶
 bt%=2¶
 wid%=8*38¶
 hi%=8*9¶
 offs%=0¶
 ¶
 opt&=2^0+2^16¶
 req&=AllocRemember&(0,400,opt&)¶
 IF req&=0 THEN ERROR 7¶
 ¶
 add&=req&¶
 ¶
 t1&=add&¶
 FOR loop2=0 TO bt%-1¶
    st$=Quest$(loop2)¶
    MakeHeader add&,st$,1,5,offs%+3¶
    offs%=offs%+8¶
 NEXT loop2¶
 ¶
 st$=Quest$(bt%)¶
 MakeHeader add&,st$,0,5,offs%+3¶
 ¶
 st$=yes$¶
 t2&=add&¶
 MakeHeader add&,st$,0,5,3¶
 ¶
 st$=no$¶
 t3&=add&¶
```

```
      MakeHeader add&,st$,0,5,3¶
      ¶
      res&=AutoRequest&(WINDOW(7),t1&,t2&,t3&,0,0,wid%,hi%)¶

      CALL FreeRemember(0,-1)¶
      ¶
END SUB¶
¶
SUB MakeHeader (ptr&,Text$,md%,le%,te%) STATIC¶
¶
   SHARED add&¶
   Text$=Text$+CHR$(0)¶
¶
   POKE ptr&,1¶
   POKE ptr&+1,0¶
   POKE ptr&+2,2¶
   POKEW ptr&+4,le%¶
   POKEW ptr&+6,te%¶
   POKEL ptr&+8,0¶
   POKEL ptr&+12,SADD(Text$)¶
   IF md%=0 THEN¶
      POKEL ptr&+16,0¶
   ELSE¶
      POKEL ptr&+16,ptr&+20¶
   END IF¶
   ¶
   add&=ptr&+20¶
END SUB¶
```

Program
description

First the routine must "know" which text you want displayed. Three texts lie in the routine; the main text, and additional texts from which it can select. The last two texts are displayed in one line, and are surrounded by borders. These make up the gadgets which you click. After establishing the text, you must set the window size. If the requester window is too small, the text simply spills over or gets overwritten, making it hard to read.

The text must be placed in memory in a certain structure, with a memory range reserved for this structure. The operating system function AllocRemember sets this range aside. It allows selection of a memory range based on preset criteria.

PUBLIC	2^0
CHIP	2^1
FAST	2^2
CLEAR	2^{16}

Any type of memory can be used, just as long as it is cleared beforehand. If no memory is available, then an error message appears.

Assume for the moment that enough memory is available. Then the text goes into the reserved area. This text must still appear in a certain format. BASIC programmers can use POKEs for this formatting. This command is useful for the use and design of your own programs only—AmigaBASIC normally doesn't require any POKEing.

The first loop brings the information text into the reserved memory range. Then the two gadgets transfer to RAM. If everything runs correctly, then the `AutoRequest` function can begin its task. It first takes the addresses of the first text, the two gadget texts and the requester's size. These return a value and then a result of 1, if the first gadget is clicked by the user.

This value can then be followed by branches to the main program. Either the system repeats the loading procedure, because of an incorrect diskette or non-existent file, or the loading procedure stops and returns the user to the main program.

9.2.2   Trapping user input errors

Now you have a requester that checks for existing files. An even more important aspect of error trapping is keeping the user's input correct. User entry has its own problems and errors.

The simplest and best solution is to write an input routine that reads the input, retains the desired characters and ignores the rest, without returning an error message. The routine must ascertain which characters are "legal" and which ones aren't. This can be accomplished by calling a string which contains valid characters, and a routine that lists the valid number of characters. The subroutine handles the rest of the characters. When the user presses the <RETURN> key, the subroutine ends.

Most input goes to a specific position of the window for display. Coordinates set this position, saving the trouble of using the LOCATE command. You can display any text through the INPUT command.

```
' Input Routine ¶
'¶
' © by Wgb May '87¶
'¶
¶
Mainprogram:¶
¶
  DEFINT a-z¶
  KAlpha$="abcdefghijklmnopqrstuvwxyz"¶
  GAlpha$="ABCDEFGHIJKLMNOPQRSTUVWXYZ"¶
  NAlpha$="01234567890+-*/.,="¶
  ZAlpha$="  ,.?!-/;:'"¶
  Possl$=KAlpha$+GAlpha$+ZAlpha$¶
  ¶
  GetInput "Last  name:",LName$,Possl$,10,10,20,0¶
  GetInput "First name:",CName$,Possl$,10,12,20,0¶
  WRITE LName$,CName$¶
  END¶
  ¶
  ¶
SUBRoutines:¶
  ¶
  SUB GetInput (Text$,In$,Possl$,x,y,Letter,Pointer)
STATIC¶
  ¶
    Xold=POS(0)¶
    Yold=CSRLIN¶
```

```
        Length=0¶
        LOCATE y,x¶
        PRINT Text$;¶
        x=x+LEN(Text$)¶
¶
     ReadOut:¶
        Cursor x+Length,y¶
        GetInkey i$¶
        IF i$=CHR$(13) THEN GOTO Done¶
        IF i$=CHR$(8) THEN GOTO RubOut¶
        IF Letter=Length THEN GOTO ReadOut¶
¶
        f=INSTR(Poss1$,i$)¶
        IF f=0 THEN¶
           BEEP¶
           GOTO ReadOut¶
        END IF¶
¶
        PRINT i$;¶
        In$=In$+i$ : Length=Length+1¶
     GOTO ReadOut¶
¶
     RubOut:¶
¶
        IF Length=0 THEN GOTO ReadOut¶
        Length=Length-1¶
        PRINT " ";¶
        In$=LEFT$(In$,Length)¶
        GOTO ReadOut¶
¶
     Done:¶
¶
        PRINT " ";¶
        LOCATE Yold,Xold¶
        IF Pointer AND 1 = 1 THEN¶
           l=LEN(In$)¶
           In$=In$+SPACE$(Letter-l)¶
        END IF¶
        ¶
     END SUB¶
¶
¶
     SUB Cursor (x,y) STATIC¶
¶
        COLOR 3¶
        LOCATE y,x¶
        PRINT " ";¶
        LOCATE y,x¶
        COLOR 1¶
        ¶
     END SUB¶
¶
     SUB GetInkey (Key$) STATIC¶
¶
     KeyRead:¶
        Key$=INKEY$¶
     IF Key$="" THEN GOTO KeyRead¶
¶
     END SUB¶
```

Program description

Before calling this new input routine, you should define a string or set of strings containing groups of valid characters. For example, you can set up a string of lowercase characters, one of uppercase characters, another one made of numbers, and a string of other characters. These strings let you easily set which characters you want accepted. The new INPUT command accepts these strings as a constant.

GetInput itself gives the text contained in the variable as a string with all valid characters, its position, the number of characters entered, and a pointer. This pointer determines whether the input text should be filled with spaces where invalid characters appear in the text. This pointer sets to 1 if this is the case.

Unfortunately, editing numbers is impossible. You can do this, however, with the following combination:

```
GetInput "Number: ",Number$,NumChar$,10,10,8
Number=VAL(Number$)
```

When NumChar$ only contains numbers, you can make sure that no nulls stand in Number if you don't want to. At any rate, you won't get a Redo from Start error from numeric input.

Cursor placement

The subroutine stores the current cursor position at the beginning. Since this position stays the same when the program exits the routine, then it doesn't affect output. The text appears in the specified position, and the computer sets the starting position for input. The length of the text entered is still set to zero.

The read loop displays the current input position of the cursor, and the routine waits for a keypress. Any character received goes through the control functions. If you press the <BACKSPACE> key, the character most recently entered deletes whenever possible. Pressing the <RETURN> key branches immediately to the end of the routine.

Next the routine checks to see if the next character is "legal." The routine examines the string constants you set for this character. If the character is valid, it is added to the input string; if not, the Amiga BEEPs and returns to the beginning of the read loop. The routine then waits for the next character.

Adaptation

You can naturally adapt this routine to your own needs. For example, this program doesn't provide for letting the user move the cursor around within the text. It allows simple character deletion, but user input would be a lot simpler if you could insert or delete characters in the middle of the input line.

Another feature missing from this routine is the acceptance of no input at all. This can be practical when one value is used repeatedly, and needs little if any changing. You can add this to the beginning of the subroutine by predetermining the length of the parameters that must appear on the screen.

Up to now, the only way you could end a prompt or input was by pressing the <RETURN> key. You could change the pointer so that when, say, the second bit is set, input ends only when the entry contains a minimum of one character.

9.3   Errors and corrections

This section deals with corrections. Up until now, this chapter has assumed that correction is the last possible option for incorrect input. Most of the time no one takes this route, since real-time error checking in BASIC simply takes too much time. The self-generated input routine showed that examining every character can take up to three seconds to see if the character is good, bad or indifferent. This can't be helped.

For example, say you only want one word out of a hundred possible words entered. The system checks every single character as it appears in the combination. When you end the input, it checks all available words against this input, and you can display an error message or branch to the input as needed.

Most of the time, responses occur in which you have no say whether or not all values are recognized. Here, checking is only possible as a last resort. If the program establishes that a value is invalid, then it can simply be corrected. The program doesn't go on immediately after this. The user must again switch on correction to see if the value just entered is valid or not.

You can see that this is a fairly complicated subject. The entire matter of error-free user input is difficult, and unfortunately you can't hold a patent on this kind of routine. Every program has its own features, and its own error sources. As a programmer, you must be sympathetic to the user, and consider every place in a program where an error can happen. This means that testing should occur wherever an error can occur—better that than a program break later on.

9.3.1   Blocking out menu items

One answer to bypassing errors is to force inaccessible menu items to appear in ghost print. Programming with the MENU command leaves all menu items open to selection. This makes designing menus fairly simple. But what if you want to deactivate menu items so that the entire menu becomes inactive? You can save yourself a lot of work using MENU number,item,0 to deactivate individual items. This gets to be time-consuming when you call this command to create an entire menu in ghost print.

That's where this program comes in. It uses a SUB routine named Able, which lets you assign the desired status to multiple menu:

items. You can deactivate an entire block if you wish, or assign checkmarks to an active block of menu items. The function is a practical
replacement for the MENU command.

```
' PullDownTest¶
'¶
' © by Wgb in June '87¶
'¶
¶
DEFINT a-z¶
¶
MainProgram:¶
¶
 GOSUB MenuDefinition¶
 PRINT"All menus active."¶
 Pause 5¶
 ¶
 PRINT "Disk menu inactive."¶
 Able 1,0,0,0¶
 Pause 5¶
 ¶
 PRINT "Drawing type set."¶
 Able 2,4,0,2¶
 Pause 5¶
 ¶
 PRINT"Single-color drawing only."¶
 Able 3,1,5,0¶
 Able 3,1,0,1¶
 Pause 5¶
 ¶
 PRINT"GET from Brush menu available only."¶
 Able 4,1,4,0¶
 Able 1,0,0,1¶
 Able 3,1,5,1¶
 Pause 5¶
 ¶
 PRINT"Press a key to end the program."¶
 Able 1,0,0,0¶
 Able 2,0,0,0¶
 Able 3,0,0,0¶
 Able 4,0,0,0¶
 Able 5,1,2,0¶
 ¶
 WHILE INKEY$=""¶
  SLEEP¶
 WEND¶
 ¶
 MENU RESET¶
 ¶
END¶
 ¶
 ¶
MenuDefinition:¶
 ¶
 RESTORE MenuData¶
 ¶
 READ Number¶
 FOR i=1 TO Number¶
    READ Items,Length¶
    FOR j=0 TO Items¶
       READ Item$¶
       IF j>0 THEN¶
          Item$=LEFT$(Item$+SPACE$(Length),Length)¶
          IF i=2 OR i=3 THEN¶
          Item$=" "+Item$¶
         END IF¶
       END IF¶
       MENU i,j,1,Item$¶
```

```
      NEXT j¶
    NEXT i¶
  ¶
  RETURN¶
  ¶
  SUB Able(MenuNr,Item,Number,Types) STATIC¶
  ¶
  FOR i=Item TO Item+Number¶
    MENU MenuNr,i,Types¶
  NEXT i¶
  ¶
  END SUB¶
  ¶
  SUB Pause (Seconds) STATIC¶
  ¶
  Elapsed&=TIMER+Seconds¶
  WHILE TIMER<Elapsed&¶
  WEND¶
  ¶
  PRINT¶
  ¶
  END SUB¶
  ¶
  MenuData:¶
  ¶
   DATA 5¶
   DATA 7,15,Disk¶
   DATA New,Load,Load as¶
   DATA Save,Save as¶
   DATA Disk Command,Quit¶
   ¶
   DATA 7,9,Draw¶
   DATA Freehand,Line,Lines¶
   DATA Circle,Rectangle,Polygon¶
   DATA Fill¶
   ¶
   DATA 6,11,Color¶
   DATA One Color,Multicolor,Palette¶
   DATA Shadow,Wipe,Transparent¶
   ¶
   DATA 6,9,Brush¶
   DATA Load,Load as,Save¶
   DATA Save as, Clear,Get¶
  ¶
   DATA 4,11,Extras¶
   DATA Workbench,Coordinates¶
   DATA Blend Out,End¶
  ¶
  add&=ptr&+20¶
```

Program description

First all variables are defined as integers. You may wonder why this program declares just these few variables. The reason is that when you define these at the beginning, the speed increases greatly—all math operations run as integer arithmetic. Besides, no problems crop up during the subroutine calls. If whole-number constants appear there, then the Type Mismatch error occurs (the subprograms want real number variables). Then you must either add integer signs to the constants in the command line, or adapt the variable types in the SUB program.

After variable definition, the main program branches to the SUB program MenuDefinition, which reads the menu texts from the DATA statements at the end of the listing.

283

Now look at the SUB program itself. After the DATA statements generate the menu data, the corresponding number goes to the outermost loop. This loop reads all the data concerning the number of menu items per menu and the length for each text. The last value is very important, since after defining a menu you can open the corresponding array. It has a maximum X-length based upon the longest text. You can only activate the individual menu items that actually contain characters. Every line that contains less than the maximum number of characters fills in with blank spaces. You can also activate the spaces at the end of every menu item.

With this, you can make a graphic, move the menu items to the start of the current item, and place a REM character in front of the line, filling the Item$ variable with SPACE$. When you select the menu item, make sure you realize that this was done.

Look at the inner loop of the SUB routine. This takes the abovementioned number of menu items from the DATA statements, and defines them with the MENU function. Menus 2 and 3 can have checkmarks before their items, when two spaces precede the texts of these menus. The addition of spaces following the texts changes when the number of menu items is greater than null. The menu title must not be corrected in this case.

Now on the main program itself. It displays the text stating that all menus are active. From this the user can determine the branch to a subroutine which waits for a given number of seconds then returns to the main program.

The design of this routine is fairly simple. First the computer calculates the time number which must be assigned to the given number of seconds. Then this waits in a delay loop until the current time is reached.

The main program displays another text that says that the Disk menu is inactive. After this, the most important subroutines execute. The parameters state that the first menu's title, as well as the other menu titles, should be set with zeros. This sets all the other menu items to zero.

The SUB routine is easy to call, but designed with ease of use in mind. For each parameter, a loop executes which assigns the specific item types to all menu items.

10
Effective programming

10   Effective programming

"How can I program more effectively?" Good question. The chances are good that anyone reading this book has some knowledge of programming. But since every programmer has his own style, the question of effective programming can't be answered simply. This chapter tries to point out some ideas that will help your programming style.

Style in programs

Before going on to the examples, here are a few things to bear in mind. Three different people authored this book. Every one of these men has his own style, but the ideas for style here come from only one of the authors. The following personal "style sheet" was used on the program examples in Chapter 4:

1)   Indent commands in every loop by three spaces

2)   Indent every main program command or every label by one character

3)   Place all subroutines at the end of a listing

4)   Place all DATA statements after the subroutines

5)   Indent any commands in an IF construct by two characters

These are personal opinions about style. These rules assume that you only write one command to a program line.

When you use multiple commands on a program line, the readability of the program suffers. Programming style is much more than the amount of money you get for writing a program. To some degree, a program is a work of art. The most important aspect of a program is that it works, and not necessarily how it looks. However, when you write a program that's several hundred lines long, or when you want to adapt this program for commercial sale, you should write it so that anyone can understand it if they look at it.

Style is but a small part of effective programming. As already mentioned, readability serves the user and the programmer, but it's incidental. The program's function is the primary factor. An effective program accomplishes in one line what could normally take ten lines of program code. Or, an effective program executes a formula in seconds that might take other programs a week.

10.1   Benchmarks

Tests for measuring program speed and efficiency are called *benchmarks*.
These benchmarks measure the time involved in a program run. You
can then edit the program and try the benchmark again.

10.1.1   Benchmark: variable types

Why are there different variable types? For one thing, you can't store
text in the same way you store numbers. To see some other reasons
why there are so many different types of variables, type in and run the
following program:

```
' Benchmark used for testing the differences¶
' between different variable types¶
'¶
' © by Wgb, June '87¶
¶
PRINT "Benchmark 1 tests for the differences between
different"¶
PRINT "variable types, using the following loop:¶
PRINT¶
PRINT "                FOR i=1 to 10000¶
PRINT "                    a=a+1¶
PRINT "                NEXT i¶
PRINT¶
¶
t1a=TIMER¶
¶
FOR i%=1 TO 10000¶
   a=a+1¶
NEXT i%¶
¶
t1b=TIMER¶
PRINT "Short integer floating variable          (%)
:";t1b-t1a¶
CLEAR¶
¶
t2a=TIMER¶
¶
FOR i&=1 TO 10000¶
   a=a+1¶
NEXT i&¶
¶
t2b=TIMER¶
PRINT "Long integer floating variable        (&) :";t2b-t2a¶
```

```
CLEAR¶
¶
t3a=TIMER¶
¶
FOR i=1 TO 10000¶
    a=a+1¶
NEXT i¶
¶
t3b=TIMER¶
PRINT "Single-precision floating-point variable   :";t3b-
t3a¶
CLEAR¶
¶
t4a=TIMER¶
¶
FOR i!=1 TO 10000¶
    a=a+1¶
NEXT i!¶
¶
t4b=TIMER¶
PRINT "Single-precision floating-point variable (!) :";t4b-
t4a¶
CLEAR¶
¶
t5a=TIMER¶
¶
FOR i#=1 TO 10000¶
    a=a+1¶
NEXT i#¶
¶
t5b=TIMER¶
PRINT "Double-precision floating-point variable   (#)
:";t5b-t5a¶
```

Program description

All the other benchmarks in this chapter are based on this program. First some text commentary appears, telling the user what the program does. The text then disappears.

The time variable t1a declares the starting time (t1a=TIMER), then the program executes a loop. The time variable with the index b sets the ending time. The computer figures out the execution time of the loop from the difference between the starting and ending time. This appears on the screen with a text. To avoid any outside influence, all variables clear and the routine starts all over again.

This tests out the execution time of the same loop, using variables of different types. The final result shows which variable types allow faster execution, and which variable types slow execution time.

See the table below. These are the values we received when we ran this benchmark, but try the program out yourself:

int	long int	simple float	simple !	double
10.92188	11	13	13	13.80078
10.89844	11	13	13	13.9375
10.89844	10.96094	13.10156	16.59766	13.83984
11.05859	11	13	13	13.80078
10.89844	10.98047	13	13	13.80078
10.89844	10.98047	13	12.98047	13.80078
10.89844	10.98047	13	13	13.80078

As you can see from the table, the values aren't constant for every type. The next section explains why this is so.

The loop executes 10,000 times. Decimal places must be born in mind —multiply the entire set by 1000, and the values are more even.

Short and long integers

The long integer values require more time than the short integers. This is understandable since the bytes store twice their length in numbers. The disadvantage to both these variable types is that they can handle whole numbers only.

Integer variables are faster than floating-point variables. So you can distinguish the types by those marked by decimal points. There are three distinctions between two types. One is single accuracy, the other has double accuracy. The simplest means that unless a variable is designated otherwise, it handles numbers with single accuracy. You can also add an exclamation point to a variable name, which invokes double accuracy. The amazing thing is that some test runs of variables that had the exclamation points following them ran much faster than those variables without it. This speed change was inconsistent, however (see also Section 10.1.2).

You'll see that most of the time double accuracy variables run considerably slower than simple accuracy variables. If you don't need to use double accuracy, don't use it.

10.1.2   Benchmark peculiarities

Before we continue on with the next benchmark, you should know about a few of the peculiarities of benchmarks.

You may wonder why benchmarks run differently each time you run the computer. This is due to the random numbers which change through the TIMER variables every time a program starts.

Speed changes

Some benchmark tests give values that can be incredibly different from each other. Some changes are due to timing, but many returned values can look totally illogical. Most of the time, these odd values can't be figured out. In a few cases, the BASIC version and the time delay used cause the changes.

Here are some hints for you. If you want your BASIC programs to run faster, then don't start BASIC from the Workbench. This takes up extra memory and another task—these things absorb execution time.

BASIC from the CLI

When you stop the Workbench and the CLI window appears, type in any characters until the disk drive runs a moment. Put the diskette into the drive and erase your random characters using the <BACKSPACE> key.

To start BASIC, type a quotation mark, the diskette drive specifier, a colon and the name amigabasic ending with a quotation (i.e., "df0:amigabasic"). Press the <RETURN> key. BASIC loads.

This method saves you a lot of time. The only thing you may really miss is the user-friendly nature of the Workbench. When you want to load a program, then you must type in the program name instead of clicking the icon. In the long run, though, the quotation marks are a lot faster.

10.1.3   Benchmark: DEF for variable declaration

The Amiga has two ways that the user can assign variables. You can either put a declaration character after each and every variable (e.g., %, &, !, #), or you can define all the variables at the beginning of the program with one character for a specific type.

The program following tests which of the two versions run faster. The return of illogical values may occur as mentioned in the last section.

```
' Benchmark for testing the time differences between¶
' variables declared using DEF to set the variable¶
' type¶
¶
PRINT "This benchmark tests for the differences in
execution¶
PRINT "times between variables. The first loop uses the¶
PRINT "variable definitions within the loop, while the
second¶
PRINT "loop uses the DEFinition statement.¶
PRINT¶
¶
CLEAR¶
t1a=TIMER¶
```

```
¶
FOR i%=1 TO 10000¶
    a=a+1¶
NEXT i%¶
¶
t1b=TIMER¶
¶
PRINT "Variable with character:";t1b-t1a¶
¶
CLEAR¶
¶
DEFINT i¶
t2a=TIMER¶
¶
FOR i=1 TO 10000¶
    a=a+1¶
NEXT i¶
¶
t2b=TIMER¶
¶
PRINT "Variables using DEF    :";t2b-t2a¶
```

characters	DEF
10.9375	10.94141
10.94141	10.94141
10.90234	10.94141
10.91791	10.91791
10.92188	10.91791
10.90234	10.90234
10.91797	10.90234
10.91797	10.91797
10.94141	10.94141
10.92188	10.91797
10.91797	10.91797

This table shows you that a definition with DEF is considerably faster. This especially applies to programs in which almost all variables are of one type, and in which very few others are used.

The speed advantage lies in not using the character for the variable type. For every variable, the interpreter has one less character to read. You see how that works. The effect only works most naturally when these lines execute within a loop, for example.

10.1.4   Benchmark: variable definition time

This means a great deal, since BASIC must set up a list of variables
used. When a variable is defined at the beginning of a program, this
variable goes to the beginning of the list. When other variables follow,
and the program must search for them in this list.

Type in the following program, or just look at the table. The best thing
to do is make your own table.

```
' Benchmark for testing speed between variables¶
' definitions both at the beginning and later on¶
' in program loops¶
'¶
' © by Wgb, June '87¶
'¶
¶
PRINT "The variables used in the first loop are
predefined.¶
PRINT ¶
PRINT "The second loop inserts other variables, even¶
PRINT "though the loop doesn't use these variables.¶
PRINT "The loop formula:¶
PRINT¶
PRINT "for i=1 to 10000¶
PRINT "    a=a*1.1¶
PRINT "next i¶
PRINT¶
¶
a=0¶
t1a=TIMER¶
¶
FOR i=1 TO 10000¶
    a=a*1.1¶
NEXT i¶
¶
t1b=TIMER¶
¶
PRINT "1st loop    :";t1b-t1a¶
¶
CLEAR¶
b=0 : c=0 : hello=0 : me=0¶
a=0¶
t2a=TIMER¶
¶
FOR i=1 TO 10000¶
    a=a*1.1¶
NEXT i¶
¶
t2b=TIMER¶
¶
PRINT "2nd loop    :";t2b-t2a¶
```

1st variable	successive variables
10.45703	10.46094
10.45703	10.46094
10.46094	10.45703
10.46094	10.48047
10.48047	10.46094
10.46094	10.48047
10.46094	10.48047
10.48047	10.46094

As you can see, there is virtually no difference when a variable is defined, even if the variable is unnecessary.

10.1.5   Benchmark: Variable name lengths

The earlier computers manufactured by Commodore only read two-character variable names. AmigaBASIC allows you to use much longer variable names, which means that you could write variable names that meant something in your programs (e.g., you could assign a variable named BorderColor to represent the screen border color number).

Longer variable namesare easier for the user to read. But do they affect the program's execution time? The longer names take up more memory, so it stands to reason that a longer name takes more time to handle.

This benchmark tests out the nature of these variables. The first loop executes a set of computations using long variable names. The second loop performs the same computations with very short variable names.

```
' Benchmark for testing speeds of loops ¶
' using shorter or longer variable names¶
¶
' © by Wgb, June '87¶
'¶
¶
PRINT "The first loop uses very long¶
PRINT "variable names. The second loop¶
PRINT "uses variable names consisting of¶
PRINT "single characters."¶
PRINT¶
¶
t1a=TIMER¶
¶
FOR IndexCounter=1 TO 10000¶
    PartialResult=IndexCounter^2-3*IndexCounter¶
    EndResult=PartialResult-1/3*PartialResult¶
NEXT IndexCounter¶
¶
```

```
t1b=TIMER¶
¶
PRINT "1st loop:";t1b-t1a¶
¶
CLEAR¶
¶
t2a=TIMER¶
¶
FOR i=1 TO 10000¶
    t=i^2-3*i¶
    e=t-1/3*t¶
NEXT i¶
¶
t2b=TIMER¶
¶
PRINT "2nd loop:";t2b-t2a¶
```

long name	short name
111.457	111.4609

Here again, there's very little difference between the two types. Most of the time, the shorter variable names are only a little faster. It is recommended that you use longer names for variables. This may take up a bit more typing time on your part, but you get much more information about the variables.

10.1.6   Benchmark: single-line loops

One question that has always been asked is whether a programmer should run loops over the course of several lines, or just squeeze loops into one line. Many programmers don't like compressed programs; but try out this benchmark first, and see which is faster.

The following program performs an addition. It continues this addition until the program reaches a specific value. This occurs within a structured loop containing several lines. The second route has the entire loop within one line. Which is faster?

```
' Benchmark for testing speed differences between¶
' line set-ups¶
'¶
' © by Wgb, June '87¶
'¶
¶
PRINT "This program tests the same command sequence in
both single-line¶
PRINT "and multiple-line program format using the
formula:¶
PRINT¶
PRINT "1. WHILE a<10000¶
```

```
PRINT "      a=a+1¶
PRINT "    WEND¶
PRINT¶
PRINT "2. WHILE a<10000 : a=a+1 : WEND¶
PRINT¶
¶
a=0¶
t1a=0 : t1b=0 : t2a=0 : t2b=0¶
¶
t1a=TIMER¶
¶
WHILE a<10000¶
  a=a+1¶
WEND¶
¶
t1b=TIMER¶
a=0¶
t2a=TIMER¶
¶
WHILE a<10000 : a=a+1 : WEND¶
¶
t2b=TIMER¶
¶
PRINT "1. (multiple lines):";t1b-t1a¶
PRINT "2. (single line)   :";t2b-t2a¶
```

3 lines	1 line
18.4375	18.96094
18.41797	18.96094
18.39844	18.96094
18.39844	18.96094
18.42188	18.96094
18.41797	18.96094
18.33984	18.87891
18.35938	18.90234

You may be surprised to learn that the tightly packed line is somewhat slower than the separate ones. Why this is so, we don't know. But this means that you can write neat, structured programs without sacrificing speed.

10.1.7   Benchmark: subroutine positioning

Older Commodore computers ran faster when program jumps occurred at the beginning of the program. This was because the BASIC operating system looked for subroutines in a program starting at the beginning of the program.

This program tests out execution times based on the positions of subroutines.

```
' Benchmark for testing speed differences based ¶
' on the positioning of subroutines within an ¶
' AmigaBASIC program.¶
¶
GOTO Mainprogram¶
¶
Subroutine1:¶
¶
  a=a+1¶
  ¶
RETURN¶
¶
Mainprogram:¶
¶
PRINT "This program tests for the speed difference (if
any)¶
PRINT "between programs using subroutines at the
beginning¶
PRINT "and end of program code.¶
PRINT¶
¶
t1a=TIMER¶
¶
FOR i=1 TO 10000¶
    a=a+1¶
NEXT i¶
¶
t1b=TIMER¶
PRINT "Normal loop time                      :";t1b-t1a¶
CLEAR¶
t2a=TIMER¶
¶
FOR i=1 TO 10000¶
    GOSUB Subroutine1¶
NEXT i¶
¶
t2b=TIMER¶
PRINT "Time with subroutine at beginning:";t2b-t2a¶
CLEAR¶
t3a=TIMER¶
¶
FOR i=1 TO 10000¶
```

```
     GOSUB Subroutine2¶
NEXT i¶
¶
t3b=TIMER¶
PRINT "Time with subroutine at end      :";t3b-t3a¶
END¶
¶
Subroutine2:¶
¶
  a=a+1¶
  ¶
RETURN¶
```

normal	start	end
13.05859	19.78105	19.75781
13.01953	19.71875	19.72266
13	19.71875	19.71875
13	19.69922	19.72266
13	19.71875	19.71875

To make this comparison, the first loop performs the innermost tasks. Then the inner section goes to the subroutine at the beginning. Finally the same subroutine is accessed at the end of the program.

The loop not contained within a subroutine is the fastest loop of the bunch. A program jump takes considerably longer, but the time difference between the two subroutines is very interesting. Placing the subroutines at the end of the program seems to work better than placing them at the beginning.

10.2   Short libraries

Effective programming also means that the programmer uses as little memory as he possibly can. This extra memory can be used for more important assignments.

Memory and libraries

Library files can take up a great deal of memory. The most important libraries are already in the system when you boot the Amiga. All other libraries are called from the Workbench diskette as needed. BASIC calls these libraries according to name, parameters and offset of every function.

A library file must have memory reserved for it, which doesn't really have another purpose. Every byte is important, though. You don't want to waste memory, especially with only 512K available.

Many libraries are frequently unnecessary, but BASIC calls them anyway. You can remove these unnecessary libraries from the list, and have the Amiga load the .bmap files that it absolutely requires.

The following program uses this principle. After entering the function names and their parameters in the DATA statements, you can start the program and create your own personal program library. You should know which libraries are required by which program. No two programs can use the same library files. Insert a comment using the Info function of the Workbench that states to which program this library belongs.

```
REM ----------------------------------¶
REM - Universal  .bmap  linker   for -¶
REM - creating abbreviated Libraries -¶
REM ----------------------------------¶
¶
Header:¶
¶
PRINT¶
PRINT"      .bmap creator for user-created  abbreviated
libraries"¶
PRINT"      (See Amiga Tricks &  Tips from Abacus for a
complete"¶
PRINT"      list  of  library  command  data  for  this
program)"¶
¶
FunctionValues:¶
¶
DATA graphics¶
¶
DATA Move,9,1,2,240¶
DATA PolyDraw,10,1,9,336¶
```

```
DATA SetDrawMode,10,1,354¶
¶
DATA end¶
¶
REM ----------------------------------------------------------¶
REM - The above DATA statememts state the following:    -¶
REM - DATA graphics = name of the short library  file   -¶
REM - Move, PolyDraw and SetDrawMode = the commands     -¶
REM - placed in the short library file                  -¶
REM ----------------------------------------------------------¶
¶
RESTORE FunctionValues¶
¶
READ LibName$¶
¶
OPEN LibName$+".bmap" FOR OUTPUT AS 1¶
¶
ReadLibFunc:¶
  READ Routine$¶
  gencount=gencount+1¶
  IF Routine$="end" THEN ShutDown¶
¶
  counter=0¶
¶
ReadLoop:¶
  READ value(counter)¶
  IF value(counter)<20 THEN¶
    counter=counter+1¶
    GOTO ReadLoop¶
  ELSE¶
    offset=value(counter)¶
    counter=counter-1¶
  END IF¶
¶
  offset=65536&-offset¶
  off1=INT(offset/256)¶
  off2=offset-(256*off1)¶
¶
  lib$=Routine$+CHR$(0)+CHR$(off1)+CHR$(off2)¶
¶
  FOR loop=0 TO counter¶
    lib$=lib$+CHR$(value(loop))¶
  NEXT loop¶
¶
  lib$=lib$+CHR$(0)¶
¶
  ges$=ges$+lib$¶
¶
GOTO ReadLibFunc¶
¶
ShutDown:¶
¶
  LOCATE 7,6¶
  PRINT gencount-2;" functions written to the short
library."¶
  PRINT#1,ges$¶
```

```
CLOSE 1¶
LOCATE 9,6¶
PRINT "        "LibName$+".bmap written to diskette."¶
LOCATE 12,6¶
END¶
```

The sample listing above shows a library which could be used with a grid-based graphic program. It contains the most important graphic functions needed: Move, SetDrawMode and PolyDraw. Think of the memory and loading time saved by loading a short library, instead of loading the entire library set.

Changing the libraries

You can make even more changes. If you don't want to call the functions under their usual names, you can change the name in the DATA list, and reboot the program. Only the offsets are necessary to call the libraries.

Changing the names for the entire library set isn't so easy. First you must copy the source library with the new names on the Workbench diskette, giving you a copy of the same library (hopefully you'll have enough memory). Change the .bmap filenames. Then the entire library is no longer a problem.

Below are the complete DATA statements for the dos, exec, graphics and intuition libraries. These let you create your own individualized .bmap files.

exec.library

```
DATA exec

DATA InitCode,72
DATA InitStruct,10,11,1,78
DATA MakeLibrary,10,11,12,1,2,84
DATA MakeFunctions,90
DATA FindResident,96
DATA InitResident,102
DATA Alert,108
DATA Debug,114
DATA Disable,120
DATA Enable,126
DATA Forbid,132
DATA Permit,138
DATA SetSR,1,2,144
DATA SuperState,150
DATA UserState,1,156
DATA SetIntVector,1,10,162
DATA AddIntServer,1,10,168
DATA RemIntServer,1,10,174
DATA Cause,10,180
DATA Allocate,10,1,186
DATA Deallocate,10,11,1,192
DATA AllocMem,1,2,198
DATA AllocAbs,204
```

```
DATA FreeMem,10,1,210
DATA AvailMem,2,216
DATA AllocEntry,9,222
DATA FreeEntry,9,228
DATA Insert,9,10,11,234
DATA AddHead,9,10,240
DATA AddTail,9,10,246
DATA Remove,10,252
DATA RemHead,9,258
DATA RemTail,9,264
DATA Enqueue,9,10,270
DATA FindName,9,10,276
DATA AddTask,10,11,12,282
DATA RemTask,10,288
DATA FindTask,10,294
DATA SetTaskPri,10,1,300
DATA SetSignal,1,2,306
DATA SetExcept,1,2,312
DATA Wait,1,318
DATA Signal,10,1,324
DATA AllocSignal,1,330
DATA FreeSignal,1,336
DATA AllocTrap,1,342
DATA FreeTrap,1,348
DATA AddPort,10,354
DATA RemPort,10,360
DATA PutMsg,9,10,366
DATA GetMsg,9,372
DATA ReplyMsg,10,378
DATA WaitPort,9,384
DATA FindPort,10,390
DATA AddLibrary,10,396
DATA RemLibrary,10,402
DATA OpenLibrary,10,1,408
DATA CloseLibrary,10,414
DATA SetFunction,10,9,1,420
DATA SumLibrary,10,426
DATA AddDevice,10,432
DATA RemDevice,10,438
DATA OpenDevice,9,1,10,2,444
DATA CloseDevice,10,450
DATA DoIO,10,456
DATA SendIO,10,462
DATA CheckIO,10,468
DATA WaitIO,10,474
DATA AbortIO,480
DATA AddResource,10,486
DATA RemResource,10,492
DATA OpenResource,10,498
DATA GetCC,528

DATA end
```

intuition.library

```
DATA intuition

DATA AddGadget,9,10,1,42
DATA AllocRemember,9,1,2,396
DATA AutoRequest,9,10,11,12,1,2,3,4,348
DATA BeginRefresh,9,354
DATA BuildSysRequest,9,10,11,12,1,2,3,360
DATA ClearDMRequest,9,48
DATA ClearMenuStrip,9,54
DATA ClearPointer,9,60
DATA CloseScreen,9,66
DATA CloseWindow,9,72
DATA CloseWorkBench,78
DATA CurrentTime,9,10,84
DATA DisplayAlert,1,9,2,90
DATA DisplayBeep,9,96
DATA DoubleClick,1,2,3,4,102
DATA DrawBorder,9,10,1,2,108
DATA DrawImage,9,10,1,2,114
DATA EndRefresh,9,1,366
DATA EndRequest,9,10,120
DATA FreeRemember,9,1,408
DATA FreeSysRequest,9,372
DATA GetDefPrefs,9,1,126
DATA GetPrefs,9,1,132
DATA InitRequester,9,138
DATA IntuiTextLength,9,330
DATA ItemAddress,9,1,144
DATA MakeScreen,9,378
DATA ModifyIDCMP,9,1,150
DATA ModifyProp,9,10,11,1,2,3,4,5,156
DATA MoveScreen,9,1,2,162
DATA MoveWindow,9,1,2,168
DATA OffGadget,9,10,11,174
DATA OffMenu,9,1,180
DATA OnGadget,9,10,11,186
DATA OnMenu,9,1,192
DATA OpenScreen,9,198
DATA OpenWindow,9,204
DATA OpenWorkBench,210
DATA PrintIText,9,10,1,2,216
DATA RefreshGadgets,9,10,11,222
DATA RemakeDisplay,384
DATA RemoveGadget,9,10,228
DATA ReportMouse,9,1,234
DATA Request,9,10,240
DATA RethinkDisplay,390
DATA ScreenToBack,9,246
DATA ScreenToFront,9,252
DATA SetDMRequest,9,10,258
DATA SetMenuStrip,9,10,264
DATA SetPointer,9,10,1,2,3,4,270
DATA SetWindowTitles,9,10,11,276
DATA ShowTitle,9,1,282
```

```
              DATA SizeWindow,9,1,2,288
              DATA ViewAddress,294
              DATA ViewPortAddress,9,300
              DATA WBenchToBack,336
              DATA WBenchToFront,342
              DATA WindowLimits,9,1,2,3,4,318
              DATA WindowToBack,9,306
              DATA WindowToFront,9,312
              DATA SetPrefs,9,1,2,324
              DATA AllohaWorkbench,9,402

              DATA end
```

dos.library

```
              DATA dos

              DATA xClose,2,36
              DATA CreateDir,2,120
              DATA CurrentDir,2,128
              DATA DeleteFile,2,72
              DATA DupLock,2,96
              DATA Examine,2,3,102
              DATA ExNext,2,3,108
              DATA GetPacket,2,162
              DATA Info,2,3,114
              DATA xInput,54
              DATA IoErr,132
              DATA IsInteractive,2,216
              DATA Lock,2,3,84
              DATA xOpen,2,3,30
              DATA xOutput,60
              DATA QueuePacket,2,168
              DATA ParentDir,2,210
              DATA xRead,2,3,4,42
              DATA Rename,2,3,78
              DATA Seek,2,3,4,66
              DATA SetComment,2,3,180
              DATA SetProtection,2,3,186
              DATA UnLock,2,90
              DATA WaitForChar,2,3,204
              DATA xWrite,2,3,4,48
              DATA CreateProc,2,3,4,5,138
              DATA DateStamp,2,192
              DATA Delay,2,198
              DATA DeviceProc,2,174
              DATA xExit,2,144
              DATA Execute,2,3,4,222
              DATA LoadSeg,2,150
              DATA UnLoadSeg,2,168

              DATA end
```

11
Machine
language calls

11.   Machine language calls

AmigaBASIC is a wonderful programming language, but it runs too
slow for many applications. The clearest solution may be to write the
program that needs the most speed in machine language and call it from
AmigaBASIC. There are some problems with this idea, which this
chapter explains.

First on to the assembler itself. We use *AssemPro Amiga* from
Abacus.

The first important factor is the addressing type used to assemble your
own machine language programs. When you want to use machine language calls from AmigaBASIC, you must use PC-relative addressing.
Normal code can be called from the Workbench or the CLI, but you can
count on a system error when calling normal machine code from
AmigaBASIC. The term "PC" refers to the Program Counter, rather
than personal computer. Why PC-relative? Look at what happens when
the Amiga loads and runs machine language. The Amiga is
multitasking, which means it can run several programs at the same
time. These programs must all start at different memory locations. It
naturally follows that the addresses used by the program cannot be
loaded at the same locations, or else the entire system crashes. After
loading, the operating system converts all addresses used to the required
memory locations.

When you load a machine language routine from AmigaBASIC, and no
other task is in the system, no address changing occurs. The program
should run as it comes from the diskette, but AmigaBASIC cannot set
the address in which the routine should lie, since it only sets absolute
addressing for itself.

Be sure that your assembler only uses offsets for the current address.

11.1   Loading and running machine language

Here's the step by step process for controlling machine language from AmigaBASIC. First the routine should be loaded into memory. You can do this in one of two ways: Load direct from diskette, or execute the routine from DATA statements from AmigaBASIC itself.

There are several ways to load programs from diskette:

1)   For long machine language or BASIC programs:

```
DECLARE FUNCTION xOpen& LIBRARY  'don't
DECLARE FUNCTION xRead& LIBRAY   'forget to
LIBRARY "dos.library"            'call libs

File$="Myroutine"+CHR$(0)
handle&=xOpen&(SADD(File$),1005)
reader&=xRead&(handle&,Address&,Lenght&)
CALL xClose(handle&)
```

2)   The DOS library must be opened for loading. The following works:

```
OPEN "Myroutine" FOR INPUT AS 1
a$=INPUT$(LOF(1),1)
CLOSE 1
```

This routine must already be set up in a string.

3)   Short routines let you read a file byte for byte into any variable, or POKE it direct into memory.

If you prefer to use DATA statements from within AmigaBASIC, look at the Data Generator program in Section 6.3.1.

If your program lies in a specific memory range (e.g. chip RAM), use the AllocMem routine from the Exec library to reserve memory. The simplest option is to read a routine into a string. You can use array variables if you wish.

11.2   LED shocker

Imagine this: You run a program. For a moment, nothing appears on the screen. Suddenly the **POWER** LED on the Amiga blinks—a system crash!

No, not a system crash; the machine language program below made the LED flash:

```
start:                  ;beginning of program
 move.l d0,-(sp)        ;Reserve data register from stack
 move.l 8(sp),d0        ;Value from data register 0
 cmp.l  #1,d0           ;Value = 1?
 beq LEDON              ;Branch to LEDON
LEDOFF:                 ;Otherwise do this
 or.b     #2,$bfe001    ;Set bit 1
 bra DONE               ;Jump to DONE
LEDON:                  ;Turn LED on
 andi.b #253,$BFE001    ;Clear bit 1
DONE:
 move.l (sp)+,d0        ;Remove d0 from stack
 rts                    ;Return to AmigaBASIC
 END                    ;end of program
```

If you don't want to type it in on your assembler, or you don't have an assembler, see the program in the next section.

11.3 Passing values

AmigaBASIC calls a machine language program with the variable name which contains the starting address of the program. This is done by the CALL command:

CALL address& (parameter_1,...,last_parameter)

The interpreter places the last parameter on the stack, then accesses the first parameter and places the return address on the stack. You can access the correct address from the stack. Here's a graphic layout of the stack:

Line number	Stack setup		
0	stack pointer	=	return address
	stack pointer+4	=	parameter_1 (just one)
1	stack pointer	=	data register 0
	stack pointer+4	=	return address
	stack pointer+8	=	parameter_1
11	stack pointer	=	return address
	stack pointer+4	=	parameter_1

Note that every register on the stack pointer increments by 4 when set for parameters.

How does AmigaBASIC handle the results of this routine through a function? The addresses of the variables which later contains the result are given. This simplifies the entire program, since you must at least use array variables.

Now on to the program itself. These DATA lines were created using the Data Generator program in Section 6.3.1.

```
REM ##############################¶
REM #    L E D - S h o c k e r    #¶
REM #----------------------------#¶
REM #   (W) 1987 by  S. Maelger   #¶
REM ##############################¶
¶
RESTORE datas¶
datastring$=""¶
FOR i=1 TO  40¶
READ a$¶
a$="&H"+a$¶
datastring$=datastring$+CHR$(VAL(a$))¶
NEXT¶
¶
datas:¶
DATA 2F,0,20,2F,0,8,B0,3C,0,1,67,0,0,E,0,39,0,2,0,BF¶
DATA E0,1,60,0,0,A,2,39,0,FD,0,BF,E0,1,20,1F,4E,75,0,0¶
¶
POWER&=SADD(datastring$)          :REM Load string address¶
¶
FOR i=1 TO 20                     :REM¶
¶
Mode&=0                           :REM Turn off LED ¶
CALL POWER&(Mode&)                :REM Call routine ¶
t=TIMER+.5                        :REM but not too¶
WHILE t>TIMER                     :REM fast¶
WEND                              :REM¶
¶
Mode&=1                           :REM Turn on LED ¶
CALL POWER&(Mode&)¶
t=TIMER+.5¶
WHILE t>TIMER¶
WEND¶
NEXT¶
STOP¶
```

311

12
Input and output

12.   Input and output

Users normally think of input and output (or *I/O*) as the contact between the Amiga and its *peripherals*. Peripherals are devices such as printers, joysticks and disk drives. The Amiga treats the built-in disk drive as an external device, since disk drives are considered external by most computers.

The advanced user may wonder how to communicate with these devices on a more-or-less direct basis. The Amiga has a basic I/O system. Every device has a corresponding software module which converts the basic control codes into device-specific codes. These software modules have file extensions of .device. Some of these device files lie in KickStart memory, while some are on the Workbench diskette.

You must create an *I/O request block* to handle I/O. This is placed in a reserved area of memory. This section is defined as follows:

```
add& = starting memory
address:B=byte:W=word:L=longword
```

add&+	type	definition
0	L	pointer to previous node
4	L	pointer to next node
8	L	type
9	B	priority
10	L	pointer to name string
14	L	pointer to message port
18	W	message length in bytes
20	L	pointer to device block
24	L	pointer to unit block
28	W	I/O command
30	B	flags
31	B	I/O error number
32	L	actual array
36	L	length array
40	L	data array
44	L	offset array

Along with this structure a *message port* must be created. This is a segment of memory set aside for I/O communication.

The I/O request block can be thought of as a letter traveling through the mail. When a multitasking system such as the Amiga's appears to be handling several tasks at once, it's really handling one program at a time for a moment. When one of these programs must communicate with another "simultaneously running" program, this communication travels as a message. The I/O request block is one messenger of this type. The BASIC interpreter of AmigaBASIC runs the I/O device as a program running parallel to the BASIC program. This hands the message block to the address of the other task. In reality, the data block stays in one place instead of moving around in memory. The foreign task passes final control over this memory. As long as an I/O request block shifts to another task, our own program doesn't access the memory. When the other task processes the message, control over this memory returns to our own program.

We won't bore you with the technical background involved, since that goes far beyond the scope of this book. If, however, you wish to pursue the details of this process, we recommend that you read any one of the books about Amiga system programming.

The following pages list a number of examples with which you can access disk drives and printers without a lot of programming knowledge.

12.1 Direct disk access

`Trackdisk.device` handles up to four 3-1/2" disk drives. With a little help, you can directly manipulate data stored on diskette.

Every Amiga floppy disk drive has two read/write heads, one head for each side of a diskette. The diskette is divided into 80 *cylinders* per side. Each cylinder consists of 11 sectors. Each sector contains 512 usable data bytes, as well as 16 sector processing bytes. The total file capacity is:

   2 heads*
  80 cylinders*
  11 sectors*
  <u>512 bytes=</u>
900120 bytes (880 K)

There are 28160 bytes unavailable to the user in addition to this 880K.

Now on to the programming: The following program has six high-level SUBs as well as four sublevel routines. All you'll need for now are the first six SUBs.

Disk access   `OpenDrive` opens any disk drive. This SUB asks for the number of the disk drive (0=internal drive, 1-3=external drives). `CreateBuffer` reserves segments of memory. This routine asks for the variable containing the starting address of the memory to be allocated, as well as the desired buffer's size in bytes. `DiscardBuffer` releases the memory reserved by `CreateBuffer`. The only argument required is the starting address of the buffer. `WorkDrive` sends an I/O command to any open drive. `CloseDrive` closes a disk drive. `MotorOff` turns off the disk drive motor.

The following program lets you open any disk drive and view any one of 1760 sectors. The program displays the data found in hexadecimal notation.

```
'###############################¶
'#                             #¶
'# Program: Disk - Monitor     #¶
'# Author:    tob              #¶
'# Date:      8/8/87           #¶
'# Version:   1.0              #¶
'#                             #¶
'###############################¶
¶
```

```
DECLARE FUNCTION OpenDevice% LIBRARY¶
DECLARE FUNCTION AllocMem& LIBRARY¶
DECLARE FUNCTION AllocSignal% LIBRARY¶
DECLARE FUNCTION FindTask& LIBRARY¶
DECLARE FUNCTION DoIO% LIBRARY¶
¶
LIBRARY "exec.library"¶
LIBRARY "graphics.library"¶
¶
var:       '* Variable¶
           DIM SHARED reg&(3,1)¶
¶
main:      '* Demonstration program¶
           PRINT TAB(20);"DISK MONITOR"¶
           PRINT¶
           LINE INPUT "Which drive (0 - 3)? ...."; dr$¶
           dr% = VAL(dr$)¶
¶
           OpenDrive dr%¶
           CreateBuffer d0&, 512&¶
¶
           LINE INPUT "Which sector (0 - 1759)?
....";sec$¶
           sec% = VAL(sec$)¶
           WorkDrive dr%, 2, sec%, d0&¶
           MotorOff   dr%¶
¶
           WHILE sec$ <> "end"¶
             CLS¶
             PRINT "Sector ";sec%¶
             PRINT¶
             c% = 3¶
             FOR loop1% = 0 TO 512 - 1 STEP 25¶
               FOR loop2% = 0 TO 24¶
                 check% = PEEK( d0& + loop1% + loop2%)¶
                 h$       = HEX$(check%)¶
                 IF LEN(h$) = 1 THEN¶
                   h$ = "0" + h$¶
                 END IF¶
                 he$  = he$ + h$¶
                 IF check% < 31 THEN¶
                   d$ = d$ + "?"¶
                 ELSE¶
                   d$ = d$ + CHR$(check%)¶
                 END IF¶
                 IF loop2% + loop1% = 512 - 1 THEN¶
                   loop2% = 24¶
                 END IF¶
               NEXT loop2%¶
               LOCATE c%, 1¶
               c% = c% + 1¶
               out$ = he$ + "   " + d$¶
               CALL Text(WINDOW(8), SADD(out$),
       LEN(out$))¶
               he$ = ""¶
               d$  = ""¶
```

```
                NEXT loop1%¶
                LOCATE 1,20¶
                LINE INPUT "Which sector (0 - 1759, end)?
....";sec$¶

                sec% = VAL(sec$)¶
                WorkDrive dr%, 2, sec%, d0&¶
                MotorOff  dr%¶
                WEND¶
¶
                DiscardBuffer d0&¶
                CloseDrive dr%¶
                CLS¶
                PRINT "All OK."¶
¶
                LIBRARY CLOSE¶
                END¶
¶
SUB OpenDrive (nr%) STATIC¶
    IF reg&(nr%, 0) = 0 THEN¶
      CreatePort "disk.io", 0, port&¶
      IF port& = 0 THEN ERROR 255¶
      CreateStdIO port&, io&¶
      dev$ = "trackdisk.device" + CHR$(0)¶
      er%  = OpenDevice% (SADD(dev$), nr%, io&, 0)¶
      IF er% <> 0 THEN¶
        RemoveStdIO io&¶
        RemovePort  port&¶
        io&   = 0¶
        port& = 0¶
        ERROR 255¶
      ELSE¶
        reg&(nr%, 0) = io&¶
        reg&(nr%, 1) = port&¶
      END IF¶
    ELSE¶
      io&   = reg&(nr%, 0)¶
      port& = reg&(nr%, 1)¶
    END IF¶
END SUB¶
¶
SUB CloseDrive (nr%) STATIC¶
    IF reg&(nr%, 0) <> 0 THEN¶
      io&   = reg&(nr%, 0)¶
      port& = reg&(nr%, 1)¶
      CALL CloseDevice(io&)¶
      RemoveStdIO io&¶
      RemovePort  port&¶
      reg&(nr%, 0) = 0¶
      reg&(nr%, 1) = 0¶
    END IF¶
END SUB¶
      ¶
```

```
SUB MotorOff (nr%) STATIC¶
    io& = reg&(nr%, 0)¶
    IF io& <> 0 THEN¶
      POKEW io& + 28, 9¶
      POKEL io& + 36, 0¶
      e% = DoIO% (io&)¶
    ELSE¶
      BEEP¶
    END IF¶
END SUB¶
¶
SUB CreateBuffer (add&, size&) STATIC¶
    IF size& > 0 THEN¶
      size& = size& + 4¶
      opt&  = 2^16¶
      add&  = AllocMem& (size&, opt&)¶
      IF add& <> 0 THEN¶
        add&  = add& + 4¶
        POKEL add& - 4, size&¶
      END IF¶
    ELSE¶
      BEEP¶
    END IF¶
END SUB¶
¶
SUB DiscardBuffer (add&) STATIC¶
    IF add& <> 0 THEN¶
      size& = PEEKL (add& - 4)¶
      add&  = add& - 4¶
      CALL FreeMem (add&, size&)¶
    END IF¶
END SUB¶
¶
SUB WorkDrive (nr%, command%, sector%, buffer&) STATIC¶
    td.sector% = 512¶
    io&        = reg&(nr%, 0)¶
    td.offset& = sector%*td.sector%¶
    IF io& <> 0 THEN¶
      POKEW io& + 28, command%¶
      POKEL io& + 36, td.sector%¶
      POKEL io& + 40, buffer&¶
      POKEL io& + 44, td.offset&¶
      er% = DoIO% (io&)¶
    ELSE¶
      BEEP¶
    END IF¶
END SUB¶
¶
'--- sub level routines for advanced use only ---¶
¶
SUB CreateStdIO (port&, result&) STATIC¶
    opt&    = 2^16¶
    result& = AllocMem&(62, opt&)¶
    IF result& = 0 THEN ERROR 7¶
    POKE  result& +  8, 5¶
```

```
        POKEL result& + 14, port&¶
        POKEW result& + 18, 42¶
    END SUB¶
    ¶
    SUB RemoveStdIO (io&) STATIC¶
        IF io& <> 0 THEN¶
          CALL FreeMem(io&, 62)¶
        ELSE¶
          ERROR 255¶
        END IF¶
    END SUB¶
    ¶
    SUB CreatePort (port$, pri%, result&) STATIC¶
        opt&  = 2^16¶
        byte& = 38 + LEN(port$)¶
        port& = AllocMem&(byte&, opt&)¶
        IF port& = 0 THEN ERROR 7¶
        POKEW port&, byte&¶
        port& = port& + 2¶
        sigBit% = AllocSignal%(-1)¶
        IF sigBit% = -1 THEN¶
          CALL FreeMem(port&,byte&)¶
          ERROR 7¶
        END IF¶
        sigTask& = FindTask&(0)¶
    ¶
        POKE  port& + 8 , 4¶
        POKE  port& + 9 , pri%¶
        POKEL port& + 10, port& + 34¶
        POKE  port& + 15, sigBit%¶
        POKEL port& + 16, sigTask&¶
        POKEL port& + 20, port& + 24¶
        POKEL port& + 28, port& + 20¶
        FOR loop% = 1 TO LEN(port$)¶
          char%  = ASC(MID$(port$, loop%, 1))¶
          POKE port& + 33 + loop%, char%¶
        NEXT loop%¶
        CALL AddPort(port&)¶
        result& = port&¶
    END SUB¶
    ¶
    SUB RemovePort (port&) STATIC¶
        byte&  = PEEKW(port& - 2)¶
        sigBit% = PEEK (port& + 15)¶
        CALL RemPort(port&)¶
        CALL FreeSignal(sigBit%)¶
        CALL FreeMem(port&-2, byte&)¶
    END SUB¶
```

Variables

reg&()	contains important internal I/O addresses (e.g., I/O-request and I/Oport)
dr%	disk drive number (0-3)
d0&	512-byte buffer
sec%	sector number (0-1759)
loop1%	loop

```
loop2%        loop
check%        character read (decimal)
h$            character read (hexadecimal)
he$           line read (hexadecimal)
d$            line read (decimal)
c%            current screen line
```

OpenDrive()

```
nr%           number of open drive (0-3)
port&         message port address
io&           I/O block address
dev$          trackdisk.device ended with null
er%           I/O error; 0=no error
```

Create-Buffer()

```
size&         buffer size in bytes
opt&          options: 216 = CLEAR MEMORY
add&          address of found memory
```

WorkDrive()

```
td.sector%    =512: bytes per sector
io&           I/O block address
td.offset&    byte offset from sector 0: multiple of 512
er%           I/O error code
```

CreatePort()

```
port$         name of new port
pri%          priority of new port (-128 to 127)
result&       address of found port (output)
opt&          memory option: 216 = CLEAR MEMORY
byte&         size of needed memory
sigBit%       signal bit
sigTask&      address of AmigaBASIC task handler
char%         ASCII code of character read
```

Program description

First the program establishes the number of the disk drive the user wants accessed. `OpenDrive` opens this drive. Next the program internally checks for whether the drive is already open, and whether an entry already lies in `reg&()`. If not, `CreatePort` turns to a message port named `disk.io`. The starting address lies in `port&`. If no port exists (`port&=0`), then an error occurs. Otherwise, `CreateStdIO` opens a port, passing the address over to the already existing port. The starting address of the I/O block goes to `io&`. The drive opens through the `Exec` function `OpenDevice%()`. When this routine returns a value greater than or less than 0, the drive cannot be opened. Possible reasons: Another task has control of the drive; an `Open` was not preceded by a `Close`; the drive doesn't exist; the drive is not connected. In such a case the port and I/O block are released, the variables return to null status and an error message appears on the screen. The address of the new port and the new I/O block goes into `reg&()`.

The program opens a buffer large enough to hold the data of one diskette sector (minimum size). This 512-byte buffer is created by `CreateBuffer`; the buffer's starting address appears in `d0&`. The user is asked for the sector he wants to view. The `SUB WorkDrive` reads this sector and places it in the buffer `d0&` (CMD READ, the read command, =2). This `SUB` fills the I/O request blocks the necessary values, and calls the `Exec` function `DoIO%()`, sent to the disk drive through the command block.

After `WorkDrive` finishes its work, the diskette motor must be switched off. `WorkDrive` turns the motor on, but not off. The reason: Multiple disk access can be tiring when you have to turn the disk drive on and off every time you need to go to the diskette. The `MotorOff` `SUB` turns the motor off. The `Motor` command (=9) in the I/O block writes the contents sent from `DoIO%()`.

Now comes the data in memory starting from `d0&`. Two loops read the values from the buffer and place these on the screen in decimal and hexadecimal notation. The program then asks for additional sectors. You either enter a number (0-1759) or the word "end" to quit. The first response calls up a new sector, the second response releases the buffer and closes the disk drive `CloseDrive` (the program tests for open disk drives through `reg&()`). If there is an open drive, the addresses of the I/O and portblock are read. `RemoveStdIO` and `RemovePort` release this structure, and the drive closes through `CloseDevice()`. Finally the program deletes the entries from `reg&()`.

12.1.1   The `trackdisk.device` commands

When you want to examine your own programs, you should use the `WorkDrive` SUB to access these programs. This SUB gives you the following commands:

Read data   Command number: 2
                Command call: `Workdrive number%, 2, sector%,`
                                    `buffer&`

If your buffer is larger than 512 bytes, you can naturally load more than one sector at a time. The entry within the I/O array 36 must be changed: For example, `5*td.sector%` instead of `td.sector%` when your buffer can handle that much data.

Write data   Command number: 3
                Command call: `Workdrive number%, 3, sector%,`
                                    `buffer&`

Writes the buffer contents to the given sector on the diskette.

Note: If you don't know what you're doing when writing to diskette, you could destroy the disk data. If you want to change the data on a sector, read the sector with command 2, edit the buffer and write the sector back to diskette.

You can write more than one sector at a time (see `Read data` above).

Motor   Command number: 9
                Command call: `Workdrive number%, 9, 0, 0`

Manipulates I/O array 36: 0=motor off, 1=motor on. `IO_Actual` returns the current status.

Format disk   Command number: 11
                Command call: `Workdrive number%, 11, track%,`
                                    `trackbuf&`

This command writes a completely new track to diskette. One track consists of 11 sectors. `track%` must therefore be a multiple of 11. The track buffer must be large enough for 11 sectors. The command ignores all data previously stored on this track and can even overwrite hard errors.

12.1.2   Multiple disk drive access

The SUBs on the previous program are constructed in such a way that
you can access up to four disk drives at a time. You must open every
drive using the OpenDrive command and close each one individually
later. In addition, every drive must have its own buffer available for
copying data. You can naturally use a single buffer.

12.1.3   Sector design

A sector shows just a small part of a diskette's true contents. From this
we can see the design of sectors (numbers are given in longwords [four-
byte arrays]):

Root block (sector 880)

0	type (=2)
1	0
2	0
3	hashtable size (512-224)
4	0
5	checksum
6-77	hashtable: sector numbers in which main directory files or subdirectories lie
78	= FFFFFFFF (-1) when bitmap is valid
79-104	number of sector containing the bitmap (normally one sector). Every bit of the bitmap corresponds to a diskette sector and indicates whether the sector is free (bit set) or occupied (bit unset).
105	day of last date diskette was altered
106	minutes
107	ticks (1/50 second)
108-120	diskette name: BCPL string: first byte gives the number of characters in a string (maximum 30)
121	day of date this diskette was initialized
122	minutes
123	ticks
124	0
125	0
126	0
127	root-ID = 1

User directory block

0	type (=2)
1	header key (number of this sector)
2	0
3	0
4	0
5	checksum
6-77	hashtable: sector numbers in which main directory files or subdirectories lie
78	reserved
79	protection bits (EXEC, DEL, READ, WRITE)
80	0
81-104	commentary string (BCPL string)
105	day of date diskette was created
106	minutes
107	ticks (1/50 second)
108-123	directory name: BCPL string
124	next entry with equal has value
125	sector number of root directory
126	0
127	user directory (=2)

File header block

0	type (=2)
1	number of this sector
2	total number of data sectors for this file
3	number of used data block slots
4	sector number of first data block
5	checksum
6-77	sector numbers of data blocks
78	unused
79	protection bits (EXEC, DEL, READ, WRITE)
80	total file size in bytes
81-104	commentary string (BCPL string)
105	day of date diskette was created
106	minutes
107	ticks (1/50 second)
108-123	filename: BCPL string
124	next entry with equal hash value
125	sector number of root directory
126	0 or sector number of first extended block (file list block)
127	file type (=FFFFFFFD)

File list block

0	type (=1)
1	number of this sector
2	total number of data blocks in list
3	number of used data block slots
4	first data block
5	checksum
6-77	sector numbers of data blocks
78-123	unused
124	0
125	sector number of root directory
126	next extended block
127	file type (=FFFFFFFD)

Data block

0	type (=8)
1	number of this sector
2	sequence of data block
3	number of data in bytes
4	sector number of next data block
5	checksum
6-127	data

12.2   Memory handling

The memory system of the Amiga is extremely flexible. This is because the memory locations can be changed to fit the situation, instead of having fixed memory. Unlike its predecessors, the Amiga has no specific memory set aside for machine language user applications. This kind of memory layout makes no sense to a multitasking computer, where several programs must share memory.

Here are the most popular methods of memory handling.

12.2.1   Reserving memory through variables

Every time you assign a value to a variable you take a piece of working memory and reserve part of the stack for this value. The amount of memory reserved depends on the variable type. For example, a long integer variable like f& would reserve 4 bytes. Now you can use this memory for other purposes as well. The starting address comes from the BASIC VARPTR command:

```
VARPTR (f&)
```

You need more than four bytes to use variable arrays (DIM f&(100) reserves 400 bytes) or strings (a$=SPACE$(100) reserves 100 bytes). The starting address of the string comes from the call:

```
SADD (a$)
```

It should be mentioned here that the starting address of string memory is variable. Every new string definition can move old strings around in memory. Every memory access changes the starting address in memory. This means that the memory is not well suited for set data structures. The following method is a more practical route.

12.2.2   Allocating memory

The AllocMem() command gives you as much memory as you ask for, as long as that much memory is free. You can choose between three options:

Public memory	2^0
Chip memory	2^1 (DMA and special purpose chips)
Fast memory	2^2 (all other applications)
Clear memory	2^{16} (automatically clears memory)

The following SUBs reduce memory handling to a minimum.

```
'####################################¶
'#                                  #¶
'# Programm: Memory Handler         #¶
'# Author:   tob                    #¶
'# Date:     8.12.87                #¶
'# Version:  2.0                    #¶
'#                                  #¶
'####################################¶
¶
DECLARE FUNCTION AllocMem& LIBRARY¶
¶
LIBRARY "exec.library"¶
¶
demo:      '* reserve 4500 bytes¶
           PRINT "Memory left after reserving 4500
bytes: ";¶
           PRINT FRE(-1)¶
¶
           GetMemory mem&, 4500&¶
¶
           PRINT "Current memory status: ";¶
           PRINT FRE(-1)¶
¶
           FreeMemory mem&¶
¶
           PRINT "Ending memory status: ";¶
           PRINT FRE(-1)¶
¶
           LIBRARY CLOSE¶
           END¶
¶
¶
SUB GetMemory (add&, size&) STATIC¶
   IF size& > 0 THEN¶
     opt&  = 2^16¶
     size& = size& + 4¶
     add&  = AllocMem&(size&, opt&)¶
     IF add& <> 0 THEN¶
       POKEL add&, size&¶
       add& = add& + 4¶
     END IF¶
   END IF¶
END SUB¶
¶
```

```
SUB FreeMemory (add&) STATIC¶
   IF add& > 0 THEN¶
      add& = add& - 4¶
      size& = PEEKL (add&)¶
      CALL FreeMem(add&, size&)¶
   END IF¶
END SUB¶
```

Program description

The principle should be obvious from the example. It uses Get-Memory to reserve a memory segment of any size for your use. Two variables return the address variable in which you'll find the starting address of the memory segment (or 0 if there isn't enough memory available) and the size of the desired segment. Reserving 1000 bytes is as simple as:

GetMemory myMem&, 1000&

You'll find the starting address of the segment in the variable myMem&:

PRINT myMem&

When you no longer need the memory, you can return it to the system with the call:

FreeMemory myMem&

You cannot go past the memory size allocated for this segment, since GetMemory actually has up to four bytes of memory reserved holding the bytes beyond the segment size.

Appendices

A.   AmigaBASIC tokens

Token (hex.)	value (dec.)	AmigaBASIC command
80	128	ABS
81	129	ASC
82	130	ATN
83	131	CALL
84	132	CDBL
85	133	CHR$
86	134	CINT
87	135	CLOSE
88	136	COMMON
89	137	COS
8A	138	CVD
8B	139	CVI
8C	140	CVS
8D	141	DATA
8E (3A)	142 (58)	ELSE
8F	143	EOF
90	144	EXP
91	145	FIELD
92	146	FIX
93	147	FN
94	148	FOR
95	149	GET
96	150	GOSUB
97	151	GOTO
98	152	IF
99	153	INKEY$
9A	154	INPUT
9B	155	INT
9C	156	LEFT$
9D	157	LEN
9E	158	LET
9F	159	LINE
A1	161	LOC
A2	162	LOF
A3	163	LOG
A4	164	LSET
A5	165	MID$
A6	166	MKD$
A7	167	MKI$
A8	168	MKS$
A9	169	NEXT
AA	170	ON
AB	171	OPEN

Token (hex.)	value (dec.)	AmigaBASIC command
AC	172	PRINT
AD	173	PUT
AE	174	READ
AF	175	REM
AF E8 (3A)	175 232 (58)	'
B0	176	RETURN
B1	177	RIGHT$
B2	178	RND
B3	179	RSET
B4	180	SGN
B5	181	SIN
B6	182	SPACE$
B7	183	SQR
B8	184	STR$
B9	185	STRING$
BA	186	TAN
BC	188	VAL
BD	189	WEND
BE EC	190 236	WHILE
BF	191	WRITE
C0	192	ELSEIF
C1	193	CLNG
C2	194	CVL
C3	195	MKL$
C4	196	AREA
E3	227	STATIC
E4	228	USING
E5	229	TO
E6	230	THEN
E7	231	NOT
E9	233	>
EA	234	=
EB	235	<
EC	236	+
ED	237	−
EE	238	*
EF	239	/
F0	240	^
F1	241	AND
F2	242	OR
F3	243	XOR
F4	244	EQV
F5	245	IMP
F6	246	MOD
F7	247	\
F8 81	248 129	CHAIN
F8 82	248 130	CLEAR
F8 83	248 131	CLS
F8 84	248 132	CONT
F8 85	248 133	CSNG

Token (hex.)	value (dec.)	AmigaBASIC command
F8 86	248 134	DATE$
F8 87	248 135	DEFINT
F8 88	248 136	DEFSNG
F8 89	248 137	DEFDBL
F8 8A	248 138	DEFSTR
F8 8B	248 139	DEF FN
F8 8C	248 140	DELETE
F8 8D	248 141	DIM
F8 8E	248 142	EDIT
F8 8F	248 143	END
F8 90	248 144	ERASE
F8 91	248 145	ERL
F8 92	248 146	ERROR
F8 93	248 147	ERR
F8 94	248 148	FILES
F8 95	248 149	FRE
F8 96	248 150	HEX$
F8 97	248 151	INSTR
F8 98	248 152	KILL
F8 99	248 153	LIST
F8 9A	248 154	LLIST
F8 9B	248 155	LOAD
F8 9C	248 156	LPOS
F8 9D	248 157	LPRINT
F8 9E	248 158	MERGE
F8 9F	248 159	NAME
F8 A0	248 160	NEW
F8 A1	248 161	OCT$
F8 A2	248 162	OPTION
F8 A3	248 163	PEEK
F8 A4	248 164	POKE
F8 A5	248 165	POS
F8 A6	248 166	RANDOMIZE
F8 A8	248 168	RESTORE
F8 A9	248 169	RESUME
F8 AA	248 170	RUN
F8 AB	248 171	SAVE
F8 AD	248 173	STOP
F8 AE	248 174	SWAP
F8 AF	248 175	SYSTEM
F8 B0	248 176	TIME$
F8 B1	248 177	TRON
F8 B2	248 178	TROFF
F8 B3	248 179	VARPTR
F8 B4	248 180	WIDTH
F8 B5	248 181	BEEP
F8 B6	248 182	CIRCLE
F8 B8	248 184	MOUSE

Token (hex.)	value (dec.)	AmigaBASIC command
F8 B9	248 185	POINT
F8 BA	248 186	PRESET
F8 BB	248 187	PSET
F8 BC	248 188	RESET
F8 BD	248 189	TIMER
F8 BE	248 190	SUB
F8 BF	248 191	EXIT
F8 C0	248 192	SOUND
F8 C2	248 194	MENU
F8 C3	248 195	WINDOW
F8 C5	248 197	LOCATE
F8 C6	248 198	CSRLIN
F8 C7	248 199	LBOUND
F8 C8	248 200	UBOUND
F8 C9	248 201	SHARED
F8 CA	248 202	UCASE$
F8 CB	248 203	SCROLL
F8 CC	248 204	LIBRARY
(F8)(D1)	(248)(209)	placed after target of SUB program call without CALL
F8 D2	248 210	PAINT
F8 D3	248 211	SCREEN
F8 D4	248 212	DECLARE
F8 D5	248 213	FUNCTION
F8 D6	248 214	DEFLNG
F8 D7	248 215	SADD
F8 D8	248 216	AREAFILL
F8 D9	248 217	COLOR
F8 DA	248 218	PATTERN
F8 DB	248 219	PALETTE
F8 DC	248 220	SLEEP
F8 DD	248 221	CHDIR
F8 DE	248 222	STRIG
F8 DF	248 223	STICK
F9 F4	249 244	OFF
F9 F5	249 245	BREAK
F9 F6	249 246	WAIT
F9 F7	249 247	USR
F9 F8	249 248	TAB
F9 F9	249 249	STEP
F9 FA	249 250	SPC
F9 FB	249 251	OUTPUT
F9 FC	249 252	BASE
F9 FD	249 253	AS
F9 FE	249 254	APPEND
F9 FF	249 255	ALL
FA 80	250 128	WAVE
FA 81	250 129	POKEW
FA 82	250 130	POKEL
FA 83	250 131	PEEKW

Token (hex.)	value (dec.)	AmigaBASIC command
FA 84	250 132	PEEKL
FA 85	250 133	SAY
FA 86	250 134	TRANSLATE$
FA 87	250 135	OBJECT.SHAPE
FA 88	250 136	OBJECT.PRIORITY
FA 89	250 137	OBJECT.X
FA 8A	250 138	OBJECT.Y
FA 8B	250 139	OBJECT.VX
FA 8C	250 140	OBJECT.VY
FA 8D	250 141	OBJECT.AX
FA 8E	250 142	OBJECT.AY
FA 8F	250 143	OBJECT.CLIP
FA 90	250 144	OBJECT.PLANES
FA 91	250 145	OBJECT.HIT
FA 92	250 146	OBJECT.ON
FA 93	250 147	OBJECT.OFF
FA 94	250 148	OBJECT.START
FA 95	250 149	OBJECT.STOP
FA 96	250 150	OBJECT.CLOSE
FA 97	250 151	COLLISION
FB FF	251 255	PTAB

B.   Other tokens

Token	Definition
$01	Variable number follows in hexadecimal notation (High/ Low = 2 Byte), e.g.: ($01) $00 $00 = Variable 0
$02	Label number follows in hex (H/L = 2 Byte), e.g.: ($02) $01 $00 = label 256
$03	Jump to label with the following number (H/M/L = 3 B.), e.g.: ($03) $00 $00 $0A = to label 10
$0B	An octal number follows (hexadecimal in High/Low format = 2 bytes). e.g.: ($0B) $00 $06 = &O 6
$0C	A 2-byte hexadecimal number follows in H/L format, e.g.: ($0C) $F8 $EC = $ F8EC
$0E	Jump to the line with the following line number (H/M/L), e.g.: ($0E) $00 $27 $10 = after line 10000
$0F	A positive integer with a value from 10 to 255 follows, e.g.: ($0F) $FF = 255
$11- $1A	A positive integer with a value from 0 to 9 follows, e.g.: $11 = 0, $12 = 1 ... $19 = 8, $1A = 9
$1C	A 2-byte integer with leading character follows, e.g.: ($1C) $80 $A0 = -160
$1D	A 4-byte floating-point number follows, e.g.: ($1D) $3C $23 $D7 $0A = 0.01
$1E	A 4-byte integer follows, e.g.: ($1E) $00 $00 $80 $00 = 32768&
$1F	An 8-byte floating-point number follows, e.g.: ($1F) $3E45 $798E $E230 $8C3A = 0.00000001

Index

Optional Diskette

For your convenience, the program listings contained in this book are available on an Amiga formatted floppy disk. You should order the diskette if you want to use the programs, but don't want to type them in from the listings in the book.

All programs on the diskette have been fully tested. You can change the programs for your particular needs. The diskette is available for $14.95 plus $2.00 ($5.00 foreign) for postage and handling.

When ordering, please give your name and shipping address. Enclose a check, money order or credit card information. Mail your order to:

Abacus Software
5370 52nd Street SE
Grand Rapids, MI 49508

Or for fast service, call **616/698-0330.**

AMIGA
Books

BeckerText

Powerful Word Processing Package for the Amiga

BeckerText *Amiga* is more than just a word processor.

BeckerText *Amiga* gives you all of the easy-to-use features found in our **TextPro** *Amiga*, plus it lets you do a whole lot more. You can merge sophisticated IFF-graphics anywhere in your document. You can hyphenate, create indexes and generate a table of contents for your documents, automatically. And what you see on the **BeckerText** screen is what you get when you print the document—real WYSIWYG formatting on your Amiga.

But **BeckerText** gives you still more: it lets you perform calculations of numerical data <u>within</u> your documents, using flexible templates to add, subtract, multiply and divide up to five columns of numbers on a page. **BeckerText** can also display and print multiple columns of text, up to five columns per page, for professional-looking newsletters, presentations, reports, etc. Its expandable built-in spell checker eliminates those distracting typographical errors.

BeckerText works with most popular dot-matrix and letter-quality printers, and even the latest laser printers for typeset-quality output. Includes comprehensive tutorial and manual.

BeckerText gives you the power and flexibility that you need to produce the professional-quality documents that you demand.

When you need more from your word processor than just word processing, you need **BeckerText** *Amiga*.

Discover the power of **BeckerText**. Available February 1988.

Suggested retail price: **$150.00**

Features

- Select options from pulldown menus or handy shortcut keys
- Fast, true WYSIWYG formatting
- Bold, italic, underline, superscript and subscript characters
- Automatic wordwrap and page numbering
- Sophisticated tab and indent options, with centering and margin justification
- Move, Copy, Delete, Search and Replace
- Automatic hyphenation, with automatic table of contents and index generation
- Write up to 999 characters per line with horizontal scrolling feature
- Check spelling as you write or interactively proof document; add to dictionary
- Performs calculations within your documents—calculate in columns with flexible templates
- Customize 30 function keys to store often-used text and macro commands
- Merge IFF graphics into documents
- Includes *BTSnap* program for converting text blocks to IFF graphics
- C-source mode for quick and easy C language program editing
- Print up to 5 columns on a single page
- Adapts to virtually any dot-matrix, letter-quality or laser printer
- Comprehensive tutorial and manual
- Not copy protected

AssemPro

Machine Language Development System for the Amiga

Bridge the gap between slow higher-level languages and *ultra-fast* machine language programming: AssemPro *Amiga* unlocks the full power of the AMIGA's 68000 processor. It's a complete developer's kit for rapidly developing machine language/assembler programs on your Amiga. AssemPro has everything you need to write professional-quality programs "down to the bare metal": editor, debugger, disassembler & reassembler.

Yet **AssemPro** isn't just for the 68000 experts. **AssemPro** is easy to use. You select options from dropdown menus or with shortcut keys, which makes your program development a much simpler process. With the optional Abacus book *Amiga Machine Language* (*see page 3*), AssemPro is the perfect introduction to Amiga machine language development and programming.

AssemPro also has the professional features that advanced programmers look for. Lots of "extras" eliminate the most tedious, repetitious and time-consuming m/l programming tasks. Like syntax error search/replace functions to speed program alterations and debugging. And you can compile to memory for lightning speed. The comprehensive tutorial and manual have the detailed information you need for fast, effective programming.

AssemPro *Amiga* offers more professional features, speed, sheer power, and ease of operation than any assembler package we've seen for the money. Test drive your **AssemPro Amiga** with the security of the Abacus 30-day MoneyBack Guarantee. Available January 1988.

Suggested retail price: **$99.95**

Features

- Integrated Editor, Debugger, Disassembler and Reassembler
- Large operating system library
- Runs under CLI and Workbench
- Produces either PC-relocatable or absolute code
- Create custom macros for nearly any parameter (of different types)
- Error search and replace functions
- Cross-reference list
- Menu-controlled conditional and repeated assembly
- Full 32-bit arithmetic
- Advanced debugger with 68020 single-step emulation
- Written completely in machine language for ultra-fast operation
- Runs on any Amiga with 512K or more and Kickstart version 1.2
- Not copy protected

Machine language programming requires a solid understanding of the AMIGA's hardware and operating system. We do not recommend this package to beginning Amiga programmers